2048 4248

SELLING YOUR SERVICES

1866 - 1991

125th

ANNIVERSARY

Henry Holt and Company / New York

Proven
Strategies for Getting
Clients to Hire You (or Your Firm)

ROBERT W. BLY

Published by Henry Holt and Company, Inc.,
115 West 18th Street, New York, New York 10011.
Published in Canada by Fitzhenry & Whiteside Limited,
195 Allstate Parkway, Markham, Ontario L3R 4T8.

Library of Congress Cataloging-in-Publication Data
Bly, Robert W.
    Selling your services : proven strategies for getting clients to
hire you (or your firm) / Robert W. Bly.—1st ed.
        p. cm.
    Includes index.
    ISBN 0-8050-1487-X (acid-free)
    1. Service industries—Marketing.   2. Professions—Marketing.
I. Title.
HD9980.5.B58   1991
658.8—dc20   90–19230
                                                                    CIP

Henry Holt books are available at special discounts
for bulk purchases for sales promotions, premiums,
fund-raising, or educational use. Special editions
or book excerpts can also be created to specification.

For details contact: Special Sales Director,
Henry Holt and Company, Inc.,
115 West 18th Street, New York, New York 10011.

First Edition

DESIGNED BY KATY RIEGEL

Printed in the United States of America
Recognizing the importance of preserving
the written word, Henry Holt and Company, Inc.,
by policy, prints all of its first editions
on acid-free paper. ∞

10 9 8 7 6 5 4 3 2 1

Contents

Acknowledgments

I'm indebted to Dr. Jeffrey Lant, Howard Shenson, Bill Bishop, Tom Hopkins, Donald Dell, Jeff Davidson, Patricia Fripp, Jerry Buchanan, Pete Silver, Hubert Bermont, John Gardner, Dottie Walters, and the other authorities on effective selling mentioned throughout the book. Their earlier efforts pointed the way.

Thanks also to my fellow service providers—friends and colleagues who, over the years, have given me countless ideas on how to build my business, get new clients, increase my income, and sell more of my services. I won't name them all here. But they know who they are. Thanks, folks!

Special thanks to Don Hauptman, Austin Hamel, Roger Parker, Joan Harris, Dr. Andrew Linick, Dr. Gary Blake, Richard Armstrong, Ed McLean, Bob Schulte, Milt Pierce, and Sig Rosenblum—successful writers, consultants, and marketers whose brains I seem to pick on an almost daily basis.

I'd also like to thank Cynthia Vartan at Henry Holt for being the best editor an author could have—once again.

Thanks to my sister and assistant, Fern Dickey, for proofing every chapter and making many helpful suggestions.

And of course, the greatest thanks to my wife, Amy Sprecher Bly, who makes it all possible.

Preface

If you are responsible for selling your services or the services of your employer, this book can help you make a lot more money.

It reveals proven techniques that can get more prospects to call you, help you close lucrative contracts with new accounts, and dramatically increase your sales and profits.

And these techniques work whether you sell to businesses or consumers—or both—and whether you render your service working behind a personal computer, on the telephone, or out of the back of a pickup truck.

In short, this book reveals the secrets of how to *sell your services*—successfully.

If you're in a marketing-driven field, such as management consulting, freelancing, or home improvements, you're already aware of how important it is to be able to outsell your competition in today's competitive environment.

If you're in a field where professionals have traditionally looked down on anything that smacks of "selling"—medicine or law, for example—then I'm sure you've observed how things are changing . . . and that in today's marketplace, you need to market and sell your services to build your practice and boost your income—like it or not. As my friend million-dollar stockbroker Jim Hansberger observes, "We are all salespeople—at least part of the time."

Now, maybe you've read some books on "selling" before. And you were disappointed—as I was.

Like me, you probably noticed that most of the advice in those other books on selling didn't really apply to you—the self-employed freelancer, consultant, entrepreneur, professional, service provider, contractor, vendor, or account representative selling *services*.

The word *salesman* instantly conjures up a clichéd image—the polished, perfectly manicured, impeccably dressed Joe Slick, who pesters people with persistent pitches and memorized techniques until they give in and sign on the dotted line and buy a gross of his widgets.

But that's not how you see yourself. For instance, you don't think of yourself as a "salesman." (I'm sure the word *salesman* isn't on your business card, for example.) You think of yourself as a skilled professional or specialist rendering professional or special services. *Selling* is the necessary but vital activity you must perform to convince clients to take advantage of the benefits your superior service offers.

And that's where you and I differ from the so-called professional salesmen whose involvement with the customer typically ends when the contract is signed. For full-time, commissioned salespeople, selling—or "closing"—is the end. It's their job, their goal.

But for you—the service provider—selling is the *means*, not the end. It's simply the first step in establishing a long and mutually profitable relationship between you and those clients who can best benefit from the unique services you provide.

Selling Your Services provides step-by-step selling guidelines and techniques designed especially for service firms

and independent service pr
how the book is organized:

In Part I, I show you hov
rather than you having to ca
ate sales leads using sale
proven inquiry-generating
stant recognition as an exp
writing, speaking, lecturin
public relations methods . .
other marketing documen
your services.

In Part II, I teach you the follow-up techniques that get
you past the secretary and in direct contact with the prospect so you can secure that all-important first meeting. For
instance, you'll learn a simple technique that prevents secretaries (and spouses) from screening your calls and virtually
forces them to connect you with the boss . . . almost every
time!

In Part III, I tell you exactly what to say to the prospect to
overcome objections, answer questions, and make him or her
want to hire you on the spot. You also learn how to quickly
and gracefully get out of situations where you are dealing
with people who are not serious about buying your services.

In Part IV, you learn how to set and get the fee you
deserve, and how to protect yourself and your client through
use of contracts, proposals, and letters of agreement. You
also learn how to get your fee even when prospects say,
"Your price is too high."

In selling your services, getting the initial order (contract) is only the beginning of the sales process, not the end,
as with many product sales. In Part V, I tell you how to
render your services to ensure maximum client satisfaction . . . how to handle difficult clients . . . and how to ensure
repeat business through superior service that dazzles clients
but takes only a minimal amount of extra time . . . and how
to sell your services during a depression or recession.

ces is as different from selling physical
...ight is from day. *Selling Your Services* deals
...pecifics and particulars of selling services, not
...s.

... this book written for service providers and service
...lers in all fields, industries, and markets? Yes.

Will you personally want to use *every* technique and
strategy presented in the book? No. Some may not be right
for your particular selling situation. Others you may not
personally be comfortable with.

And that's okay! There's still a wealth of information here
to help you get more clients and increase your sales. Even if
you get just one powerful idea or new technique that boosts
your personal income by thousands of dollars this year, then
your investment in *Selling Your Services* will have paid off
handsomely . . . don't you agree?

     —Bob Bly,
       Sales Trainer to America's Service Industries™

A Special Author's Note to Readers of *Secrets of a Freelance Writer*

If you read my earlier book *Secrets of a Freelance Writer*, you will notice some similarities between that book and the early chapters of *Selling Your Services*. That's deliberate: Both books cover the marketing of services, and so some repetition is essential if we are to present a complete course in service selling.

However, *Selling Your Services* takes up where *Secrets* left off. It provides dozens of new and more powerful sales techniques, including the specifics of *exactly* what to say to potential clients to overcome objections, make your point, and get the contract or the assignment. You'll find a wealth of new information and ideas that are brand-new.

In addition, while *Secrets of a Freelance Writer* is for writers only, *Selling Your Services* is for people selling every type of trade, technical, professional, and consulting service imaginable. So not only does the advice go deeper, but the scope is broader—as it should be.

—RWB

Selling Your Services:
An Overview

The goal of this book is to help you get more clients, sell more of your services, make a lot more money, and have a lot of fun in the process. You will learn proven techniques for generating new business leads, referrals, repeat business . . . and for getting the jobs you want at the fees you want to charge.

Let's get started.

SELLING SERVICES IS DIFFERENT FROM SELLING PRODUCTS

There are dozens of books on selling, but most focus on selling products—physical, tangible items. And they're written primarily for the professional salesperson.

This book focuses solely on selling *services*. And selling services is as different from selling products as night is from day. *Selling Your Services: Proven Strategies for Getting Clients to Hire You (or Your Firm)* provides the millions of people in the *service* sector with proven strategies on how to sell.

There are a few similarities in selling services—which

are intangibles—and selling products. But there are also many, many differences. Among the key differences in selling products versus selling services:

SELLING PRODUCTS	SELLING SERVICES
Sold by professional salespeople who don't see the buyer once the sale is made and whose only concern is bringing back an order.	Frequently sold by the person who will actually render the service. This person must build a *personal* relationship with the buyer and has to *select* prospects with good "personal chemistry"; otherwise, the relationship will fail.
Sale is finished once the order is taken and the product is delivered.	Getting a signed contract is only the first step. Clients must be continuously sold and resold before, during, and after the service is performed.
Proof of satisfaction is easy to demonstrate and is achieved when the product is delivered. The product salesperson, therefore, is not selective and will sell basically to anyone with the money to buy.	Satisfaction is subjective. Therefore, service sellers must be sure to screen prospects and select only those prospects who seem a good "fit" with the seller's personality and type of service.
Prospects are qualified according to whether they have the money and authority to buy.	Prospects are qualified according to whether their specific problems can be solved in a satisfactory manner by the service offered.

SELLING PRODUCTS

Salespeople are primarily concerned with closing the sale and do not worry about whether the prospect will become a "difficult" account—because they do not have to personally deal with customer complaints (in most cases).

Pricing is fairly standard and easy to calculate.

Visits from the salesperson are almost always free.

Salespeople use volume discounts and price bargaining as a prime negotiation tool for closing sales.

SELLING SERVICES

Salesperson will not pursue sale of a "difficult" prospect because he or she is also the one who will have to cope with this person while rendering service.

Pricing differs with each client and project and frequently requires intensive up-front effort in order to diagnose the prospect's problem, estimate the job, and prepare a quotation or proposal.

Some service providers view visits and preparation of bids or proposals as consulting work and consequently charge for these services (for example, lawyers who charge a small initial consultation fee to listen and decide whether to take your case).

Prices are not very flexible, because the service business is labor-intensive and your firm cannot lose money on the initial contract in exchange for the promise of fu-

SELLING PRODUCTS

SELLING SERVICES

ture business—as is often done in product selling.

Prospects view the salesperson as a "salesman" and do not expect him or her to be an expert.

Prospects view the salesperson as a "consultant" or expert, and their image of the service firm is dependent largely on how well this consultant performs in initial meetings.

Salesperson is paid commissions, creating a powerful incentive to sell as much product as possible.

Salesperson must render services sold (or at least part of them), so may be hesitant to sell more than he or she can handle.

Product salespeople are trained to overcome objections and sell to the prospect despite protestations that he or she does not want to buy.

In service selling, an objection is not necessarily something to be "overcome" but, rather, serves as a warning signal that the person may be a bad "match" for the service and that the meeting should be ended.

Customer is buying an "off-the-shelf" item that is mass-produced and not tailored to specific needs.

Customer is buying (and expects to get) a service that is highly customized and tailored to specific needs.

Today the United States has made the transition from a *product-producing* to a *service-providing* economy. According to a recent article in *Executive Business Magazine*, in 1970, 35 percent of the American work force was employed in manufacturing; today that percentage has dropped to 20 percent.

Meanwhile, the share of employment represented by services and service-related industries rose from 48 percent to 60 percent during a recent seventeen-year period. The U.S. Bureau of Labor Statistics reports that approximately 21 million Americans are employed in manufacturing while approximately 36 million work in service businesses. In an article on the "hottest jobs in the next decade," published in the June 1990 edition of *Money* magazine, twenty-three out of the twenty-five "fast-track careers" profiled were in service or service-related areas; only two dealt primarily with manufacturing.

What's more, approximately 250,000 new small businesses are started each year, which means a lot more potential clients for you—but also a lot more competition. According to the U.S. Small Business Administration, there is a total of 3.8 million businesses in the United States, and 99.5 percent of these have fewer than five hundred employees.

Because of this shift from a manufacturing to a service economy, most books, courses, cassettes, and other programs on "selling" that focus on *goods* rather than service, information, or ideas are outdated and not applicable in today's sales environment.

Further, even manufacturing companies are becoming service sellers. As buyers see less and less difference between manufactured products, *service* has become the factor that most influences their choice of vendor.

Selling service has now become both a profit center in its own right (*Software Success* newsletter, for example, found that 85 percent of software companies surveyed expect to make a profit from support services) as well as an integral component of any hard-good "product." So everyone—even salespeople who traditionally think of themselves as "merchandise movers"—is in fact a "service seller." The ability to provide and sell service is now critical to the success of every corporation, small business, and self-employed entrepreneur in the United States.

Here is just a sampling of the types of businesses engaged in actively selling their services in today's marketplace:

Accountants
Ad agencies
Architects
Attorneys
Automobile repair services and gas stations

Banks and financial services institutions
Barbers
Bed and breakfast inns
Builders and home remodelers
Business and management consultants

Camps
Career counselors
Career training firms
Carpenters
Child care, baby-sitting, preschool centers
Computer programmers, custom software developers,
    data-processing consultants
Construction firms
Consultants
Contractors

Dating services
Dentists
Desktop publishing bureaus
Diaper services
Doctors
Dry cleaning and laundry establishments

Editorial services
Electricians
Electronic repair shops
Engineering and consulting engineer services
Environmental testing services
Executive search firms

Financial planners
Franchise owners
Freight forwarders
Fund-raising consultants
Funeral parlors, morticians

Graphic artists

Hair and beauty parlors
Health spas and exercise clubs
Hospitals and clinics
Hotels, motels, clubs, restaurants

Insurance agents
Interior decorating, design, planning services
Investment advisers

Laboratories and testing services
Literary agents

Maintenance and service firms
Masons
Meeting planners
Metalworking and fabrication services
Musicians and entertainers

Painters
Pharmacists
Photographers
Printers
Proofreaders
Psychiatrists and psychologists (therapists)

Real estate agents
Roofers

Sewer and drain cleaning services
Speakers
Stockbrokers

Tanning salons
Tax preparers
Telephone and telecommunication services
Temporary employment services
Training and development consultants
Transportation firms
Travel agents
Typesetters

Utilities

Veterinarians
Videotape rental stores

Watch and jewelry repair services
Wedding consultants
Word processing services
Writers

X-ray, ultrasound, NMR, diagnostic services

If you don't see your profession or trade on the list, don't worry, because it's just a representative sampling. There are literally hundreds of other fields where service providers must sell their services to prospects and clients—and this book applies to all of them.

THE FIVE-STEP SERVICE SELLING PROCESS™

No matter what the service you're selling, selling it successfully depends on carefully following a well-defined method. I call it the Five-Step Service Selling Process.

Although there may be variations depending on your industry, trade, or profession—for instance, people in your field may place more emphasis on a particular step than people in different businesses—this process is almost universal throughout the world of service providers.

Here, in a nutshell, are the five steps to selling your services—successfully. Please observe that the book you are now reading is intentionally divided into five parts, each part addressing a step in the process (check the contents page for details).

Step 1: Generate initial interest in your services

The first step in selling your services is to get one or more prospects (a prospect is a potential client) to express interest in learning more about your services.

This interest may be immediate and intense—that is, the prospect has the need, has the money, is ready to buy, and essentially just wants to look you over and find out the cost of the job before hiring you. Or it may be casual—the prospect merely wants to see a brochure or ask a few exploratory questions about the nature of what you do and whom you work for.

This initial interest can be generated in a variety of ways. Two major ways are through direct marketing techniques and by becoming well known in your field or local business community.

With direct marketing techniques, such as print advertising or direct mail, you can announce your services and get prospects to call or write you for more information.

Visibility-enhancing public relations techniques, such as public speaking, writing articles for local newspapers and business magazines, or giving seminars, are other ways to generate interest. Using this method, you will get people to come to you because they perceive you as the expert in your field.

In many service businesses, prospects will request that you send some printed information on your services by mail. An effective brochure or package of sales materials helps answer the prospect's questions and converts the prospect from "mildly interested" to "very interested"—which is precisely what you want.

Step 2: Follow up the initial interest to get an appointment or generate a meaningful discussion about your services and how you can help the prospect achieve his or her goals

Once the prospect has expressed some initial interest, you have to follow up. The purpose of follow-up is to (1) bring those people who are genuine potential clients for your services closer to buying and (2) eliminate those people who expressed interest but are not serious prospects for your services.

The first task under this step is to qualify prospects—that is, determine which people represent genuine prospects for your type of services. A genuine prospect has the means to afford your services (money or purchasing authority) and has a problem or requirement that your services can effectively handle.

In addition, if you are to work successfully with this person, there has to be at least some minimal level of "chemistry" between you. Otherwise, the engagement to render services will be fraught with aggravation, disagreements, arguments, and tension.

As part of the qualifying process, once you determine that certain people are *not* good prospects for your services (that is, they are difficult people, cannot afford your fee, or have a situation better served by another firm), you need to part politely with them. I will give you a few simple techniques you can use to separate yourself from nonprospects as quickly as possible, without creating the impression you are giving them the brush-off.

The next task in this step is to follow up with those people who are good prospects for your service. This involves calling and convincing prospects either to meet with you in person or to speak with you at length over the telephone to discuss their needs and how your service can solve their problem for them. The end result of step 2 is an appointment for an in-person meeting or telephone conference.

Step 3: The initial meeting or discussion

This is the sales meeting. It can take place face to face or over the telephone. Its purpose is simple: to convince prospects to hire you to perform services. The end result of this step is a tentative commitment from a client to retain you to provide your services to handle his project or solve his problem. Sales professionals call getting this commitment closing the sale.

In product selling, the initial meeting is called a sales call, because it involves a salesperson calling on a prospect for the sole purpose of selling something. But in service selling, the person doing the calling—you—is not a professional salesperson, but a highly trained specialist in your specific field. For that reason, your visit has value to the client apart from its sales objectives.

For instance, if you go to a prospect's home to give an estimate, your estimate has value, because it was prepared by you, an expert, and thus gives the prospect information on whether other estimates received are accurate or within a reasonable range.

If you are a designer, and during the meeting you throw out some quick design concepts to impress the potential client with your expertise, these have value to the client, who may actually use them even though you have not yet been engaged to perform services.

For this reason, those of us who sell services do not refer to the initial meeting as a "sales call." We use a variety of other terms, including estimate, analysis, needs assessment, consultation, critique, review, demonstration, briefing, and diagnosis. These terms accurately reflect the value of the diagnostic services that are performed during the initial meeting.

Because these diagnostic services are so valuable, more and more service providers are charging for them. According to consultant Howard Shenson, ten years ago or so only 25 percent of prospects expected to pay consultants for diagnostic services performed in the initial analysis and early stages of problem solving. Now, realizing the tremendous value of such services, 75 percent of prospects expect to pay consultants for them.

While this ratio may not hold true for your field, look around you. Many of your peers are beginning to charge more, earlier, in the initial stages.

Tip: If you *don't* charge for the initial meeting or conversation, stress in your literature your "free, no-obligation" analysis, estimate, consultation, or whatever. The initial meeting is valuable to the client, and if it's free, that's a selling point. Incidentally, one of the major questions many service providers have is "Should the first meeting be fee or free?" I'll help you determine that in chapter 7.

Step 4: Getting the assignment or project

Getting the assignment or project is the true and final "close" of the sale. It involves coming to an agreement concerning price, deadline, and other terms, then getting a signed written agreement—a contract, purchase order, or letter of agreement—and some deposit or advance payment covering a portion of your total fee (typically ranging from 10 to 50 percent of the total). Only when you have the signed agreement and deposit check in hand can you truly say you have made the sale.

But the service-selling process doesn't really end with the contract, as is the case with selling products. There is one final step to successfully selling your services. . . .

Step 5: Keeping the client "sold" after the sale is made

Most contracts allow cancellation by the client at intermediate phases or steps of the project. If that happens, you collect only your fee up to that point (or more, or less, depending on the wording of your particular contract). What this means, however, is that you really haven't completed the sale until the job is done *to the client's satisfaction.*

Therefore, customer service is an essential ingredient of selling your services successfully. To collect your fees, get lucrative referrals, and receive repeat business (additional assignments) from your clients, you have to perform your service so that the client is satisfied.

Selling Your Services walks you through these five essential steps. Also, an additional chapter—chapter 16—provides an immediate action plan for boosting your sales in a recession, slow economy, or during a slump in sales or business downturn in your industry. If things are slow and you are hurting for business, I suggest you turn to that chapter and read it immediately.

SELLING SERVICES TO BUSINESSES VERSUS SELLING TO CONSUMERS

Does this Five-Step Service Selling Process work regardless of whether you sell to consumers or businesses? Yes. The principles are the same, and the advice given in the book, except where noted, applies both to consumer and business-to-business selling.

However, there are *some* differences in selling to consumers and selling to businesses, and it pays to be aware of them. Specifically, here are the six key differences in consumer versus business-to-business marketing and selling:

1. *Business buyers need to buy. Consumers don't.* Business buyers need to buy. Not *your* service, necessarily. But something to solve a problem, handle an application, or fulfill a need the firm has. The proof of this is the existence of the purchasing agent, whose sole function is to purchase things.

Rarely do business buyers buy things for fun, or for the sake of spending money, or on impulse. They buy because it's their job to take care of a specific set of problems, and your service addresses one of those problems.

With consumers, it's more of a mixed bag. In some cases—plumbing emergencies, termite infestations, illness, tooth decay, radon, asbestos, a lawsuit—the consumer has an immediate need and no choice but to seek some sort of treatment (your service). However, most consumer items are really more luxuries than necessities. You don't really need that redwood deck, car detailing service, pedicure, or family room. And many other of the services you buy, you buy as time-saving luxuries—after all, you could really wash your car, mow your lawn, trim your hedges, caulk your windows, fix your doorbell, and shovel your walk yourself, if you so desired.

Business buyers must buy—99 percent of the time. This is not true for consumers, who *must* buy perhaps only 20 to 30 percent of the time, and buy because they *want* to buy the other 70 to 80 percent.

2. *Business buyers are sophisticated.* For instance, if you're selling telephone repair services to Fortune 500 corporations, you'll be talking to a telecommunications manager who's been dealing with voice and data transmission for her whole career—and probably knows more about it than you do. You can't go in unprepared. The prospect is going to ask tough, technically detailed questions. If you can't answer them, she'll think you're an ignorant bozo and show you the door.

This is why so many firms selling technical services use two-person selling teams: a sales representative to get in the door and a technical expert to answer nitty-gritty questions and work with the prospect's technical staff to accurately assess the project requirements.

Consumers, by comparison, are not sophisticated. They don't know much about what you do—it's generally a mystery to them—and they probably don't have the time or inclination to learn the details. While the business buyer wants to know the nuts-and-bolts details—*how* your service or program works—the consumer doesn't.

Consumers are mainly interested in results—the ends, not the means. Trying to explain details or educate them is often unnecessary, frequently bores them, and may in fact *lose* you the sale.

Are there exceptions? Sure. Hobbyists, for example. Computer hackers. Do-it-yourselfers. Enthusiasts. They are interested and want as much "how-to" information as you can give them. But average customers *don't* want to be overloaded with information. If you can convince them that you know what you are doing, are reliable, are charging a fair price, and that your services meet their needs, they'll hire you. They don't need to know *how* you do it; they just need to be convinced that you *can* do it.

3. *Business buyers will read a lot of copy. Many consumers won't.* This directly affects how you design and prepare your marketing materials, a subject covered in detail in chapter 3. At this point, just remember that business buyers, who are sophisticated, require a lot of detailed information before making a decision. So you can be fairly certain that they will read at least a portion of the detailed sales brochures, booklets, proposals, and sales sheets you prepare.

We hear, on the other hand, how the illiteracy rate is increasing in the United States, how people are suffering from "information overload," how everybody has too much to read and too little time in which to read it. Today's consumer is busy. Grandma may have delighted in poring over the

latest Sears catalog, but today's moms are too busy making
dinner and taking care of the kids after coming home from
full-time jobs. For this reason, copy aimed at consumers
should be concise and to the point. Make it simple. Make it
scannable. Make it easy to read.

4. *Multiple buying influences*. Most consumer purchases
are made by one person (the prospect) or by two people (the
prospect and the prospect's spouse). At times, children, par-
ents, relatives, or friends may form a minibuying committee
that holds sway over the prospect's decision. But in most
cases, if you can convince the prospect that your proposition
is worthwhile, you've made the sale.

In business, it's an entirely different ball game. Most
business purchases of more than $100—for either goods or
services—are made by committee. And, as Dr. Ing F.
Porsche, founder of the Porsche automobile company, observes, "Committees are, by nature, timid. They are based
on the premise of safety in numbers; content to survive
inconspicuously, rather than take risks and move independently ahead" (as quoted in *Consulting Opportunities Journal*, volume 8, number 1).

As a result, service providers must seek out, reach, and
direct their selling efforts at the *real* decision maker within a
corporation . . . or, if this is not possible, they must at least be
aware that any tentative decision made by a person lower
down on the corporate hierarchy is not firm and may be
reversed for numerous reasons—or for no reason—by an
executive higher up on the ladder.

You may have to sell many "buying influences" (different
people) within the organization on using you before you get
the contract. Generally, the broader the scope of the project
and the bigger the fee, the more people involved with the
review and approval process.

One way to avoid problems is to identify, by name and job
title, the person who is the real decision maker for purchasing your type of service. For instance, in my case, I know

that in a large corporation, a person with the title of advertising manager will usually have the authority to retain me to write ads and brochures, so I'm comfortable when I get an inquiry from such a person. On the other hand, I am wary of inquiries from a product manager, because such a person typically does not make the final decisions as to who writes marketing materials. In such cases, I ask for the name of the advertising manager and permission to contact him or her and send a duplicate set of my sales materials—because I know I must sell the advertising manager to get the contract.

5. *Business services are (slightly) more complex.* Services are generally (but not always) more complex than products; services offered to businesses are generally (but not always) more complex than services offered to consumers.

This is a problem because complexity frightens many potential buyers: If they are confused by your offer, or don't understand exactly what it is you'll be doing—or what they'll be getting out of it—they hesitate. And the longer prospects put off a decision, the more unlikely they are to buy.

The solution is to understand exactly what it is you *do* offer people—what your services are, how they work, what clients get for their money (and what they do not get), what the "deliverable" is (for example, do clients get a report, service contract, waterproof coating, new kitchen cabinets? What exactly do you give clients?), and what result or benefit clients can expect from your services (increased productivity, improved employee communication, fewer headaches, and so on).

Once you've thought through these issues, you need to develop a standard way of presenting them to prospects so that people understand them, are not frightened or put off by them, and in fact are enticed by them. You can do this in a variety of formats: as an oral sales presentation, a slide show, a videotape or filmstrip, an audiocassette, a written proposal, a fact sheet, a list of questions and answers, a marketing brochure.

The key point is: The more complex your service, the more important it is to do a good job of communicating it to potential clients. Business services are typically more complex than consumer services, and business buyers typically want more information—more details—before making a final decision.

6. *Business buyers buy for their firms—and for themselves.* Consumers are motivated almost solely by their own personal agenda. Is this good for me? Do I need it? Can I afford it? Will I like it? Can I trust these guys? Can someone else do it better or cheaper? If you can provide satisfactory answers to these questions, you stand an excellent chance of making the sale.

Business buyers, by comparison, are motivated simultaneously by two separate and distinct agendas: business/corporate and personal.

On the corporate side, business buyers want to buy what is best for the company. After all, that's what they collect a salary for. If they buy well for the company, they will be perceived as people who perform their job competently, and raises and promotions should be (theoretically, at least) forthcoming.

If, on the other hand, business buyers make a *wrong* buying decision—if your service turns out to be too expensive, or isn't performed to the satisfaction of the buyer's firm, or fails to deliver the desired result—it will reflect negatively on the buyers. The buyers' supervisors will say the buyers made a bad decision and are therefore not good at their job. They may be passed over for a raise or promotion. They may even be demoted or fired.

For example, there's an old saying among corporate information systems managers: "No one ever got fired for buying IBM." Many data-processing professionals will choose IBM products because IBM has a reputation for service and quality that is almost beyond question.

If you buy IBM and there's a problem, you can say, "Well,

I bought it from IBM." Others will think, *He bought IBM, so it's not his fault there's a problem. Who could have predicted it?* But if you take a chance on an unknown computer manufacturer and have a problem, your colleagues will think, *What an idiot! He bought the computer from XYZ Computers. Who ever heard of XYZ? If it was me, I would have bought IBM.*

Besides wanting to do right by their companies, however, business buyers are also motivated by personal agenda. Your services may satisfy the business agenda of increasing sales, boosting productivity, enhancing efficiency, reducing labor costs, or saving money. But if they conflict with your prospect's personal agenda—working less, eliminating headaches, no overtime, avoiding hassles and problems—you will have great difficulty convincing him or her to buy.

Remember in the 1950s how people used to joke about the so-called efficiency experts who would come into a manufacturing plant, make time-and-motion and similar studies, then submit (for a fat fee) a plan on how to increase efficiency and eliminate waste—a plan that usually recommended firing half the staff and replacing them with robots? Well, say you offer a similar consulting service in the area of productivity or labor efficiency (I have one client who does just that!).

In your sales presentation your immediate instinct is to stress "My methods can help you cut your labor force by 25 percent—which means big savings and lots more profit!" Now, the prospect's business agenda may call for increasing profits. But his or her personal agenda says, *I don't want to see my friends/staff/colleagues fired—and I certainly don't want to hire some hot-shot consultant whose report might put my job in jeopardy!*

If there is a conflict between business and personal agenda, the conflict may prevent you from making the sale. Remember, business buyers buy for their companies . . .

and for themselves. You must satisfy both the corporate/
organizational and the personal agenda.

A SPECIAL NOTE

As you master each step in the Five-Step Service Selling
Process, keep in mind that the activities in each phase are
designed to move buyers *one step closer* to the sale, not for
you to get an immediate job.

Unlike fast-food hamburgers or a six-pack of beer, which
consumers might buy on impulse, consumers examine the
purchase of a service more closely. It's a *multistep* buying
process, and as outlined earlier, each step has a specific goal:
to generate initial interest, to secure an appointment, to get
a tentative commitment, to obtain a signed contract and
deposit check, or to keep the client satisfied.

One of the biggest mistakes many service providers make
is to try to shorten the process, skip steps, or force prospects
to a decision before they're ready to buy. You must perform
each step in the Five-Step Service Selling Process completely and successfully if you are to get that contract.

Be realistic. Do a thorough, patient selling job and you
will be rewarded with substantial business. Don't think,
"I'm so great that I don't have to sell prospects; once they see
me (or my work) they'll be automatically sold." That attitude
and approach may have worked for some people in the 1980s.
But it is far less likely to work today. The business world is
more competitive than ever. Especially in the service sector.
Today more and more service firms offering similar services
compete with each other in the marketplace. And clients are
becoming choosier and more demanding about who they hire
and what they buy.

"I believe each of us is born with a certain destiny," says
Jerry Buchanan, founder of the TOWERS Club, a support
organization for entrepreneurs. "There is some one great

work we were born to accomplish. If we fail to recognize our calling, or if we do recognize it but fail to attempt its achievement, then this lifetime has been a wasted effort."

For many of us in the service sector, that "calling" is to render the service we provide our clients to the best of our abilities. Not to be able to perform our professional services because we are unsuccessful at *selling* those services to prospects would make our lifetime a wasted effort.

You may not think of yourself as a salesperson. Right now you may not enjoy selling. Perhaps you even think of it as something undignified, beneath your status as a respected professional in your field. Maybe selling is distasteful to you. Even scary. But the purpose of your existence—or at least the reason for your business—is to do what you do best: that is, perform your service for the benefit of your clients. If you're a doctor, you cure the sick. If you're a consultant, you solve problems. If you're a handyman, you make dilapidated homes livable again.

But let me tell you something. You are going to have to learn to sell—and sell well—to survive and prosper in the 1990s and beyond. To compete in today's marketplace, it's not enough to offer a superior service. You must be able to market and *sell* your service effectively, as well.

That's what *Selling Your Services* teaches. It's all here. Step-by-step instructions and guidelines, tips and techniques. Follow my Five-Step Service Selling Process, and you'll soon be selling so much of your services, you'll have all the business you can handle and be booked up many weeks or months in advance with lucrative, enjoyable, profitable assignments.

And there's one more thing:

You may not think of selling as fun, but it is. It's as exciting, challenging, and creative as anything you've ever done in your career.

Why is this so? Because, unlike some professional salespeople who peddle products that are second rate or propositions that cheat the public, you know you are selling something that is a fantastic value and enormously beneficial, and that you wholeheartedly endorse and are enthusiastic about—namely, *you*! (Or, more specifically, the service you provide.) When you believe in and feel good about the "product," selling is not something to be ashamed of. No. In such a situation, it's a wonderful experience, a thrilling adventure, and an activity of tremendous value to the public that benefits from the services you perform.

In fact, let me go out on a limb and make a prediction: After reading this book and putting my Five-Step Service Selling Process into practice for several months, not only will you sell more of your services, expand your client roster, and make more money—but you'll also come to find that selling is, for you, a fun and exciting activity.

You'll smile as you shake hands with more new clients and receive signed contracts and fat deposit checks in the mail . . . knowing that both you and the client will profit handsomely from the transaction. And you'll reach a point where the challenge of getting good clients to hire you pleases and satisfies you as much as or more than anything you've ever done—or will do—in your career.

Power Prospecting: How to Generate Initial Interest in Your Services

CHAPTER ONE

Techniques for Generating Sales Leads

Once you decide to begin actively marketing and selling your services, how will potential clients learn about the availability of those services?

If you're lucky, perhaps your phone will start ringing right away, without any effort on your part. If that happens—congratulations! You will have all the business you need, and you can skip this chapter.

But for most service providers, self-promotion is an essential activity. Just as Ford must advertise to sell cars, you must advertise and promote yourself and your service business if you expect people to call you with assignments.

How much of your time will be spent marketing and selling your services? It varies by industry and individual. Many established service providers spend between 10 and 25 percent of their time on self-promotion. Beginners must devote even more effort to establishing a reputation, getting clients, and making a name in the local community.

Self-promotion is the subject of this chapter. How do you promote yourself? Does direct mail work for service providers? Does it pay to advertise? How can you get people to hire you? I'll show you what techniques can work for you, including telemarketing/cold calling, referrals, testimonials, direct mail, advertising, and networking.

TELEMARKETING

Telemarketing, as it applies to selling services, means picking up the telephone, calling strangers, and asking them if they'd be interested in getting a free estimate or learning more about your services.

Does this type of "cold-call" telemarketing work? For most service providers, no. I never make cold telephone calls to a list of prospects, and for the most part, I advise you to do likewise.

There are several reasons why cold telephone calling is so ineffective. First, it puts you in the weak, unseemly position of appearing to be "begging" for the work. At best, prospects perceive you as someone who isn't very busy and needs work. At worst, it annoys the heck out of prospects, making them totally unreceptive to your message.

The main reason I don't recommend cold telephone calling is because of a principle taught to me by marketing expert Pete Silver. Pete says that when marketing your services, it's better to get prospects to come to *you*, rather than you going to them. Cold telephone calling violates this principle.

Despite what I've just told you, cold-call telemarketing campaigns are actively conducted by thousands of firms, most notably home improvement companies (siding, windows, doors, roofing) and financial services firms (gold coins, stockbrokers, mutual funds, and other investments).

Stockbroker Andrew Lanyi, a twenty-nine-year veteran of Wall Street, says he has made over 1 million cold calls in his career. It must be working, since Andrew now earns over $1.5 million a year—almost eight times more than the President of the United States.

If you do decide to make cold calls, have someone else in your office do it or hire someone to make the calls for you. Andrew Lanyi, for example, now has a staff of three people who do the initial calling, telephoning prospects listed in directories and corporate reports. The team spends all day calling prospects, qualifying them (a Lanyi client must invest a minimum of $50,000), and setting them up for a call from Andrew.

COLD CALLING

Even less effective than making cold calls over the phone is cold calling in person. In my observation, making cold calls simply doesn't work.

If you are selling to consumers, knocking on doors puts you on a level of the Avon lady, Fuller Brush salesman, vacuum cleaner salesmen, and other door-to-door peddlers. You want your potential clients to respect you—to think of you as a professional, not a peddler. You'll destroy any chance of that if you just show up on their doorstep. Also, consumer advocates have alerted homeowners to scams perpetrated by door-to-door con artists, so making a cold call at buyers' homes automatically puts them on the alert and creates a negative impression.

If you sell to businesses, making a cold call—showing up in the corporate lobby without an appointment and asking to see Suzy Smith or John Jones—is equally as bad. It shouts loud and clear to the prospect that you are a person whose time is not valuable—who is not busy and successful.

Also, cold calls are annoying. When I was an advertising manager, I hated it when magazine space reps showed up unannounced. To be polite, I always saw them, but I only half listened to their feeble pitches (the people who made such cold calls were invariably the most incompetent salespersons, with no real understanding of my business or my needs), and never placed ads with them. The ones I re-spected always phoned for an appointment well in advance.

Don't make cold calls—especially in person.

REFERRALS

Referrals—also known as word-of-mouth—are a great way to get new business. One advantage of getting leads through word-of-mouth is that prospects are already favorably in-clined to hire you, because they have been told great things about you by the person who gave them your name.

Whether referrals are frequent and common depends on the type of service business you're in. In my field, direct-mail copywriting, some clients happily refer colleagues to writers and artists, while other clients keep the names of the free-lancers they use a closely guarded secret.

When my wife was pregnant, our doctor referred us to a qualified Lamaze instructor. I discovered that natural child-birth experts get almost all of their business as a result of referrals from gynecologists, obstetricians, and hospitals. If referrals are a major source of business in your profession, it's important to learn who does the referring—and to con-tact them and let them know of your service.

So, although referrals generally produce sales leads of good quality, you cannot control or significantly increase the quantity of referrals. For the most part, referrals either happen or they don't. Therefore, you can't count on referrals as your only source of new business, and you need to develop other methods of generating sales leads.

However, this doesn't mean you are totally helpless when it comes to generating referral business. There are some clients who might refer you but simply never think to do so and never get around to it. These can be sources for refer-rals, with a little prodding from you.

One referral technique that's especially useful when the

client is a large organization is to ask for referrals to other clients within that organization.

Typically, most of us are thrilled when we're working for Manager X or Division A of a large Fortune 1000 corporation; this represents lucrative business. But few of us, myself included, ever stop to realize that now that we've got an "in" at the company, other managers and divisions that could buy our service will be much more likely to use us—especially with a referral from Manager X.

To get this referral, say to your client, "Mr. Client, I have a question. Who else in [name of company] do you think could benefit from my service?" When the client gives you one or two names, ask for the complete information, including spelling, title, address, and phone number.

Then say, "Mr. Client, when I get in touch with [name of referred lead], can I mention your name?" When the client says yes—and he will—you can now legitimately call other prospects within the corporation and say "[Name of client] told me that you use [type of service you offer] and that I should get in touch with you."

If you are uncomfortable about having this phone conversation, a less aggressive way of asking for referrals is to send a letter. A model letter you can use follows.

date

Mr. Joe Jones, Title
XYZ Company
Anytown, USA

Dear Mr. Jones:

I'm glad you like the [name of project] I recently completed for you.

Like you, I'm always on the lookout for new business. So I have a favor to ask.

Could you jot down, on the back of this letter, the

names, addresses, and phone numbers of a few of your colleagues who might benefit from knowing more about my services?

(Naturally, I don't want anyone whose business competes with yours.)

Then just mail the letter back to me in the enclosed reply envelope.

I may want to mention your name when contacting these people. Let me know if there's any problem with that.

And thanks for the favor!

Regards,

Steve Miller

TESTIMONIALS

Testimonials can benefit many self-promotions—including brochures, direct mail, ads, and press releases. A testimonial is a statement from a satisfied client praising you and your services. A typical testimonial might read:

> "Thanks for the training program on 'People Skills for DP Professionals.' The techniques you taught have already improved relations between users and software developers in our organization and have helped us get through a major bottleneck on one important new system."
>
> May Stoddard, Manager of Training
> Big Company, U.S.A.

Some testimonials are received unsolicited; for example, a client might send you a letter thanking you for a job well done. Naturally, this makes a good testimonial. However, before you use it, get the client's permission—in writing. Otherwise, clients may become angry if they see themselves quoted in your next ad or brochure without consent, and you will have damaged your relationship.

Getting permission is easy. To quote a client, send a standard permission letter similar to the one that follows.

date

Mr. Sam Smith
Anytown, USA

Dear Sam:

I never did get around to thanking you for your letter of 6/7/91 (copy attached). So . . . thanks!

I'd like to quote from this letter in the ads, brochures, direct-mail packages, and other promotions I use to market my catering services—with your permission, of course. If this is okay with you, would you please sign the bottom of this letter and send it back to me in the enclosed envelope. (The second copy is for your files.) Many thanks, Sam.

Regards,

Jean Wilson

YOU HAVE MY PERMISSION TO QUOTE FROM THE ATTACHED LETTER IN ADS, BROCHURES, MAIL, AND OTHER PROMOTIONS USED TO MARKET YOUR SERVICES.

Signature_____   Date_____

I always send a self-addressed stamped envelope and two copies of the letter. This way recipients don't have to copy the letter or address and stamp their own envelopes.

"But what if clients don't send me nice letters?" you may ask. That's okay—most clients won't, because most people don't bother to send notes and thank-you letters nowadays. However, this doesn't prevent you from asking satisfied clients to endorse your services with a testimonial. The following letter solicits favorable comments from clients.

date

Mr. Andrew Sprecher
Anywhere, USA

Dear Andrew:

I have a favor to ask of you.

I'm in the process of putting together a list of testimonials—a collection of comments about my services, from satisfied clients like yourself.

Would you take a few minutes to give me your opinion of my catering service? No need to dictate a letter—just jot your comments on the back of this letter, sign below, and return to me in the enclosed envelope. (The second copy is for your files.) I look forward to learning what you *like* about my service . . . but I also welcome any suggestions or criticisms too.

Many thanks, Andrew.

Regards,

Jean Wilson

YOU HAVE MY PERMISSION TO QUOTE FROM MY COMMENTS AND USE THESE QUOTATIONS IN ADS, BROCHURES, MAIL, AND OTHER PROMOTIONS USED TO MARKET YOUR SERVICES.

Signature_____   Date_____

Note that this letter asks for an "opinion" instead of a testimonial and that it urges the recipient to give criticisms as well as positive comments. In this way you are not just asking for a favor; you're getting information that will help you service the client better in the future. You are not the only one who profits; both you and the client do.

DIRECT MAIL

When other service providers ask me "What is the most effective self-promotion for you?" I answer without hesitation: direct mail.

You can quickly write an effective sales letter and mail it to prospective clients. It is a relatively inexpensive promotion, and it gives you great control over cost, because you can mail as few or as many letters as you wish.

Direct mail can be as simple as a one-page letter or as complex as a multicomponent package with see-through windows, color brochures, order forms, reply envelopes, computer-personalized letters, and other inserts. It can be produced using only a typewriter or word processor, or you can add color, glossy stock, photographs, drawings, pop-ups, and three-dimensional objects.

In my experience, cheap and simple is best for service providers who mail limited quantities on a limited budget. My standard package consists of a one-page letter (a typed form letter printed on one side) and a reply card mailed in my regular #10 business envelope.

Although I could personalize each letter using my computer, I prefer a form letter because it's faster and easier to produce and mail. If I personalized, I could mail letters only when I wasn't using my computer to do client work. A form letter can be pulled off the shelf and stuffed in an envelope any time, in seconds.

If you need a lot of leads, you can mail in large quantities.

I like to "test" any new letter by mailing to one hundred prospects. If the letter generates a good response, you can use it in larger quantities—say, five hundred or so at a time. If the letter fails to produce any replies, go back to the typewriter and try again.

Also, there's no law that says you have to mail in large quantities. Whenever I learn of potential clients—say, an ad agency with a new account, or a company launching a new product—I can look them up in a business directory, address an envelope to the appropriate person, and drop a form letter in the mail. This is much quicker than writing a personal letter from scratch and allows me to reach many new prospects I might not otherwise have time to contact.

The following is a simple one-page form letter I mailed to prospects listed in business directories. Mailed with a reply card in a standard #10 business envelope, the letter generated a 7 percent response.

HOW AN ENGINEER AND FORMER AD MANAGER CAN HELP YOU WRITE BETTER ADS AND BROCHURES.

For many people, industrial advertising is a difficult chore. It's detailed work, and highly technical. To write the copy, you need someone with the technical know-how of an engineer and the communications skills of a copywriter.

That's where I can help.

As a freelance industrial and high-tech copywriter who is also a graduate engineer, I know how to write clear, technically sound, hard-selling copy. You'll like my writing samples—ads, brochures, catalogs, direct mail, PR, and AV. And you'll like having a writer on call who works only when you need him.

Here are my qualifications:

I have an engineering background (BS, chemical engineering, University of Rochester). I started out writing brochures and AV scripts for the Westinghouse Defense Center. After I left Westinghouse, I became advertising manager for Koch Engineering, a manufacturer of process equipment.

In my freelance work, I've handled projects in a wide variety of industries including computers, software, chemicals, industrial equipment, electronics, publishing, banking, health care, and telecommunications. My articles on business communications have appeared in *Business Marketing*, *Computer Decisions*, *Amtrak Express*, *Chemical Engineering*, and *Audio-Visual Directions*. And I'm the author of *The Copywriter's Handbook* (Henry Holt), *A Dictionary of Computer Words* (Dell/Banbury), and nine other books.

Now I'd like to help *you* create ads, brochures, and other promotions. Call me when your creative team is overloaded, or when the project is highly technical.

I'd be delighted to send you a complete information kit on my copywriting services. The package includes a client list, fee schedule, biographical information, and samples of my work. Just complete and mail the enclosed reply card and the kit is yours—at no cost or obligation to you, of course.

Sincerely,

Bob Bly

P.S. Mail the reply card *today* and I'll also send you a free copy of the much-reprinted article, "10 Tips for Writing More Effective Industrial Copy."

You can either adapt my letter to suit your needs, or write your own letter from scratch. If you want to write your own letter, here's an outline you can use:

1. Begin with an opening statement that grabs attention.

You can promise a benefit, as I do in my headline.
Or you might get attention by stating a fascinating
fact, quoting a statistic, or asking a provocative question.

2. Next identify the reader's problem. Then offer your
   services as a solution. I do this in the three opening
   paragraphs of my letter.

3. Elaborate on your background, showing why you are
   uniquely qualified to solve the client's problem. Explain why your services are superior, or why you have
   the best qualifications for the job. In my letter, this
   section follows the sentence "Here are my qualifications."

4. Call for action. Ask the reader to phone or write or mail
   back a reply form. Offer a reason for the reader to respond, such as free information, a free consultation, a
   free meeting, a free analysis, or free estimate. Tell readers the specific action you want them to take and spell
   out the benefits they will receive if they respond *now*.

5. Always include a reply card the reader can use to
   reply and request more information. The typical headline for such a card is "YES, I'd like to know more
   about how [name of service] can provide [major bene-
   fit]." The reply card does not have to be a business
   reply card; you can put a box in the front upper-right
   corner that says, "Place stamp here." However, using
   a business reply card enhances your image a bit and
   may also lift response slightly.

6. The reply card should leave ample room for the prospect to fill in name, title, and company name (if mailing to businesses), address, city, state, and phone
   number. Under the headline, the reader should be
   able to indicate the desired action by checking a box.
   Typically this might read:

   [   ] I'm interested. Please call me to
         arrange a FREE estimate.

[   ] Please send more information by mail.

The first offer is called the "hard" offer. It is for prospects who have an immediate need, and checking it results in a phone call or visit by the seller. The second offer is called the "soft" offer, because it enables the prospect to find out more without making personal contact with you. Typically, 90 percent of prospects will check the soft offer; only 10 percent will have an immediate need and check the hard offer.

Of the prospects who check either offer, 10 to 25 percent will eventually become clients within a time frame ranging from a month to a year or longer. The rest, for one reason or another, will not become clients. Some were not really interested but were just curious. Some people just like to get brochures in the mail and will respond to any offer. Some had a need but did nothing about it or chose someone else. And your service may not have been right for others.

7. Mail your sales letters in regular #10 business envelopes. Type the recipient's name, title, company, and address directly on the envelope. Do not use labels. A recent article in the *Wall Street Journal* reports that many corporate mail rooms dump mailers sent to titles rather than individual names, so always use the prospect's name.

The advantage of having a tested sales letter—one that will generate a certain percentage response every time you mail it—is that you can quickly produce as many sales leads as you need, whenever you need them. For example, if your letter generates a 3 percent response, mailing one hundred letters will, on average, produce three inquiries. If your goal is to get ten sales leads, you will need to mail three hundred to four hundred letters. As a rule, you'll get the majority of responses to your letter within two to four weeks after you mail it.

PERSONAL LETTERS

If you have the time and feel that direct mail is too imper-
sonal for your taste, you could write personalized letters
targeted to specific prospects. The key is to personalize not
only with the person's name but with specific details that
show your knowledge of the business, industry, products,
and goals.

For about two months in 1981, I tried to start a small ad
agency in New York City. One freelance writer sent me a
letter that began "Dear Mr. Bly: Congratulations on your
new business. May you have great success and pleasure
in it." I found this opening effective because it flattered me
and showed me that the writer knew something about my
company.

One way to personalize without writing a brand-new letter each time is to write a basic "boilerplate" (standard)
letter that you can then tailor to a particular reader by
adding a few details. If you write an entirely new letter to
every prospect, you may get good response but you won't be
able to get many letters in the mail. The overall effect may
be a reduction in total leads produced instead of an increase.

You can use my letter (shown earlier) as a model, or try
something totally different. The important point is that you
are not committed to your first effort, nor will a bad sales
letter ruin your reputation. At worst, it simply won't get any
response. The important thing is to try a variety of ap-
proaches and learn which works best for you.

ADVERTISING

Another way to get people to call and ask about your services is to advertise in newspapers, magazines, and directories. While your own experience and judgment may suggest
where to run your initial ads, you can't really predict which

publication will work best. As with direct mail, you should test your ads—both the content and where you place them. Only by testing do you know which ad and which publications will get the best response.

Although I have run larger ads, I have found that small classified and display ads work best for me. In any case, I recommend that you test small versions of your ad first. If the smaller ad gets good results, you can do a larger version based on the same theme. But if the ad flops, rewrite and try again before spending more money on a bigger version.

Where should you advertise? Obviously, in publications read by your prospective clients. And which are these? It depends on your business, on the services you offer, and the market you want to reach.

A useful reference for people who advertise is the Standard Rate and Data Service (SRDS), 3004 Glenview Road, Wilmette, IL 60091, (708) 256-6067. SRDS publishes comprehensive directories listing all magazines and newspapers, plus advertising rates for each publication. SRDS directories are available at most local libraries.

However, common sense and experience are at least as useful as SRDS in planning your advertising. In what publications do other service providers in your area advertise? What publications are your clients reading? What publications do *you* read?

You should advertise in publications read by your *prospects*, not by other vendors. If you are a painter, for example, advertise in the town newspaper, not in *Professional House-Painter's Bulletin*.

One good indication that a publication is worth trying is that your competitors are already advertising in it. If no one in your field advertises in a magazine or newspaper, there may be a very good reason for that. Advertise where others do—or, as advertising expert Joe Barnes puts it, "Fish where the fish are biting."

Don't neglect small, local publications, such as the news-

letters of local business associations or bulletins produced by
professional groups and associations. Weekly newspapers,
penny savers, and town shoppers are excellent for local service businesses such as real estate agents, insurance agents,
financial planners, painters, roofers, and other contractors.

Once, for $2, I placed a thirty-five-word ad in *IABC Em-
ployment Letter*, a newsletter published by the local chapter
of the International Association of Business Communicators.
The first (and only) call I received resulted in an immediate
$5,000 assignment to write an annual report.

Once you have been in business for a time, you will begin
to receive many solicitations in the mail asking you to advertise in a variety of professional directories. If you decide to
try an ad, insist that it be placed in a separate category for
your specific type of service. Don't allow your ad to be placed
in a category that's too generic; otherwise, no one will find it.

For example, if you are an executive recruiter, insist on a
category titled "Executive Recruiters." Don't allow the directory to place your ad under the broader category "Management Consultants"; no one thinks of looking under
"Management Consultants" for a headhunter.

Some business publications have separate sections for
classified and display ads offering business services. People
turn to these sections when they are looking for a service, so
your best bet is to put your ad in that section under the
appropriate category. However, you might also want to test
an ad outside of the special section.

My advertising strategy is to run a small classified ad in
the special services section of *Adweek*, one of the leading
trade publications covering my industry (advertising). My
ad runs all year long. That way, people can always find my
name when they turn to the section to look for a writer. I also
have developed ads for other publications that I run periodically when I want to increase the flow of new business
leads.

WRITING THE AD

In a small ad, you don't have room for a lot of sales talk, so you must stick to the essentials. The ad must communicate in a clear, direct fashion: who you are, the services you offer, type of clients you serve, the next step, and how to get in touch with you.

If you are advertising in a magazine where no other service providers in your industry or profession are running ads, you can gain attention simply by stressing your service in the headline. Because there are no other ads for this service, people interested in your type of service will be drawn to the headline. For instance, if you are the only collection agency advertising in a local business magazine, your ad might read as follows:

COLLECT THOSE OVERDUE BILLS!

We help you get the money owed you to increase your cash flow. To turn old invoices into cash fast, call Watson & Crick Collections, phone XXX–XXXX.

On the other hand, if many other collection agencies advertise in this publication, you would need something special to make yours stand out from the crowd.

Some ad writers would elect to use a clever headline. I prefer to target readers by stressing a benefit or specialty. For instance:

BUSINESS-TO-BUSINESS COLLECTION SPECIALISTS

We use proven techniques that get business customers to pay bills while retaining good customer relations. You get cash *without* losing valued clients. For details call Watson & Crick Collections, phone XXX–XXXX.

Stressing the offer of a free booklet or report can also be a successful tactic:

10 NEW WAYS TO COLLECT OLD BILLS!
Free booklet explains collection secrets that turn your old unpaid invoices into cash—fast! For your copy, call or write Watson & Crick Collections, 100 Main St., Anytown, USA, phone XXX–XXXX.

There are two additional points to keep in mind with small ads. First, although repetition helps create an awareness of your name, most ads gradually lose their impact over time. When the number of responses begins dropping off, you might consider running a new ad. (But save the old one. You may want to rerun it later.)

Second, competition will hurt your response. When I was one of only a few writers advertising in *Adweek*, response was great. As more and more writers took out ads surrounding mine (many of them lifting sections of my headline and copy and using it in their own ads!), response dropped off. When the competition gets thick, you must work extra hard to make your ad stand out. On the other hand, *no* competition may indicate that the publication doesn't work for your type of offer. But you can always test it and see.

On occasion I have run larger ads in select publications. You can get more response and attention with a larger ad, but the price of the space can be stiff. Although some of my big ads were successful, I find that the smaller ads are more cost effective in most cases. The exception is in highly targeted business directories or local and regional business publications where small businesspeople can afford even a full-page ad.

Some additional tips for making ads generate more response:

1. The headline should either stress a benefit ("IN-CREASE PRODUCTIVITY!"), the nature of your service and your specialty ("ROOF REPAIR FOR VICTORIAN HOMES"), or an offer of free information ("NEW FREE BOOKLET TELLS HOW TO REDUCE LONG-DISTANCE PHONE BILLS").

2. Ask for action. Tell the reader to phone, write, or send a fax for more information.

3. Offer free information, such as a brochure, catalog, report, pamphlet, or booklet.

4. Show a small picture of your brochure or booklet.

5. Describe the contents or special features of your free information ("Includes 12-month lawn care maintenance schedule").

6. Give your literature a title that implies value. "Information kit" is better than "sales brochure." "Resource guide" is better than "catalog."

7. Include your fax number in your ad, if you have one and are aiming at business audiences.

8. Put a heavy dashed border or other unusual border treatment around your small ad to make it stand out.

9. Offer a free consultation, analysis, recommendation, study, cost estimate, computer printout, critique, and so on.

10. Talk about the value and benefits of this free offer.

11. Test different small ads. Keep track of how many inquiries each ad pulls. Then run only those ads that pull best.

12. Put your name in the ad as well as your company name. Invite the reader to contact you personally.

13. Use a testimonial from a satisfied client as a headline or in body copy.

14. Use your photo in the ad to personalize the message.

15. Consider using a toll-free hotline. Pete Silver, a professional speaker, has a toll-free number, 800–MR–SPEAKER.

NETWORKING

Networking is a new name for an activity that has been going on for a long time: doing business through personal contacts. The purpose of networking is to meet as many people as possible who can, in some way, help advance your career. And the reason these other people are networking is to find someone who can help them—perhaps you. "I go to luncheons and meetings even when I'm busy," says entrepreneur Joan Harris. "These give me high visibility which translates into lots of new contacts, referrals, and actual business."

Is it necessary to network? I'm living proof that it isn't. I've served more than a hundred satisfied clients, have a steady flow of new-business leads at all times, and only a few have come to me through networking, meetings, or social contacts (most are through direct mail, publicity, public speaking, articles, or word of mouth). I used to tell beginning service providers, "Don't bother with networking; you don't need to do it and it's a waste of time."

Now, however, I'm starting to "come out of my shell" (as some of my colleagues have observed) and am making much more of an effort to meet people, make contacts, and join and participate in professional societies and informal groups— even though I'm shy and an introvert by nature.

Why? There are several benefits. First, if yours is a one-person business, work is a solitary activity, and loneliness can be a problem. One way to cope with isolation is to force yourself to get away from the office every now and then. It can be mentally stimulating and refreshing to have lunch with a group of service providers or attend an evening lecture sponsored by a local business club. You meet new people, make friends, and exchange ideas.

Forming a "network"—a group of people you know and who know you—can open up many new doors for you. For instance, at one luncheon I met a man who recently opened his own printing business. We established a good rapport, and he now does most of my printing for me, paying closer attention to my jobs than other printers I had found through local Yellow Pages ads.

Networking builds a base of "people resources" you can count on to help you with many situations. Now I can turn to my card file and find artists, writers, printers, photographers, lawyers, accountants, and many other professionals who can be of service to me or my clients. I know I'll get immediate attention from these people because we've already established a personal relationship, no matter how brief.

Often I will refer one person in my network to another person who can help. For example, an audiovisual producer called and asked if I knew someone who could direct an industrial film for her. I was able to give her the name of an independent director I had met. The referral ended the producer's search and put some money in the director's pocket. And, while I never asked for it, I'm sure both of these people would be glad to return the favor some day.

Finally, networking can also lead to more business for you. Most often, someone you meet through networking may keep your card and someday give your name to a prospective client. Or sometimes you meet a potential client directly. In either case, the more people who know your name, the better.

The advantage of networking over advertising is that people you meet through networking are more likely to remember you because of the face-to-face contact.

Before I got involved in networking, I kept an eye on the "meetings" section of several trade journals and promised myself I'd go . . . *when* I had the time. As it turned out, I never had the time and never went to any meetings. If you're like me, a good way to get started in networking is to join several clubs or associations. Paying the membership dues somehow makes me feel that I should at least attend a meeting or two to get my money's worth. (I am currently a member of the Business/Professional Advertising Association and the American Institute of Chemical Engineers.)

Another way to force yourself to go is call up a friend and invite him or her to a luncheon or evening meeting. Do it several weeks in advance. Making the commitment early helps prevent you from backing out at the last minute.

Ten Tips for More Productive Networking

1. Always bring a handful of business cards. Exchange cards with everyone you meet.
2. Don't be a wallflower. Try to walk over to people and make conversation.
3. Get a drink from the bar and hold onto it, even if you don't drink (drinking mineral water and club soda is "in" these days). Having a glass in hand can help shy people overcome nervousness.
4. Do not sell while networking. Your purpose is to make contacts, not get a client to sign a purchase order.
5. If you've never attended a meeting of a particular group before, go with a friend who can introduce you to people in the group.
6. Dress in proper business attire. Your comfortable, well-worn "work-at-home" clothes are not appropriate for a business gathering.
7. The best way to make friends and get people talking is to ask them questions. Instead of telling all about yourself, ask other people about what *they* do.
8. When you get home, follow up by sending people a short note that says "It was a pleasure meeting you—let's keep in touch." You might also enclose another business card, a brochure about your services, or a reprint of a recent article you wrote.

9. Keep a "contact file" of business cards, organized alphabetically or by type of business.
10. When making referrals, think of people in your contact file first. Sending some business to a person is a good way of cementing the relationship between you.

Networking can result in referrals not only from service providers in other fields but from people working in your own field and offering similar services—even direct competitors. There are certain jobs you will take on your competitor won't, and vice versa. If you know each other and are aware of your respective specialties, you can refer business to each other.

For instance, as a writer, I get numerous calls from people who want me to write instruction manuals. I don't do instruction manuals, but I refer those leads to three writers I know who do. In return, they've referred me for work they knew they couldn't handle but that was right up my alley.

Networking, advertising, cold calling, telemarketing, referrals, and writing letters are all action-oriented marketing techniques focused on generating an immediate, direct response—an inquiry from a potential client with an immediate or future need for your services.

As important and powerful as they are, these direct-response methods are only half of a total new business marketing effort. The other half consists of the soft-sell, visibility-building publicity techniques, such as writing articles, being interviewed by the media, and giving speeches. These methods are covered in the next chapter.

CHAPTER TWO

Publicity
Techniques That Work

How do you promote yourself? Does sending out press releases work for service providers? How can you get the media to pay attention to you? I'll show you what techniques can work for you, including article-writing, giving speeches, teaching, seminars, newsletters, premiums, sending out press releases, and getting the media to write about you.

ARTICLES

A full-page ad in a business publication can cost $2,200, $4,500, even $5,500 or more. And small display ads in your local newspaper can run several hundred dollars per insertion. But how would you like to get that space for *free*? That's what article-writing can do for you.

Next to direct mail, writing articles for the trade press is the most effective self-promotion I have used. Recent articles that have appeared under my byline include: "31 Ways to Get More Inquiries from your Ads" (*Business Marketing*), "29 Good Story Ideas for Your Corporate Newsletter" (*Busi-*

ness Marketing), "23 Tips for Creating Business-to-Business Mailings that Work" (*Who's Mailing What!*), "How to Get Your Technical Feature Article Published" (*Business Marketing*), "22 Rules for Successful Self-Promotion" (*Direct Marketing*), "10 Ways to Improve Your Trade Show Direct Mail" (*Exhibitor*), "How to Improve Your Presentation Skills" (*CPI100*), "How to Write Business Letters that Get Results" (*Amtrak Express*), "Why Engineers Can't Write" (*CPI100*), "10 Ways to Stretch Your Advertising Budget" (*Business Marketing*), "Marketing to Engineers" (*Direct Marketing*), and "How to Write Sales Brochures" (*Writer's Digest*).

These articles have several things in common. To begin with, they are all short. When writing an article for publication, I try to limit the length to 1,500 words so that it can be reprinted on one or two sides of a single 8½- by 11-inch sheet using my office copier. However, if the subject deserves a more comprehensive treatment, I'll write a longer piece.

Second, most of the articles are written in list form—twenty-two rules, ten tips, thirty-one ways. List articles are easy to organize, easy to write, and—importantly—easy to read. I can write a short list article in less than an hour. Yet editors tell me that of all the articles I publish, these list articles are the most popular with their readers.

Third, the articles all deal with subjects related to the services I offer my clients. This is intentional. One of the best ways to demonstrate your expertise in a subject is to write and publish an article about it. For instance, if you specialize in producing slide presentations, you can impress clients by sending them a reprint of an article you wrote on the topic of audiovisual presentations.

Sit down now with pencil and paper and try to generate a list of article ideas that relate to your particular business and specialties. Pin this list to your bulletin board, and make an effort to sell at least one of these articles to an editor within the next two months.

I use reprints of my articles as supplementary sales literature. If a client asks me about public relations, I send my
article on publicity. If a client wants me to write a speech, I'll
send a reprint of my article on how to give a good presentation. If a client calls and asks, "What do you know about
catalog marketing?" I'll send reprints of columns I wrote
on catalog copy for *The Business-to-Business Catalog
Marketer.*

Another way to get the most out of your articles is to
enclose reprints along with your direct-mail letters. You can
send the article with your regular direct-mail letter. Or the
article itself can be the focus of the mailing.

In one mailing I mailed reprints of an article to one
hundred clients and prospects, each with a handwritten note
that said "Hi, Jim (or Jane or Joe). Here's an article you
might find interesting . . . and (I hope) helpful. Regards,
Bob." This is a great way to keep in touch with clients or
impress prospects. People need information and respond
well to it.

For small quantities of article reprints, you can photocopy. If you need one hundred or more, have them offset at a
local print shop. For quantities of five hundred or more, the
publication may be willing to sell you reprints on glossy
stock. Be sure to have your name, address, and phone number appear on every article reprint—and every other promotion you send out.

When writing self-promotion articles, which publications
should you target? You can write for:

- local daily and weekly newspapers
- penny savers and shoppers
- trade publications read by those in your own profession
- trade publications in industries in which your clients
  work
- local business publications
- local consumer magazines

- national business magazines
- national consumer and general-interest magazines

Although, ideally, you hope that a great number of potential clients read the publication in which your article appears, this isn't always necessary. Why not? Because the article has great value as a *reprint*. If your prospects aren't likely to read it in the magazine, you can always rent a list of names and mail it to them.

Several directories list magazines by category (advertising, sales and marketing, writing, business) and by industry (chemical, pulp and paper, food processing, construction). Two of the best are *Bacon's Publicity Checker*, published by Bacon's Publishing Company, 332 South Michigan Avenue, Chicago, IL 60604, (312) 922–2400 or (800) 621–0561, and *Writer's Market*, published by Writer's Digest Books, 1507 Dana Avenue, Cincinnati, OH 45207, (513) 531–2222.

But a better place to start is with the magazines you now read, because you're already familiar with their editorial style and content. For example, if a local business magazine has a monthly column written by a different person each month, write to the editor suggesting an idea for the column.

If you've written for magazines before, you already know the procedure for proposing an article. If you haven't, take a look at *Writer's Market*; it contains some helpful guidelines. The best book I've ever read on how to publish magazine articles is *The Freelance Writer's Handbook* by Gary Provost (New York: New American Library, 1982). I also recommend *How to Write Articles That Sell* by L. Perry Wilbur (New York: John Wiley & Sons, 1981).

Must you be a professional writer to produce an article editors will run? No. In fact, for many types of how-to and informative articles, editors would rather get contributions from experts and professionals—you—than from a reporter

or journalist who is researching the subject as an outsider
and lacks the intimate knowledge to make the article accurate and meaningful. So don't worry. People like you are
approaching editors—and getting articles published—all
the time.

The best approach is to send editors a brief letter outlining your article idea. Give the title of the article, the major
points you will cover, why this information is important to
the publication's readers, and your qualifications for writing
the piece. The following is a query letter that was successful.
It sold because it took a general topic—technical writing—
and slanted it toward the specific audience reading the
magazine—chemical engineers.

date

Mr. Kenneth J. McNaughton
Associate Editor
CHEMICAL ENGINEERING
McGraw-Hill Building
1221 Avenue of the Americas
New York, NY 10020

Dear Mr. McNaughton:

When a chemical engineer can't write a coherent report,
the true value of his investigation or study may be dis-
torted or unrecognized. His productivity vanishes. And
his chances for career advancement diminish.

As an associate editor of *Chemical Engineering*, you
know that many chemical engineers could use some help
in improving their technical writing skills. I'd like to
provide that help by writing an article that gives your
readers "Ten Tips for Better Business Writing."

This 2,000-word piece would provide ten helpful tips—
each less than 200 words—to help chemical engineers
write better letters, reports, proposals, and articles.

For example, engineers and managers need to be more

concise in their writing. Too many engineers would write about an "accumulation of particulate matter about the peripheral interior surface of the vessel" when they're describing solids buildup. And how many managers would use the phrase "until such time as" when they simply mean "until"?

My book, *Technical Writing: Structure, Standards, and Style*, will be published by the McGraw-Hill Book Company in November. While the book speaks to a wide range of technical disciplines, my article will draw its examples from the chemical engineering literature.

I hold a B.S. in chemical engineering from the University of Rochester, and am a member of the American Institute of Chemical Engineers. Until this past January, I was manager of marketing communications for Koch Engineering, a manufacturer of chemical process equipment. Now I'm an independent copywriter specializing in industrial advertising.

Ken, I'd like to write "Ten Tips for Better Technical Writing" for your "You and Your Job" section.

How does this sound?

Sincerely,

Bob Bly

Always enclose a #10 self-addressed stamped envelope with your query. If you don't hear from the editor within ten weeks, write a follow-up. If you still don't hear, write another letter saying you are withdrawing the article from consideration. Then try another publication.

Say you get an assignment to write an article. If, after you submit it, the editor calls or writes to say that she liked the article, be prepared to suggest another article you can write for her publication. An editor who is enthusiastic about your writing is your best prospect for future article sales.

Once you write several articles for an editor, you may get

to the point where you don't need to write query letters. If you have a good relationship with an editor, you may be able to call her, give a quick outline of your idea, and get an immediate go-ahead over the phone. It's a real advantage to have at least one editor who will publish your articles on a regular basis. This way you always have a forum where you can get new ideas into print.

A big question service providers ask me is "Should I get paid for my articles?" Unlike consumer and general-interest magazines, which pay high rates for articles, many local shoppers and specialized trade journals do not pay. And those that do pay offer small fees, called honorariums, which typically range from $50 to $100 per magazine page.

One reason trade journals don't pay is that they figure you are writing the article to promote yourself. Therefore, they are giving you free publicity in exchange for your article.

Naturally, if a trade journal offers to pay for your article, you should accept—gladly. But should you insist on payment from magazines that don't regularly pay for articles? It depends on your goals.

When I started freelancing, I didn't care if I got paid for a trade journal article. The important thing, I reasoned, was to get publicity and reprints for self-promotion. My procedure was to ask what the magazine paid and accept that rate, even if it was zero.

Of course, if you feel strongly that writing articles is a paid activity, then you can try to negotiate a payment. Some editors may agree to it, while others will refuse. One strategy that has worked well for me is to barter: I write the article and take a free ad in the magazine instead of a cash fee.

Tip: Run your ad in the same issue in which your article appears. Ads get better responses when you also have an article in the magazine. Why? Because many people who read your article may become interested in knowing more about you. When they see your ad, it becomes easy to get in touch with you.

If you can propose a regular *column* in a magazine or newspaper widely read by your prospects, that's an even better promotion than an occasional article. Readers get used to seeing your column, and you gradually become famous in your community or profession. One column I used to write brought me an additional $40,000 in annual revenue from prospects who called as a direct result of the column.

A LITTLE-KNOWN TECHNIQUE FOR MAKING ARTICLE-WRITING MORE EFFECTIVE

Seeing your name in print is a wonderful ego boost, and it certainly impresses your clients. But there's a simple technique you can use to turn published articles into direct-response ads for your services that generate immediate inquiries and leads. How? By adding a *resource box*.

A *resource box* (the term was invented by Dr. Jeffrey Lant) is a more complete description of you than usually appears in the author's bio published at the end of an article. Instead of "Joe Jones is a management consultant based in New Jersey," a resource box contains a brief but complete description of your services plus complete information— name, address, phone number—on how readers can get in touch with you. For example:

Joe Jones is a management consultant specializing in customer training for supermarkets, restaurants, and other clients in the retail food industry. For a free copy of his newsletter, "The Customer Service Connection," call or write Joe Jones, Happy Drive, Anywhere, USA, phone XXX XXX–XXXX.

To get the resource box published with your article, don't specifically ask the editor if you can have one. Just type it on the last page of every article you submit. About 10 to 25 percent of the time, editors will use it without question. Editors who object initially usually can be swayed. For instance, if you're not getting paid for the article, you can say you'll waive your usual several-hundred-dollar fee for an article if they print the complete resource box as is. Some editors will accept this.

"Sure, the resource box is longer than the usual blurb," says Jeffrey Lant in his book, *Money Making Marketing* (Cambridge, MA: JLA Publications, 1987). "Sure, some publications won't give it. But fight for it. The essence of marketing is getting the prospect to trust you and to make it easy for him to take action when he does."

The majority of editors will not allow a resource box. In that case, your fall-back position is to ask for a free ad instead of payment for the article. What size ad? The biggest they'll allow. My rule of thumb is to ask for ad space with a dollar value equal to twice the fee the article is worth. But I'll swap an equal value if the editor is tough about it.

Should you write the article if the editor won't give you payment, a free ad, or a resource box? Initially, yes—the publicity is good, and you can use the reprints. Once you've published a lot of articles and have a number of editors regularly seeking articles from you, you can get tough about this with any new editor who asks for a contribution.

PUBLIC SPEAKING

Another great way to build your reputation and get your name around is by giving lectures. If you've written articles or books, or have gained a reputation locally as an authority in your field (either local or national), it is inevitable that at some point, someone will invite you to speak.

And if you're not invited? Then invite yourself. Write a letter to the program directors of local business organizations. Propose a topic and offer yourself as a speaker.

Most talks are given at lunch or dinner meetings of local clubs, trade associations, professional societies, or civic, community, or business groups. For instance, I have spoken before dozens of groups, including local chapters of the Women's Direct Response Group, Business/Professional Advertising Associations, Publicity Club of New York, Financial Advertising and Marketing Association, American Chemical Society, Society for Technical Communications, and Women in Communications, to name just a few.

The best place to speak is at any function where potential clients will be in attendance. If you get invited to speak, don't hesitate to ask about the meeting. How many people will attend? What companies are they from? What are their titles? Are they homeowners or renters? Giving talks to people who are not in a position to hire you may be fun, but it won't build your business.

Your topic should be directly related to your business. If you specialize in writing subscription promotions, and you are addressing a group of circulation managers, one possible topic might be "The Six Most Common Mistakes Made in Subscription Promotion—and How to Avoid Them."

The talk should not be a sales pitch for you or your services, however. It should provide the audience with interesting and helpful information on the topic. By giving your audience good advice, you establish yourself as an expert who they may want to use for further consultation on a paid basis.

Don't feel obliged to be entertaining or funny when you speak. Instead, concentrate on giving the clearest, most informative presentation you can. Speak in a relaxed, natural manner. And just be yourself.

Most presentations run fifteen to thirty minutes, with extra time for a question-and-answer period. Practice your speech at home and make sure it fits the time limit allotted for your presentation. Speakers who do not rehearse until they know their material "cold" are inviting disaster. And audiences hate it when speakers run over the time limit.

When you give a talk, bring along extra copies. At the beginning of your speech, let people know that copies are available. But don't hand them out until after you've finished. If you distribute the speech in advance, people will read it and ignore you.

An alternative to making copies of your speech is to distribute a handout summarizing key points or a recent article you've written on the topic of your talk. All handouts and reprints should have your name, address, and phone number printed on them so people can get in touch with you.

A big advantage of public speaking over writing articles is that speaking allows you to make contact with people on a more personal level. You make more of an impression speaking at a small or medium-size gathering because people get to see you, hear you, meet you, and shake hands with you. Mixing with the crowd before and after your talk, exchanging handshakes and business cards, is a good way to make contacts for new business.

A disadvantage of public speaking is that you reach far fewer people with a lecture than with an article. Thirty people at a luncheon might hear your speech on how to write more clearly. Yet thirty thousand people might read (or at least glance at) an article on that same topic published in a town shopper. Speeches take at least as much time to research and write as articles. And they must also be rehearsed a number of times. This is why I personally prefer articles to speeches, although I use both promotions.

A good way to maximize the promotional effectiveness of your speech is to tape-record it and distribute audiocassettes of the program to potential clients. Many prospects will listen to your tape while driving, giving you a captive audience. If they like what they hear, you'll get hired.

Audiocassettes can be duplicated, labeled, and boxed for around $1.25 a copy or so in quantities of fifty or less. I have mine reproduced at Dove Enterprises, 907 Portage Trail, Cuyahoga Falls, OH 44221, 800 233–DOVE.

One other thing to keep in mind is that a speech can always be turned into an article. The opposite is also true. Recycle your material whenever you can. It saves time and gets your message across to the broadest audience possible.

And what about money? Some groups will offer a small honorarium for speakers; most expect you to give them your wisdom for free. If you're doing it for the publicity, then don't worry about the pay. However, if you feel strongly that you should be paid for your time, then by all means ask program sponsors for a fee. The worst they can do is say no. If they do refuse, should you still accept the engagement? Dottie Walters, publisher of *Sharing Ideas* newsletter for speakers, says you should ask yourself the following questions concerning any invitation to speak without pay:

1. Will you be speaking to a room full of prospects whose business could keep you busy for the next year?
2. Will the organization publicize your name and picture to the market you hope to penetrate?
3. Will they give you a list of the attendees on labels? With phone numbers?
4. Will they give you a letter of recommendation?
5. Is the organization so prestigious that the mere fact that you spoke there will help your career by positioning you as a highly skilled expert in the marketplace?
6. Can you mingle and meet people of influence who can lead to paid contracts?
7. Can you write ahead to the attendees and tell them you will be at the hotel the day after your program and available for professional paid consultations?

I would add to the list: Is this a speech you would want to record and offer as an audiocassette program to potential clients?

For more information on making money as a *paid* speaker, read *Speak and Grow Rich* by Dottie and Lillet Walters (Englewood Cliffs, NJ: Prentice Hall, 1989).

TEACHING

For years I taught an evening class in advertising copywriting at New York University. The class, which met from six to eight Tuesday evenings, ran ten weeks every semester. Although my "official" rate of pay from NYU was $30 an hour, when you add up the time spent commuting to and from New York, grading homework, and preparing for class, my real take-home pay was closer to $10 an hour.

When I was teaching, friends asked, "Why do you continue to teach the course for $10 an hour when you are earning $200 per hour in your service business and already have a full schedule?"

One reason is that teaching a college-level course is, in many ways, another form of self-promotion. Saying that you teach a college course in your field is a very impressive credential to parade in front of potential clients.

As a service provider, the product you are selling is *you.* Doing such things as writing articles, giving speeches, and teaching college enhances your professional reputation, thus increasing your value in the marketplace. So in that sense teaching is a business builder.

A secondary benefit, in terms of promotion, is that occasionally prospective clients called and told me they got my name from the NYU course catalog or that NYU's administrative office recommended me. While I didn't get many leads this way, a few clients have come to me as a direct result of NYU. Some former students also hired me, although of course I would not work for people while they were students in my class.

Another reason why I taught is that I enjoy it. It's fun to teach your craft to other people. And teaching is educational. I have learned a great deal about advertising as a result of preparing lectures and teaching the class.

How do you get a teaching "gig"? Some people are lucky enough to be asked to teach. If not, you can always write a letter to the head of the appropriate department at your local community college. The college already has staff for its existing courses, so your best bet is to propose a new course. For example, NYU has an extensive program of copywriting courses, so my proposal for a specialized course in business-to-business copywriting was a natural extension of their curriculum. Your letter should also outline your qualifications for teaching the class.

If you get turned down, try another department or another college. Small community colleges, especially those with evening classes for adult education, are more likely to be receptive than Ivy League colleges and universities. You might also try contacting adult community education programs sponsored by local high schools. These programs frequently offer introductory courses on a variety of topics, including auto repair, carpentry, business, computers, writing, tax preparation, and so on.

Teaching is one self-promotion activity that you should be paid for. The college is making good money from tuition paid by students attending your class and can afford a modest salary for you. Hourly rates ranging from $10 to $40 are common for businesspeople teaching evening courses for adults.

SEMINARS

Another alternative to college teaching is to get into the seminar business. One way is to write to companies that sponsor and market seminars, and offer your services as a seminar leader. Check newspaper ads and your mailbox for promotions from seminar companies that give courses in your area. One such firm is Performance Seminar Group in Norwalk, Connecticut.

Another method is to create your own seminar and give it on your own. Here you would have to market the seminar as well as teach it.

Not only does being a seminar leader get your name around in your industry, but it can be profitable in its own right. Seminar leaders hired by big companies earn anywhere from $400 to $1,000 a day and up. And if you run your own seminar business, your income can be tremendous, depending on how many people attend your program. I know several service providers who found the seminar business so lucrative that they made it their main activity!

Arranging, marketing, and giving a seminar is a complex subject, one that cannot be adequately discussed here. Instead, let me recommend a few books on the topic:

How to Create and Market a Successful Seminar or Workshop, by Howard Shenson (Howard L. Shenson, 20750 Ventura Blvd., Woodland Hills, CA 91364, 818 703–1415)

How to Expand Your Consulting Practice with Seminars, by Herman Holtz (New York: John Wiley & Sons, 1987)

Money Talks: The Complete Guide to Creating a Profitable Workshop or Seminar in Any Field, by Dr. Jeffrey Lant (JLA Publications, 50 Follen Street, Suite 507, Cambridge, MA 02138, 617 547–6372)

Speaking for Money, by Gordon Burgett and Mike Frank (Communication Unlimited, P.O. Box 1001, Carpinteria, CA 93013)

NEWSLETTERS

A number of service providers and consultants I know use a newsletter to promote themselves and keep their name in front of potential clients. Self-published newsletters, mailed regularly, are a powerful way of building your reputation and awareness of your name with a select audience (the people receiving the newsletter) over an extended period of time. And nowadays newsletters are going beyond mere image-building. Many newsletters are mailed with a business reply card, encouraging readers to send for more information on products and services.

Should you use a newsletter? Like everything else in this chapter, I say: Try it and see. It may work for you. If not, you can always stop publishing.

A simple format is best. A promotional newsletter can be produced directly on your typewriter, word processor, or desktop publishing system and duplicated at a local "quick-print" shop. There is no need to have it typeset or hire a professional artist. "The newsletter must appear to the recipient to be totally for their benefit and without any advertising," says marketing consultant and newsletter publisher Pete Silver.

How long should the newsletter be? Two sides of a sheet of typing paper is fine. Four pages is also a good length. Longer than that isn't needed. People won't read a longer newsletter unless the content is exceptionally informative or provides exclusive information.

How often should you publish? Four to six times a year seems ideal. If you publish more frequently, writing the newsletter may interfere with your other work, or you might run out of fresh material. And people tend to ignore newsletters that come out less than once a quarter.

And what about content? Your newsletter should provide solid information, tips, and advice on topics related to the professional services you sell to your clients. For instance, if

you design sales training programs for companies based in
Silicon Valley, your newsletter might be titled "The Silicon
Valley Sales Reporter." Articles would provide tips on how to
sell high-tech products.

Having said this, I must confess that I have never used a
newsletter to promote my own business. I've always felt that
if I'm going to write something, I may as well publish it as an
article so that it reaches a wider audience. And because my
schedule is fairly hectic, I don't want to commit myself to a
regular publishing schedule. But of course, you may feel
differently.

PREMIUMS

A premium is a free gift item you distribute to prospects and
customers. Most premiums are inexpensive items ranging in
price from $1 to $10 and imprinted with the advertiser's
logo, company name, address, phone number, and possibly a
short slogan or descriptive phrase.

The purpose of giving away premiums is twofold: First,
you create goodwill by giving people a gift, no matter how
small or inexpensive. And second, the gift serves as a constant reminder of you and your services.

My dad, for example, is an insurance agent. Each year he
mails an attractive wall calendar, imprinted with his company name, address, and phone number, to his clients. Posted
on a wall at home or in the office, the calendar puts my father's
name in front of his customers the whole year-round. An
advantage of premiums is that people *keep* them—unlike
advertisements and sales letters, which are read once and
then thrown away or filed out of sight and out of mind.

Typical premiums include coffee mugs, key chains, pocket
tool kits, golf caps, T-shirts, umbrellas, imprinted Post-It™
Notes, pads, golf balls, pocket sewing kits, memo pads,

pens, pencils, windbreakers, watches, clocks, balloons, and tote bags. But don't just pick an item out of a premium catalog. The best premiums are ones that are original, unusual, or that have a strong tie-in with the product or service you are offering.

Sometimes an idea for a premium just strikes your fancy and seems right. About a year ago I received a promotional mailing for an item called the BIG CLIP. The BIG CLIP is an oversized (five inches long) plastic paper clip that can be imprinted with any message.

As I always use a big paper clip to hold together the pages of the finished manuscripts and consulting reports I mail to clients, the BIG CLIP was a natural for me. I ordered 250 BIG CLIPS imprinted as follows:

> For "industrial-strength" copy . . .
> BOB BLY (201) 599–2277
> Freelance Copywriter
> 174 Holland * New Milford, NJ 07646

Now every finished assignment I mail out is held together with a BIG CLIP. One client commented: "Your oversized clip really stands out in my desk drawer. Every time I look down I see your name!"

Try a premium for yourself. Don't give people the same old coffee mug or golf cap or ball-point pen that everyone else does. Try to think of something unusual, original, unique . . . something that ties in nicely with your sales pitch.

PRESS RELEASES

Another low-cost way of getting publicity is to send out press releases to the media. A press release is a short news or feature story typed up and distributed to a list of editors who might be interested in running a story based on its contents. Unlike a feature article, the press release is mass-mailed and not exclusive to any one editor or publication. Editors understand this and receive hundreds of releases every day, so the format is perfectly acceptable to them.

Most giant corporations and big PR agencies churn out press release after press release. Most of them fail to get any attention because they are about routine, mundane matters that are of no interest to editors. A typical release of this type begins "XYZ firm has opened a new office" or "Joe Jones has been promoted from assistant vice president to vice president at Friendly Bank." Really? Who cares? At best, such ho-hum news gets a one-line mention in the "News Brief" column—hardly worth the effort.

One PR agency sent a letter to editors that began "Frank Smith, CEO of Our Company, is available for an interview. When would you like to interview him?" Most corporate executives are egomaniacs. What Frank Smith doesn't realize is that *no* editor wants to interview him—unless given a reason to do so or an angle for a news story about Frank or his firm.

The key to using press releases successfully is as follows. Most corporate PR people look for events (most of which are trivial), then write news releases about these events. Their thinking is "I need to send out so many releases this month; what can I write about?" They start with a desire to send out a release, not an idea for a story.

You should do the opposite: Start with a newsworthy story, angle, hook, or other information, then write a release to highlight this information and present it to editors. And here's the key: If you can't find something newsworthy to write about your business, *invent* it.

I'm not saying to lie or make things up. Rather, I'm saying to come up with an idea that's newsworthy, implement the idea, then write about it. The best way to illustrate this point is with the following examples.

Powerful Press Release Ideas that Work

One of the most effective public relations strategies is to send out a press release offering a free booklet, report, or other useful information.

In this type of release, the first few paragraphs announce the publication and availability of the booklet and summarize its contents, the body excerpts some of the helpful advice (in the hopes the editor will run a longer article based on it), and the closing paragraph tells how readers can obtain the booklet.

FROM: Bob Bly, 174 Holland Avenue,
New Milford, NJ 07646
CONTACT: Bob Bly—(201) 599–2277

For immediate release

NEW FREE BOOKLET REVEALS 31 WAYS TO GET MORE INQUIRIES FROM YOUR ADS

New Milford, NJ, September—A new booklet, published by independent copywriter and advertising consultant Robert W. Bly, reveals 31 strategies for creating ads that generate more inquiries, leads, sales, and profits for advertisers.

The booklet, "31 Ways to Get More Inquiries from Your Ads," is available free of charge to business executives, entrepreneurs, advertising professionals, and students. The cost to the general public is $1.

Bly said he originally wrote the booklet for companies and ad agencies that need to see more of a bottom-line return from advertising campaigns originally designed purely to build "image" and awareness.

"There's no reason an image campaign can't also generate leads as well as awareness," says Bly. "High-quality

inquiries mean more sales and profits. And they also
provide a way of measuring response. The booklet presents 31 ways to increase any ad's pulling power without
destroying the basic concept or interfering with communication of the key message."

Some of the inquiry-producing techniques presented
in the booklet include:

- Offer free information—a booklet, brochure, catalog,
  price list, order form—in every ad you write.
- Give your literature piece a title that implies value.
  "*Product guide* sounds better than *catalog*," notes Bly.
  "*Planning kit* implies greater value than *sales bro-
  chure*."
- For a full-page ad, use a coupon. According to Bly,
  "This will increase response 25 to 100 percent."
- Make the coupon large enough so that there is plenty of
  room for prospects to write in their name and address.
  "Tiny coupons drive people crazy," notes Bly.
- In a fractional ad, put a heavy dashed border around
  the ad. "This creates a couponlike appearance, which in
  turn stimulates response," explains Bly.
- Offer something FREE—such as a free product sample, free report, free video or audiocassette, free analysis, free consultation, free estimate, free seminar,
  free demonstration, or free trial.

Says Bly: "By modifying existing ads using the techniques outlined in this booklet, advertisers can increase
response to their ads 20 to 100 percent—without destroying the basic concept and theme of their campaigns."

To receive a free copy of "31 Ways to Get More Inquiries from Your Ads," send a self-addressed stamped
#10 envelope to: Advertising Inquiries, Dept. SS, 174
Holland Avenue, New Milford, NJ 07646.

Bob Bly is a freelance copywriter specializing in

business-to-business and direct response advertising and the author of eighteen books including *The Copywriter's Handbook* (Henry Holt and Co.).

I sent this release to fifty advertising trade publications, but it was also picked up by many business magazines and newsletters. I enclosed a copy of the booklet with each release that went out. The publicity generated fifteen short articles about me, which generated 2,500 requests for the booklet. (An article in *Nation's Business* generated 400 of these inquiries, and I still got an occasional request more than two years after it ran.)

Alan Caruba, a New Jersey PR counselor, wanted to gain some publicity for his business. The challenge: Caruba is one of hundreds of independent PR counselors, and there is nothing newsworthy about being in the PR business per se.

Alan's solution? Create a "PR Hotline" through which he can offer his consulting service on an hourly basis via telephone to smaller firms that either need quick advice or cannot afford to pay the traditional large monthly retainer most PR firms charge. Another interesting twist: Alan accepts MasterCard and Visa, which is an unusual way to charge for professional services. His release on the topic, which gained wide publication and generated many inquiries to the hotline, is as follows:

THE CARUBA ORGANIZATION
Box 40, Maplewood, NJ 07040
201/763–6392

For immediate release:

CHARGE PR ADVICE TO YOUR CREDIT CARD
"PR HOTLINE"—NEW BUSINESS SERVICE

Maplewood, NJ—Mike Wallace of "60 Minutes" is at the door with a camera crew! What do you do now?

"Most public relations does not involve a crisis," says
PR counselor Alan Caruba of Maplewood, NJ. "In fact,
good PR can avert such problems while helping to promote products, services, and causes of every description."

Caruba notes that "many business and professional
people neither need, nor want, to retain a full-time public
relations agency or counselor. What they need is good
advice from time to time." That's why Caruba created the
"PR Hotline," a telephone service that allows anyone with
a PR question or problem to call. One can charge the
service to either MasterCard or Visa.

At $50 for the first forty minutes or $75 for up to a full
hour, "a lot of very specific analysis and advice can be
provided," says Caruba. "Public relations can be local,
regional, or national in scope. It can represent a single
project or a long-term program."

Caruba has been dispensing advice and service to
corporations, associations, small business operations, and
individuals for more than twenty years. He is a member
of The Counselors Academy of the Public Relations Society of America and frequently lectures and writes on the
subject.

Years ago I wanted to promote myself as an authority in
advertising. As I'm not a big ad agency, however, I knew
that merely sending a release announcing my latest projects
or clients would not be effective. The business of J. Walter
Thompson is of interest to the trade press; the business of
one lone advertising consultant is not.

When I asked myself, "How can I create something newsworthy and thus get publicity for myself?" the Advertising
Hotline was the answer. The idea is simple: A nationwide
telephone hotline businesspeople can call to get quick tips
and advice on how to improve their marketing. Implement-
ing the idea was even easier: Just set up a phone line in my

basement and attach an answering machine with a long out-going message. Hotline callers were treated to a five-minute prerecorded "miniseminar on tape" on a different topic each week. Here is my release:

For: The Advertising Hotline, 174 Holland Ave., New Milford, NJ 07646
CONTACT: Amy Sprecher, (201) XXX–XXXX

For immediate release

NEW NATIONAL TELEPHONE HOTLINE PROVIDES FREE ADVERTISING AND MARKETING TIPS TO AD AGENCIES, CORPORATIONS, AND SMALL BUSINESS

New Milford, NJ, December 4th—The "Advertising Hot-line," a new nationwide telephone hotline, has been estab-lished to provide free advice, information, and tips on advertising, direct mail, publicity, and other forms of promotion to ad agencies, PR firms, large corporations, and small businesses. The Hotline number is XXX–XXXX.

"Clients and their agencies today need solid, reliable information on what works in advertising—and what doesn't," says Bob Bly, the Hotline's director. "As a free-lance copywriter, I have hundreds of people calling me asking questions such as: 'How can I get more inquiries from my quarter-page trade ad? How can I write a direct-mail package that will get a good response?' I set up the Advertising Hotline to give these folks some of the an-swers."

Unlike many other information sources, Bly points out, the Advertising Hotline is free. "A lot of companies can't afford to hire consultants, and it takes time to read a book, listen to an audiocassette, or attend a seminar," notes Bly. "The Hotline is free and takes only 5 minutes of the caller's time."

In the months to come, callers who phone the Advertising Hotline at XXX–XXXX can listen to taped "mini-seminars" on a variety of subjects. Scheduled topics include: "10 Ways to Stretch Your Advertising Budget," "How to Write Winning Sales Letters," "12 Questions to Ask *Before* You Create Your Next Advertising Campaign," "New Ideas for Your Corporate Newsletter," and "Selling Financial Services by Mail." The current topic can be heard right now by calling the Hotline at XXX–XXXX.

The hotline can be reached from any telephone in the world, 24 hours a day, 7 days a week. The taped message usually runs between 3 to 5 minutes in length. The message is changed approximately once a week.

I sent the release to fifty trade publications covering advertising, public relations, promotion, marketing, and sales. Attractively printed Advertising Hotline Rolodex™ cards were mailed with the releases to give editors the impression that the Ad Hotline was a real and ongoing activity.

Eighteen publications ran stories based on the release. At least five ran almost the entire release, practically word for word. This publicity generated thousands of phone calls to the Hotline within twelve months. Unfortunately, because of my schedule, I was unable to keep up with producing the weekly messages, and so I discontinued the hotline. But one day I may start it up again.

Gary Blake, a management consultant specializing in business and technical writing seminars, is a big believer in press releases and has gained a lot of trade and national publicity for his seminars. Each press release is centered around a unique idea or concept that editors find both intriguing and either entertaining or newsworthy.

In one recent release, Dr. Blake took a humorous approach, inventing the term *institutionalitis* to describe the overly formal, stiff, antiquated style plaguing corporate writing. But instead of just getting publicity coverage, he also generated a huge response by offering an institutionalitis poster. His release follows.

CLIENT: CONTACT:

The Communication Workshop   Gary Blake
217 E. 85th St.   (718) 575–8000
New York, NY 10028

For immediate release

SPECIALISTS URGE BYPASS, EDUCATION, AND EARLY DETECTION IN TREATING CORPORATE AMERICA'S NUMBER-ONE COMMUNICATION PROBLEM: INSTITUTIONALITIS

NEW YORK, NY, April 1—"Institutionalitis"—the use of overly formal, pompous, and antiquated phrases in business communications—is now at "epidemic proportions." That's the opinion of writing specialists at the Center for Diseased Language Control who are urging managers to treat hedgy, pompous, and antiquated phrases with methods of early detection, education, and "word bypass" surgery.

Once thought of as only a disease affecting lawyers and government bureaucrats, institutionalitis now afflicts middle managers in data processing, sales, operations, customer service, engineering, and accounting. According to studies, the problem is spread through the careless misuse of words and a tendency to write for the filing cabinet instead of for other human beings.

Says one writing specialist, "You can live with institutionalitis for years before knowing that you have it. Then, it's often too late to do anything to save your style. If left unchecked, institutionalitis can wreck a career."

According to Gary Blake, Director of The Communication Workshop, a New York City–based consulting firm specializing in the treatment of writing disorders, "A simple five-minute test can detect institutionalitis and prevent its spread. Just look at one of your letters, memos, reports, or proposals and see if you're using words and phrases like 'Enclosed please find,' 'Under separate cover,' 'pursuant to,' or 'Thanking you in advance.' Next, check for redundancies like 'end result,' 'consensus of opinion,' 'close proximity,' or 'foreign imports.' The more widespread the jargon, hedgy words, and lengthy sentences, the more advanced the disease."

"It's odd," says one writing specialist, "but institutionalitis can strike anyone—manager or support staff, young or old, educated or uneducated."

Unless you treat the diseased language, it gets worse and worse, eventually weakening the heart of an organization. Then you need to hire a writing consultant to come in and perform "word bypass surgery." This operation, which has become routine, takes place during a two-day seminar. Gradually, sufferers of institutionalitis learn to "bypass" unnecessary words and phrases. For example, a manager who had been in the habit of writing "In the majority of instances . . ." now just writes "Usually," thus bypassing several unnecessary words.

A joint statement issued by the writing doctors said that "the best prevention is education." But not just a seminar that treats the symptoms, one that treats the causes. In Dr. Blake's two-day seminar, he discusses how institutionalitis takes root in our writing and shows the advantages of using a clear, conversational writing style.

In the postseminar recovery period, managers begin to notice that their writing needs less editing, that they write faster as well as better, and that their thoughts are better organized, easier to grasp, and more persuasive.

The lucky managers who have their wordiness and stiff language caught in time usually go on to excel in their occupations. Their writing gradually becomes more and more specific, concise, and compelling. Those who are not treated, however, waste thousands of hours in corporate time writing muddy prose that needs to be endlessly edited and reedited.

Since prevention is the ultimate cure of institutional-itis, The Communication Workshop has produced a poster showing dozens of examples of the disease. Dr. Blake hopes that the poster will find its way to bulletin boards in the hallways of corporations throughout the United States. To receive a poster, send your name, title, organization, and address to The Communication Workshop, 217 East 85th Street, New York, NY 10028. Please enclose $1.50 per poster to cover postage and handling.

This press release was printed in several newspapers and trade magazines and generated more than six hundred requests for the poster.

OTHER TECHNIQUES FOR GETTING THE MEDIA TO WRITE ABOUT YOU

Press releases are probably the most effective and least costly method of getting publicity in the media. But there are a few others.

Big corporations that want to announce something newsworthy often call press conferences. I don't advise you to use this technique, however. It's too expensive, and as you are not a well-known company or PR firm, not many editors would show up.

Other service providers position themselves as experts

by sending letters to editors that say, in essence, "I am an expert in so-and-so subject, and I am very open to being interviewed by the media. So if you ever do a story on so-and-so subject, and need information, feel free to call me."

The strategy here is to offer yourself as a source. Many editors and reporters are not experts in the topics they write about and are in constant need of experts they can interview—frequently on a moment's notice. If you have expertise in a subject they cover and are cooperative and available when they need you, they'll interview you. The benefit? You get quoted as an expert source in the article, your name is given visibility, and you become known as an authority in your field.

When mailing such a letter, it's a good idea to include a printed Rolodex™ card the reporter or editor can keep on file. The tab of the card should probably identify your subject first and your name second ("Tax laws/Sue Spencer, CPA"). That way the reporter can file you by name or by topic.

Finally, don't neglect electronic media. Send press releases and pitch letters to radio and TV as well as newspapers and magazines. When being interviewed, always have some free booklet or brochure to offer listeners, and make sure you give your name and address so listeners can contact you to receive your material. You may want to clear this with the host or interviewer before you go on.

For detailed information on publicity and public relations, I recommend *The Unabashed Self-Promoter's Guide*, by Jeffrey Lant (JLA Publications, 50 Follen Street, Suite 507, Cambridge, MA 02138, 617 547–6372). It's the most detailed and thorough book I know of on the topic of how to get free publicity in print and electronic media.

CHAPTER THREE

Creating Brochures and Other Marketing Documents

Once you've generated initial interest in your service using the marketing techniques described in chapters 1 and 2, you'll need sales literature to send to these prospects. You'll also need a system for following up and keeping track of leads. This chapter:

- tells you how to design and write effective sales literature,
- provides step-by-step instructions on how to follow up with prospects who have requested your materials, and
- presents an easy-to-use system for keeping track of inquiries.

WHY YOU NEED SALES LITERATURE

Do you need a brochure, price sheet, flier, or other sales literature? It depends, to a large extent, what the standard practice is in your business. For example, most professionals who market to businesses rather than consumers find that it is necessary to have a brochure.

According to a study done by Thomas Publishing, it is extremely difficult to sell to a business without some type of sales literature describing your service. The study showed that 90 percent of corporate purchasing agents and other buyers required sellers to have a brochure in order to be put on the vendor list and allowed to bid on jobs.

Some service providers, however, do *not* use brochures. My literary agent, plumber, electrician, carpenter, and internist have all convinced me to hire them without showing me a brochure.

On the other hand, more and more service providers find that having some sort of printed literature gives them an edge in selling more of their services to more prospects. My chimney sweep, the man who cleans my gutters, my urologist, our pediatrician, the firm that removed the asbestos from my basement—all use printed promotional literature, ranging from a simple one-page flier for the gutter-cleaning service to an elaborate multipage child care guide published by the pediatrician.

Does printed literature help make the sale? I know for a fact that having sales literature played a factor in convincing me personally to hire several of the above service providers instead of their competition.

In the case of the asbestos removal, I was nervous, because I knew that a slipup could actually make the problem worse, releasing dangerous particles into the air. So I wanted a knowledgeable, reliable firm. The firm I used was the only contractor to send me a booklet explaining the nature of the problem and why I should remove the asbestos. Their information package also included extensive references and explained how they absolutely *guaranteed* I would get an asbestos-free basement. This material made me feel confident that selecting them was the right, safe, best choice.

Should you use a brochure? Just because your competitors don't doesn't mean you shouldn't. In fact, their lack of sales literature represents an opportunity for you to gain a competitive edge. Today many consumers are afraid of doing business with a firm or individual they don't know; a brochure helps establish credibility. The reason: Anyone can pay $50 for some letterhead and a business card. But a brochure causes your prospect to think "Wow, they have a brochure. They must really be in business!"

Also, by presenting your story in logical, consistent fashion, a brochure ensures that all key sales points in your pitch are delivered by you and retained by prospects. Prospects can study your brochure long after you're gone, and the copy reminds them of why you're the best.

Brochures can also help educate prospects about the situation they face or the problem they need solved. By educating prospects, you create the impression that you understand their needs, thus winning their confidence—and their trust.

Another important advantage of having a brochure is that many prospects create a reference file of information—brochures, article reprints, news clippings—related to their problem. When your brochure is dropped in this file, you know prospects will always have your name, address, and phone number in front of them when they consult the file. A brochure makes it easy for prospects to contact you when they need you.

When someone calls and asks for more information about your service, how will you respond? Perhaps at first you'll want to visit everyone who calls. But you'll soon find that this isn't practical. Some clients are too far away. Sometimes you will be too busy handling other assignments to make sales calls. And, unfortunately, many inquiries come from cranks who will just waste your time or people who, for one reason or another, will not end up hiring you.

With a brochure, you can quickly and easily respond to all inquiries with solid information and a well-thought-out sales pitch. A brochure serves to whet the appetite of those who represent genuine prospects and discourages those who are not serious about hiring you. For example, by presenting your fee schedule up front, you don't waste time talking with people who can't afford you.

Finally, the most important reason to have a brochure is that many prospects who learn about your service will say "I may be interested. Please send me your brochure." In many cases, prospects will not want—or will not be ready for—a personal visit from you. The reason: Prospects either don't have time to see you or, more likely, they are afraid you will use high-pressure sales tactics if they let you into their home or office. And most people don't like to be sold.

So the safest—and easiest—way for them to learn more about you is to say "Send your brochure." If you don't have any information to send, those prospects who want more information will be turned off, and you'll lose them.

THE SIX BASIC TYPES
OF SERVICE BROCHURES

Although there is an almost infinite variety in the types and styles of sales materials used by service providers, the literature you need falls into six basic categories. Probably you don't need all six. But you may need more than one. For example, you might want a small, simple pamphlet to mail out to prospects with casual interest, followed by a more complete package that presents the in-depth technical details to prospects who are ready to buy.

The six basic types of sales literature used by service providers are self-mailers, slim-jim brochures, fact sheets, full-size brochures, information packages, and sales pitch kits.

Let's take a look at the pros and cons of each.

Self-mailer

A self-mailer is a promotional piece sent through the mail without an outer envelope; the mailing label is affixed directly to the printed piece. Although they may be more complex, most are simple in design, constructed by folding a single sheet of paper to form four or six panels. The paper stock must be stiff enough to allow the piece to be handled by the postal system and still be undamaged when it arrives in the prospect's mailbox.

Self-mailers work well as direct-mail pieces sent to lists of cold prospects as described in chapter 1. But you should *never* use a self-mailer to fulfill an interested prospect's request for more material.

Why not? It's simple. Prospects *perceive* self-mailers to be direct-mail solicitations—"junk mail" they didn't ask for and don't want. If you send your brochure as a self-mailer, prospects will probably think it's just another unsolicited advertisement and will throw it away. They won't realize they asked for it—because it looks like direct mail, not information they requested.

Whenever you mail any information requested by a prospect, use an outer envelope. Stamp the outer envelope with a rubber stamp that says "HERE IS THE INFORMATION YOU REQUESTED." This way there's no mistaking your package for unsolicited material.

Always include a cover letter with any material you send. In the letter, thank prospects for their interest and remind them that they asked for the material you have sent. Every package I send out to prospects is accompanied by a letter that begins, "Thanks for your interest in my copywriting services. . . ."

Put your brochure in an envelope with a letter.

Never use a self-mailer as an inquiry-fulfillment piece.

Slim-jim

A slim-jim is a small brochure made by folding a single sheet of paper. You can create a six-panel slim-jim by folding a letter-size (8½- by 11-inch) sheet of paper twice. To make a mock-up, take a sheet of paper. Hold it as if you are reading a letter. Fold it twice horizontally as if you are folding a letter to fit in an envelope. Now turn it on its side 90 degrees. You've created a little booklet with six panels, including front and back cover.

You can also create an eight-panel slim-jim by folding a legal-size (8½- by 14-inch) sheet of paper three times. A four-panel slim-jim can be made by creating a six-panel slim-jim, then having the printer cut off one panel. Or you can put a perforation on one of the folds, to create a four-panel slim-jim with a tear-off reply card.

Slim-jims are so-named because they are slimmer than regular size brochures. The page size of a full-size brochure, like the type of piece you'd pick up in a new car dealer's showroom, typically measures 8½ by 11 inches or 7 by 10 inches. The slim-jim panel size is approximately 4 by 8½ inches, which allows it to fit nicely in a standard #10 business envelope. The slim-jim can thus be easily inserted with outgoing correspondence such as letters, invoices, statements, proposals, estimates, and so on.

Why do service providers like slim-jims so much? There are several advantages:

- Slim-jims are easy and inexpensive to produce.
- They fit in a standard #10 business envelope.

- Because of the small panel size, they look good without a lot of elaborate design and visuals, and can be mostly or all text.
- One panel can be a tear-off reply card, giving the prospect a convenient response vehicle.
- The amount of copy is limited, making slim-jims concise and easy to read.

PROVEN FORMULAS FOR WRITING AND DESIGNING SLIM-JIMS

Three copywriting formulas or outlines seem to work especially well for slim-jim brochures used by service providers. These are: question-and-answer, list, and who/what/when/where/why/how.

- *Question-and-answer.* Here you organize the brochure as a series of questions and answers.

First, write down all the questions your prospect is likely to ask about your service, in the order you think they'd ask them. These become the copy subheads in your brochure.

Then, under each question, write out a brief but complete answer. This becomes the body copy.

Count up the total number of questions. Say there are twelve. The headline on the cover of your brochure becomes "12 Questions About Vinyl and Aluminum Siding (or Desktop Publishing, or whatever it is you offer) . . . and One Good Answer to Each."

The last question should always be "What's the next step?" In the copy under this section, you encourage prospects to contact you for further discussion, a free estimate, or whatever the next logical step is.

The question-and-answer format is effective because, by answering prospects' questions, it alleviates their concerns, fears, and worries.

- *List format.* The list format presents the information about your service in simple 1-2-3 fashion.

To create a list brochure, make a list of the important

features of your service. Arrange the list in order of priority, with the most important features first. Then number the features. These become the subheads for your brochure.

Under each feature, write brief but complete copy elaborating on the feature, explaining what it means and its significance to buyers, and then telling the benefit prospects get from the feature. For instance, if the feature is "No job too big or too small," the benefit might be "We can solve your problem no matter what the size of your lawn or what your budget is." This description becomes the body copy under each subhead.

Next, count up the number of feature subheads. Let's say it's fourteen. Then determine the *main* benefit you offer your customers. Let's say it's productivity improvement. The headline on the front panel of your slim-jim becomes "14 Ways [name of firm] Can Help Your Company Improve Its Productivity." The back panel would have your address, phone, and the "next step" information discussed earlier.

• *Who/what/when/where/why/how.* A third way to organize your brochure is like a journalist organizes a news story—the five Ws plus H, or *who, what, when, where, why,* and *how.* You don't have to stick exactly to this formula—for example, there might be no section on *when* or *how*—but it provides a rough outline for covering all important points about your service.

For instance, the subheads in a brochure of this type might read:

Who We Are
What We Do
Who We Work For
When You Should Call Us (and When You Shouldn't)
Why Our Service is Successful for Our Clients
How Our Service Works
The Next Step

Brief explanations under each subhead become the body copy. The headline for the cover can be anything you want. One possibility is "Important Facts About [name of company]'s [type of service]."

Fact Sheet

The same copy you use in a slim-jim can be used in a fact sheet. In a fact sheet, the copy is printed front and back on an 8½- by 11-inch sheet of paper that is *not* folded but is mailed flat in a 9- by 12-inch envelope. Be sure to back it with a stiff piece of cardboard to prevent folding or wrinkling.

The advantages of the fact sheet format are that you can fit more copy into it and you can include it with other sheets mailed flat in the envelope. These can include a personally typed cover letter, a list of clients, a price list, an order form, article reprints, and so on.

To promote my consulting services, I use a fact sheet that closely follows a format suggested by Dr. Jeffrey Lant in his excellent book, *Tricks of the Trade* (Cambridge, MA: JLA Publications, 1987).

Full-size Brochures

Slim-jims work well and are used by thousands of service providers nationwide. But perhaps you want a brochure that's more substantial. There are several reasons why many service firms opt for a full-size brochure:

- There is more room for illustrations, photos, and other visuals.
- These visuals can be reproduced in a larger size for more dramatic and real-life presentation.
- There is more room for copy, enabling a fuller, more detailed explanation and sales pitch.
- The brochure can be three-hole-punched and inserted

into the three-ring binders used by many corporate purchasing departments.

- The larger brochure makes more of an impression than a tiny slim-jim.
- A slim-jim can get lost if placed into a standard-size file folder. A full-size brochure doesn't.
- A full-size brochure creates an image of size—an image some service providers may feel it's important to convey.

As mentioned earlier, the full-size brochure has a page that's approximately the size of a piece of notebook or writing paper—either 7 by 10 inches or 8½ by 11 inches. Full-size brochures can be four, six, eight, twelve, sixteen pages, or longer. They are, in essence, multipage fact sheets.

For most small to medium-size service firms, four or six pages is more than sufficient. This is also less costly to produce, because a four- or six-page brochure can be formed by folding a single piece of paper.

If the brochure is eight pages or longer, two or more pieces of folded paper must be bound. And that's more expensive. The most common binding method for brochures is "saddle-stitched"—two staples shot through the spine.

More and more often today, you see interesting alternatives to the traditional saddle-stitched, glossy, color brochure. Some service providers, for example, desktop-publish their brochures and bind them in a report cover or using a GBC™ binding. This makes the brochures look more important than mere sales or promotional materials.

The style and format should fit your business and your market—and not vice versa. If your service would benefit from color photography (as might be the case if you do landscaping, for example), a color piece might be in order. But if you sell a service that doesn't need to be illustrated, such as income tax preparation, then an all-copy, one- or two-color brochure might serve you better. Pick a style, tone, format, and design appropriate to your service and the type of customer you serve.

Information Package

Instead of telling their whole story in one booklet or brochure, some service providers send a package of materials consisting of half a dozen or more different sheets of 8½- by 11-inch paper, printed on one or both sides. Some sheets may be typeset, but most are produced using a regular typewriter or word processor.

What are the advantages of a package versus a single brochure?

First, the package looks more impressive than a single piece when it arrives on the recipient's desk.

Second, the package is more easily updated because it is modular and inexpensively printed in small quantities from a typed original. Most elements can be run off in small quantities on a photocopier. And you store the original in your computer for easy updating and revision.

Third, unlike a single brochure, which presents the same message to every prospect, the package can be tailored to the specific needs of the client. For instance, if you're a photographer and you get an inquiry from a manufacturer who needs photos of a new production line, you would send reprints of industrial photos only, not fashion or travel.

In addition, a package consisting of several elements has a greater chance of making an impression on those readers who only glance at mail before throwing it away, as the odds are they will glance at each element.

I have been using a package to respond to inquiries about my copywriting services for over nine years. My package contains the following elements:

1. A four-page cover letter written in question-and-answer format. The letter thanks the reader for his interest in my services, then covers such topics as my qualifications, background, experience, type of assignments and clients I handle, fees, deadlines, revisions, and how to order from me. The back page of the letter contains a reprint of a display ad I once ran.
2. A one-page fact sheet elaborating on my background and experience.
3. A client list (one sheet, both sides).
4. Excerpts of testimonials from satisfied clients (one sheet, both sides).
5. Reprints of two articles I've written.
6. A reprint of a one-page newspaper article written *about* me from the local town shopper.
7. A sales flier on my book *The Copywriter's Handbook*. This allows the reader to order the book direct from the publisher.
8. At least three photocopied samples of my work. I always send samples similar to the type of work the prospect needs.
9. A one-page fee schedule that gives estimated fees for typical projects and lists my terms and conditions.
10. An order form the client can use to hire me by mail (one sheet, two sides, printed on heavy blue stock to make it stand out).

I like to send a comprehensive package because it answers all questions before they are asked and tells prospects everything they need to know to make an intelligent decision about hiring me. My goal is to get people to hire me by mail, without a meeting, although I will meet with local prospects if they request it and if I have the time.

You may not want to send such detailed information,

preferring instead to encourage prospects to ask for an appointment. If getting an initial meeting with the prospect is your goal, send less material than I do—not more.

Sales Pitch Kit

A sales kit, or "pitch book," is literature you use as a presentation aid when you sit down and explain your services to prospects.

While some salespeople use preprinted flip-chart-type panels with bulleted copy, usually prepared by a marketing department or ad agency, your sales kit should be more flexible. I recommend using a three-ring binder with plastic pages. Each page is a clear plastic pocket into which you can slip a printed insert, such as a client list or photograph. The sheets are three-hole-punched for easy removal and insertion into your binder.

Do you need to have the notebooks imprinted with your company name and logo? It's not necessary, because you control the presentation and turn the pages for the prospect. So when you set up your notebook on the table, you immediately open it and flip to the first inside page. The notebook is not left behind with the prospect; you can prepare other leave-behinds, such as a price list, client roster, flier, or slim-jim brochure.

There are two advantages of using notebooks for sales presentations. First, because materials are easily inserted into the plastic pockets, the pages can be quickly and easily updated. A mass-produced brochure, on the other hand, may become dated before you use up the entire print run.

The other advantage is that you can tailor the presentation for each prospect by removing, adding, and rearranging pages. Just open the binder clips, take out pages, and move them around. You can purchase both the three-ring notebooks and the plastic sheets in most stationery or office supply stores. If not, try an art supply store.

What should go in your pitch book? In no particular order, here are some of the things you can include:

- Samples of your work (reports, printed pieces)
- Letters from satisfied clients
- Photographs of completed jobs
- Licenses, insurance certificates, permits, bonds
- Diplomas, awards, certificates
- Benefits of your service
- Description of your service
- Copy of your guarantee or warranty
- Client roster
- Copies of ads you've run
- Brochures and fliers
- Article reprints

Tailor the presentation, both when you prepare it and as
you present it. For instance, if a prospect seems bored with
an explanation of your service and doesn't want to look at
photos of your work, but is concerned about whether you are
reliable, flip to the testimonial letters, pull out your client
roster, and provide names and numbers of clients the prospect can call to check you out.

Do *not* feel you must present all of your pitch, in the
proper order, just because you worked on it. Take your cues
from prospects. Give them only what they need—and as
much as they need. The purpose is not to simply present
information. If you can tell prospects what they need to
know, answer all their questions and concerns, and address
all their fears and worries, you will make the sale.

If you continue to shove your presentation book in a prospect's face and keep blabbing after this point, you may actually talk your way out of a sale by boring him or her silly.
When you sense prospects want to move on, ask what else
they need to know. When you sense prospects are bored,
probe to find out what really interests them.

KEEPING TRACK OF LEADS

When I first got started, I received relatively few inquiries, so keeping track of them was no problem. Whenever potential clients called, I packed up my portfolio and went running to their offices. After the meetings, I pinned their business cards to my bulletin board, then followed up with calls and letters and waited for the phone to ring.

But now I simply don't have time to meet with everyone who contacts me, much less take them all on as clients. Instead, I send my sales literature.

Of course, when someone does call, it helps me to have a record of who he or she is and when I mailed my package. A filing system for leads is also helpful for follow up.

For every inquiry, I record basic information using the simple form reprinted here.

Date _____ Source of inquiry _____ Response via _____

Name _____ Title _____

Company _____

Address _____ Room/floor _____

City _____ State _____ Zip _____

Phone _____ Fax _____

Type of business:

Type of projects:

For: [   ] **immediate project**   [   ] **future reference**
    [   ] **project to be started in:** _____
                                    (month/year)

STATUS:
[   ] **Sent package on (date):** _____

[   ] **Enclosed these samples:** _____

_____

[   ] **Next step is to:** _____

[   ] **Probability of assignment:** _____

[   ] **Comments:** _____

_____

_____

CONTACT RECORD:

Date: _____ **Summary:** _____

With this form, you can quickly and easily make sure you get all the information you need about your prospect, including:

- Name, company, address, phone number.
- Floor, mail stop, or room number—for sending messengers or express delivery services.
- Source of inquiry (where did they learn about you?) and method of response (phone call or letter).
- Type of business (if you sell to business) and what the prospect needs (light carpentry, deck, basement finished, family room, dormer, and so on).
- A record of all your contacts with this prospect as you follow up by phone, mail, and in-person meetings.

The forms are punched and kept in a three-ring binder. I use section dividers to separate the forms by several categories:

1. "Projects pending"—for prospects who have a hot project and are likely to become clients within the next few weeks.
2. "Projects possible"—for prospects who might give me an assignment but are not as definite as "projects pending."
3. "Leads to follow up"—the largest section, this contains the files of everyone who inquired about my services within the past year but did not have an immediate project in mind. Most of the prospects in this section requested my literature to keep on file for future reference, in case a project comes up.

I also have a separate notebook in which I keep forms for leads that are more than a year old. This notebook is divided into two sections:

1. "Past clients"—companies that have used my services in the past but haven't hired me recently.
2. "Old leads"—people who requested my package a year ago or more but never showed any further interest.

This notebook system allows you to promote yourself to your best prospects again and again, while keeping good records of every promotional activity.

For example, if I write an article entitled "How to Sell Insurance Through Direct Mail," I can look in my notebook and send a reprint of the article to advertising managers at insurance companies who previously requested information on my services. Sometimes this type of follow-up can re-awaken the interest of a prospect who received your literature but has forgotten about you. It has resulted in many additional sales for me. Any follow-up of this type is noted under the "Contact Record" section of my form.

One other point: Many service providers keep records of this type on their computers, using personal filing or database management programs. However, I prefer my notebook. My form has plenty of room for detailed information, and I can get at my files without having to turn on my computer.

FOLLOWING UP ON SALES LEADS

Okay. Let's say you get a telephone call or letter from someone who says "I read your ad and I'm interested. What's the next step?"

The next step is really up to you, and it varies depending on your personal style of selling and the way you run your business. Here are some of the follow-up techniques used by service providers I know.

• *Meeting.* For many service providers, the goal of promotion is to get a meeting with prospects in their office or home. The purpose is to discuss your services and convince prospects to hire you for the assignment.

• *Literature/meeting.* Other service providers prefer to send a letter, résumé, and additional information through the mail. If prospects like the materials, service provider and prospect meet to discuss an assignment. If not, the service provider saves a wasted trip.

• *Literature/phone/assignment.* Service providers who need not physically visit prospects to render service and who send the more complete type of information package described earlier often try to get assignments by mail, eliminating the time-consuming process of an initial meeting. Typically, I will send my package, then follow up with a phone call. I tell prospects I am calling to make sure they received the information they requested and to see if this looks like the type of services they need. I also offer to send additional information or answer any questions.

If they respond positively, we might discuss any specific assignments they had in mind. I encourage prospects to send me authorization and background material in the mail so I can proceed with the work if they want to hire me.

• *Literature.* Some service providers send their package and do no follow-up. They take on assignments only from prospects who respond to the package without being prodded in any way. Naturally, any follow-up discussion generated in this manner will be with people who are highly motivated and enthusiastic about your services. However, unless you are so busy that you really don't need more work, you will probably have to do some type of follow-up after you send your sales materials.

Even if you are busy, I think it makes sense to follow up the mailing of your brochure or package with at least one phone call. Most prospects appreciate the fact that you cared enough to make sure they got the material they requested.

Generally you should make this follow-up call within a week or two after you mail your material. Those prospects who have a genuine interest can be convinced to go on to the next step. If a prospect has no interest, you will quickly sense this and can end the call politely.

YOUR "KEEP-IN-TOUCH" PROGRAM

A program of regular mailings and phone calls to your prospect list is a great way of keeping your name before potential customers and getting more assignments. As a small service business, you may be limited as to the time you can devote to follow-up activities. Still, most of us don't communicate frequently enough with our recent prospects, current clients, and past clients. We focus on getting fresh leads. We follow up with a phone call or two, but if the person doesn't buy, we file the lead in our notebook and forget about them.

Is this a mistake? Quite possibly. After all, people who were motivated enough to respond to your ad or mailing— or who hired you at one time and were satisfied—are likely to have some need for your type of service at some point, aren't they? If you keep in touch with those prospects and customers on a regular basis, you stand a greater chance of having them remember you—or of having your name come across their desk or mailbox—at the time when they finally get around to hiring someone to do that job they've been putting off. And when that happens, your chances of making the sale, or at least getting to bid on the job, are excellent.

On the other hand, if you don't stay in touch with prospects and clients and remind them of your existence on a regular basis, then they will more than likely forget about you. Your existence will fade from memory. And they'll never call you.

I know this is difficult to believe. But remember: When an inquiry is made, it's always much more important to the *seller* than to the *buyer.* The seller, being overly optimistic, gets excited about every lead. And the inquiry may be one of a few leads—or maybe the only lead—you've gotten all day. Or all week. So it means a lot to you.

But to buyers, asking for more information is no big deal. Their interest may be casual. They may be responding out of curiosity only, or because they like to get brochures. Or it may be one of dozens of things they've sent for recently. In fact, *they may not even remember asking for your information when you call to see if they received it.*

For this reason, you've got to be persistent if you want to make an impression.

How persistent? Jeffrey Lant says that to make the sale, you should ideally contact prospects seven times within an eighteen-month period. He calls this the "Rule of Seven," and while you may not stick with it exactly, it's a sensible guideline as to frequency of communication.

There are really two ways to keep in touch with clients and prospects. The first is with a regular, planned contact program.

In such a program, you set a regular schedule for follow-up:

- You can pick up the phone and call to say "hello" every once in a while.
- You can send a friendly keep-in-touch letter that keeps prospects up to date on your recent activities, or simply reminds them that you're available to help.
- You can send helpful materials such as a new business card, new Rolodex™ card, change of address notice, and so forth.
- You can send reprints of articles you've written.
- You can send tearsheets of other newspaper and magazine articles that would be of interest to prospects.
- You can send a letter or card to prospects on birthdays, anniversaries, Christmas, and other key holidays and events.

I think that the best method is to send articles—a combination of articles you've written plus news clippings that deal with the prospect's industry. But a phone call or letter certainly won't hurt. And a Christmas or birthday card every year is a nice touch.

With a formal follow-up program, you schedule a series of follow-ups and then stick to the schedule. You can send one a month, one every other month, four times a year—whatever you prefer. (If you follow the Rule of Seven, you average 4.7 contacts per prospect or customer per year.) The cumulative effect of all this activity is to place your name foremost in prospects' minds so that when they have an assignment, they think of you.

If you don't have a regularly scheduled program of follow-up, you can use the second method, which is an informal program of sending materials to select prospects—not your entire list—whenever something appropriate comes along. This method is far less time-consuming and works better for service providers who are busy and lack marketing support staff.

How does it work? As you are doing your regular business reading, and come across an item of interest to a particular client, clip it and mail it to him or her. I like to include a short handwritten note that simply says: "Jim: Thought this might interest you. —Bob Bly."

I'll send anything that's relevant to the client's business. This can include article reprints, press releases, even their competitor's ads and brochures. Clients and prospects will really appreciate this effort on your part to keep them informed. It will pay off in the long run.

Another extremely effective keep-in-touch technique is the Here's-my-recent-success mailing. Here you send a letter telling clients and prospects, "Here's a recent job I did for [name of client]. They were very pleased, and we achieved [describe specific results]. Here's what Joe the client said: [insert brief client testimonial]. Can I help you achieve the same success? Sincerely, Bob Service Provider."

Enclose with the letter tangible material from the job. This can be a case history article, news clip, photograph, sample, videotape, or a copy of a letter of praise from your satisfied client. Note: Be sure to show your proposed mailing to the client and get permission before sending it. Some clients are sensitive and don't want you to use their names. You must respect this wish, or you could risk losing a client.

Success-story mailings work well because most prospects hire you for the result your service achieves, not for the service itself. For example, a corporation wants greater productivity, not a study, survey, or training session. The study, survey, or training is not the end; it's the means to achieve the benefit of greater productivity. The success-story mailing gives tangible proof that you deliver not just performance of service (which isn't really what they want) but a beneficial result to your clients (which is what all clients seek).

Also, prospects distrust many of your promotional claims, viewing them as self-puffery. But in a success-story mailing, the praise is being done by a client—someone like them—and is hence much more credible and believable. It also shows them that you have at least one big proven success to your credit, which is something many novices and amateurs cannot claim.

PART TWO

Follow-Up:
How to Get Appointments
with Prospects

CHAPTER FOUR

Techniques for Prequalifying Your Prospects

In chapter 3, we discussed how to prepare sales literature, how to package and send it, and some of the mechanics of following-up and tracking leads.

In this chapter and in the next three chapters, we will explore precisely *how* to follow up—the objectives of follow-up, the ultimate goal, and what to say to prospects to get them to do what you want them to do.

IS FOLLOW-UP NECESSARY?

Should you follow-up after you mail a package to a prospective client?

As discussed in chapter 3, yes. Many prospects, especially those with genuine interest, appreciate the phone call and the fact that you cared enough to follow through.

Also, in today's competitive marketing environment, more and more of your competitors are following up—aggressively—on a higher percentage of inquiries than ever before, even for inquiries that a few years ago they would have considered "marginal." If they follow up and you don't, they'll have a better chance of making their service look superior to yours—and their criticisms of your service will go unchallenged.

HOW PROSPECTS RESPOND TO A FOLLOW-UP PHONE CALL

Prospects who are not serious or are just collecting brochures will probably not be that open or chatty when you call, but you can make these calls brief and not keep them on the phone too long.

The *best* prospects, of course, are those who are so interested that they call you after receiving your material to discuss a project before you have a chance to get back to them. These are the prospects who are most likely to become paying clients.

When should you follow up? I generally call one or two weeks from the date I mailed the package. This allows plenty of time for the material to reach the prospect (U.S. mails and intercompany mail delivery systems can be slow) and for the prospect to get to it (many prospects are busy and won't read your material until several days after they get it).

Ideally you should send the package the same day you get an inquiry . . . or at the very latest, the next day. This means having sufficient copies of your sales material printed and stored in your office. When running low, always print more so you don't run out.

SETTING THE RIGHT TONE FOR THE CALL

What's the best approach for following-up? I believe that the one thing *any* prospect in *any* business situation dislikes most is to get a phone call from someone who tries to *sell* him or her something. When you get a phone call from some high-pressure, fast-talking telemarketer trying to sell you an investment or get you to donate money, you immediately want to find a way to end the conversation and hang up the phone, don't you?

In your own selling efforts, you want to avoid creating this same kind of uneasy feeling in your prospects. Eliminate all traces of hard-sell in your follow-up approach. The basic purpose of your call should be to make sure prospects received all the information they needed and to explore their specific needs a little further—*if* they seem willing to do so.

HOW I FOLLOW UP

A little later I'll explain some universal techniques for follow-up. Right now I want to give you the specifics of my own follow-up methods, so you can get a good feel for how it's done (at least by one reasonably competent service provider and marketer) in real life.

As I've explained, I keep all inquiries in a three-ring binder. Clipped to the inside cover of this notebook is a telephone script listing the questions I ask during the follow-up call. Here are the questions:

1. *"Did you receive my package?"* If prospects say no or that they don't recall seeing it, I offer to send another right away. In a week or so, I call back and ask "Did you receive my package?" again (reminding them that they asked me to send it).

2. *"Did you have a chance to look it over?"* If prospects say no, I ask if I may call back in a week or so after they've had a chance to review my material.

3. *"Do you use this type of service from time to time?"* If they say no, then they are obviously not prospects for my service, and I end the call. If they say yes, they have

in essence told me that they are potential clients for my services.

Note: You may ask, "If they say they don't use your type of services, shouldn't you try to sell them on why they *should* be using it?" Generally I find that doing so is not worth the effort. There are more than enough prospects who are actively seeking your type of services, so why waste time with someone who doesn't believe in them?

Sales, advertising, and marketing activities of all types are generally more successful when you are "preaching to the converted." For example, if you're opening a new steak house and grill, don't advertise in *Vegetarian Times.* Instead, try to attract steak lovers. That's your real market.

In any situation, you can either (1) sell to people who use your type of services, want what you offer, and are just trying to decide whether they can afford to go ahead or who is the best service provider to pick, or (2) sell to people who don't use your type of services, fold their arms across their chest, and say, "Convince me!"

Let me tell you, option 1 is going to be easier, more pleasant, less time-consuming, and far more profitable. Doing option 2 is like shouting into gale-force winds; you won't be heard. Let the big corporations like IBM and Xerox "educate the marketplace" about new ways of doing things; little guys and gals like us have to stick to preaching to the converted.

Sell your services to individuals and firms that regularly *use* your type of services. One of my clients is a large mailing-list broker. All sales and marketing effort is aimed at major users of direct mail, such as magazines. They don't try to convince firms that don't do direct mail to try it in the hopes of renting them a few names one time. It would be a waste.

4. *"Do you have a project coming up that I can help you with?"* If prospects say yes, I ask details about the project so we can better define the scope of the assignment. Questions might include:

What type of assignment is it?

What is the scope, size, or length of the job?

Do you have a layout, outline, sketch, plan, or any idea of what you want or have in mind?

Can you send me some background material?

When do you need it? (What's the deadline?)

If they say "We don't have a project right now; we're just collecting information for our files," I ask if it would be okay for me to call in a month or so to check up on their needs at that time. I say, "When would be a good time to call back to check in with you and see how things are going and how I might be able to help?"

I also ask if I may put them on my mailing list. They are then giving me permission to contact them again. When I do call or write again, I remind them that I had promised to do so last time we spoke.

5. *"Do you have any questions I can answer?"* Often prospects have questions after reading your material, especially about fees. Answer them as completely and as honestly as you can, in a concise, straightforward, no-nonsense manner.

6. *"Is there any other information or samples I can send you?"* If prospects have a specific project in mind, they may ask for samples that more closely relate to this project than the samples or photos you originally sent them.

DON'T BE PUSHY

In telephone follow-ups, I never push, always taking my cue from the prospects' manner and demeanor.

If prospects seem friendly and eager to talk, I do a more in-depth exploration of their needs and requirements.

If prospects seem distant or annoyed that I called, I first ask, "Is this a good time to call, or am I catching you at a busy time?" If they say it's a bad time, I set a time to call back.

If they say it's an okay time but still sound as if they wish I hadn't called, I go through my questions quickly, thank them for their interest, and hang up. I *never* try to sell a prospect or push one into conversation or action against his or her will.

Note: What I'm telling you is the opposite of what most sales trainers and speakers would advise. They would tell you *never* to ask prospects if they're busy or if it's a good time to call, because this gives them the opportunity to tell you to go away. But I hold a contrary view. There is no point in trying to hold a conversation with someone who doesn't want to talk. People are busy. If you call me when I'm holding a screaming infant in one hand and cooking supper with the other, and I tell you I'm busy and it's not a good time, and you continue to keep throwing sales pitch at me, I'm going to get mad. Fast. I'll hang up. And you've ruined your reputation with me. I'll never buy from you or talk with you again, no matter how wonderful your service is.

For example, we received a telemarketing call the other night. The woman began, "This is Beatrice from Ace Family Portraits. Is Mr. Bly there?" I answered, quite testily, "Beatrice, we are leaving for a funeral in ten seconds [this was the truth]. How can I help you?"

Instead of expressing condolences and offering to call back at a more convenient time, Beatrice, acting like a programmed robot, launched into her scripted presentation without missing a beat. "Mr. Bly, we are offering a free five-by-seven-inch color portrait taken in your home of your new baby. . . ." I told her no thank you and hung up the phone. And believe me, I would never do business with this firm at any time because of Beatrice's stupidity, insensitivity, and pushy sales attitude.

You may think you're being a great salesperson by being pushy. But one of the traits *clients* value most in salespeople (and service providers) is the ability and willingness to *listen*. Sadly, most of us are good talkers and poor listeners.

In selling services, we have to establish a closer, more personal, more concrete relationship with our prospects and clients than product sellers need to. For this reason, you must always seek to take actions that are in the prospects' best interests and to their liking—not yours. In addition, if they're busy or don't want to talk for any other reason, they won't be receptive to what you say, even if they allow you to babble on for a few minutes.

So I always try to find out whether prospects are receptive to continuing the conversation. If they're not, I'd rather make a commitment to follow up at a time more convenient for them.

Generally, prospects with no interest whatsoever will tell you "I'm not interested; don't call me any more." That's fine. Why would you persist in calling people who have no need or interest in your services? They have your information; if they need you, let them call you.

On the other hand, prospects with some interest—even if it's not immediate—will probably put you off to some future date, saying "Call me in August." Your response is to (1) confirm that this is what they want and tell them you will call in August, (2) ask if you can put them on your mailing list (so you can contact them many times *before* August through mailings), and (3) to make a note in your calendar to follow through and call back in August. Of course, when you call in August, you remind prospects that they asked you to call them.

Does this work? Yes. In many selling situations, the majority of prospects calling for information have a *future* need; only a small minority have an *immediate* need. You should recognize this fact and build your follow-up program around it.

Recognize in your attitude and approach to selling your services that many people want to get some information for future reference but don't want to be contacted until they're closer to making a buying decision. By tailoring your follow-up program to accommodate this state of mind rather than fight it, you'll be much more successful in selling your services long term.

Further, if prospects say that they're not interested, don't get mad. Several times I got annoyed and said, "Then why did you request this material in the first place?" That immature attitude gets you nowhere. Always treat *everyone* with dignity and respect, even if you feel he or she doesn't deserve it. There's no benefit to acting like a prima donna, and it can harm you if word gets around.

DON'T CRITICIZE THE COMPETITION

Once in a while prospects may say, "Well, I got your package, and it looked good, but we were in a hurry and we hired so-and-so." Or "We looked at several people, but so-and-so had more experience, so we went with him."

Never belittle the other individual or firm they hired, and never imply that the prospect made a bad choice. Instead, say "I'm glad you were able to find someone who meets your needs. If you need any help in the future, please don't hesitate to give me a call." Another approach that works is to say "So you hired so-and-so for the project. What other projects do you have coming up in the next few months that I can help you with?" Make notes and call prospects back when it's time to start planning for those new projects.

HOW TO SAY NO (WITHOUT BLOWING PEOPLE AWAY)

Occasionally prospects will call you with assignments that you will not want to accept. This happens when you are too busy or when you sense that a prospect is not someone you would want to deal with.

Naturally, you don't want to tell prospects you won't work with them because you don't like their personalities. A more gracious way to get out of it is to simply say "I wish I could help you, but I've just accepted a large assignment from [name of your biggest, most well-known client] and I'm booked until [name a time three or four months from now]."

This allows you to get out of the situation gracefully while leaving the prospect with the impression that you are one busy and successful person.

An alternate approach is to quote a higher-than-normal fee when dealing with prospects you think might be unpleasant or difficult to work with, the logic being that the extra income makes up for the aggravation.

Another time you may want to say no is when prospects call and either their company is too small to afford you or they just don't have the budget for the specific assignment. The most polite approach here is also the most honest and direct one: "I'm sorry, but for the project you describe I charge X thousands of dollars. But please keep me in mind for a project where the budget will allow us to work together."

Once your reputation grows, other service providers wanting to emulate your success will call to pump you for free advice, as will small companies and organizations that can't afford to hire you but hope you will advise them at no cost. The best technique for handling these calls (and I stole this from professional speaker Patricia Fripp) is as follows:

"You could buy my time on a consulting basis for $200 an hour [or whatever your fee is]. If you want my time for free, I'll give you five minutes starting now." Then answer their questions for five minutes at no cost.

Finally, as you become more well known in your industry or community, various community groups, organizations, and professional clubs will invite you to speak on whatever your specialty happens to be. Most do not pay speakers and will not want to pay you. A polite way to handle these calls (and once more I stole this technique, this time from Dottie Walters, author of *Speak and Grow Rich!* [Englewood Cliffs, NJ: Prentice Hall, 1989]) is as follows:

After asking what their budget is for speakers, and finding out that they will not pay, you say: "I would like to help you, but I give only three free speeches a year and am booked for the next two years. But please keep me in mind for a future program."

This establishes that you are *paid* to talk (and you don't do it for free), that you were willing to help, but you are too popular and busy to accommodate them. Of course, there may be situations in which you are willing to speak for no fee (see chapter 2). If so, fine.

PREQUALIFICATION: THE MAIN OBJECTIVE OF YOUR FOLLOW-UP

There are two reasons to follow up with prospects. The first is to *qualify* prospects—that is, to determine which are good ones and which aren't. The second reason is to sell your services to those prospects who pass your initial screening test.

What is a qualified prospect? Simply put, a qualified prospect is someone who is a good potential candidate for your services—someone who is likely to buy, able to buy, and who can properly benefit from what you offer.

What do I mean by *prequalifying* the prospect? In your initial phone conversation, you want to make a quick assessment about whether a particular inquiry is worth pursuing. You might qualify the prospect more fully in subsequent meetings and phone conversations, so I call the initial screening *prequalification*.

Why prequalify inquiries before pursuit? Because this

simple initial screening, which takes about five minutes and requires asking only a few simple questions, can save you a bundle of time. It eliminates hours wasted on chasing after bad leads. And focuses your marketing and sales efforts where they should be: on convincing prime prospects to buy your service.

How to Prequalify a Prospect

Prequalification is best done over the telephone. Questionnaires sent through the mail can be a first step, and these devices can sometimes help stimulate response to your package or to cold mailings. But most of us can't really prequalify a person until we talk with him or her over the telephone.

In most instances prequalification is not done in person, because one of its benefits is that it eliminates wasting time meeting people who are not good candidates for your service.

I can't give you the exact questions to ask your prospect, because these questions are dependent on the markets you serve, the way you do business, and the services you offer. But I can offer guidelines to help you formulate your "prequalification script," similar to the list of questions (presented earlier) that I ask my own prospects.

Basically, the purpose of asking the prequalification questions is to determine whether the person fits the characteristics of a qualified prospect. A qualified prospect:

- has an immediate or future need to obtain a particular benefit or buy a particular type of service.
- has the money to do so.
- can authorize the purchase (or obtain authorization for it).
- is a person you can work with (personal chemistry).
- would significantly benefit from retaining your services.

If a person meets each of these five criteria, then he or she can be considered a prime prospect for your service, and you should actively and aggressively direct your sales and marketing efforts toward this person.

If a person meets some of these criteria, or meets all of them but only marginally, he or she can be considered a marginal prospect. You might try to sell the marginal prospect, but you wouldn't spend much time and effort doing so.

If a person does not meet these criteria, he or she does not qualify as a prime prospect for your services, and you should not waste time and effort talking to him or her. Use the techniques given in the last section to separate yourself politely from this person and not waste any more time. (Interestingly, some of the biggest nonprospects will waste huge amounts of your time, if you let them, while some of the best prospects do business efficiently with a minimum of chit-chat and small talk.)

Let's take a look at each of the five prequalifying criteria in a little bit more detail.

PREQUALIFYING CHARACTERISTIC 1: THE PERSON HAS AN
IMMEDIATE OR FUTURE NEED TO OBTAIN A PARTICULAR
BENEFIT OR BUY A PARTICULAR TYPE OF SERVICE

The prime prospect is someone who either needs you now or will in the future. Obviously, the best sales leads are from prospects with an immediate need. To determine whether the need is immediate, you simply ask, "Do you have an immediate project/assignment/problem I can help you with right now?"

If there is no immediate project, try to determine if there is a future need. Ask, "Do you use this type of service from time to time?" ("This type" refers to the type of service you render as described in your sales materials.)

Naturally, most prospects will say "Yes, I use your type of service from time to time" or "I haven't used this type of service yet, but I'm thinking of doing so." Otherwise, why would they have requested your brochure?

It's also a good idea to determine *when* they'll have a need by asking them. However, when doing so, don't say "Will you have a project in the future I can help you with?" because prospects' tendency is to answer "I don't know"—which leaves you in a weak position for follow-up.

Instead, assume they will have a need (they already said they use your type of service from time to time), and instead ask *when* they will have a project. For example: "Do you anticipate holding a training seminar for your salespeople within the next three months? within six months? this year?" Prospects will generally answer with some time frame, and your response is to offer (and promise) to contact them again around that time.

A few prospects may indeed tell you that they *don't* use your type of service. For example, "No, we've never had an outside sales trainer do a training program for our sales reps, but I saw your ad and just was curious."

In this case, they might not think they need your services, but they certainly need the *benefit* your services provide—namely, better-trained salespeople who sell more products and open more new accounts. So you will need to explain a bit about how your services work, what the benefits are, and the results you have achieved for your other clients.

For instance, a sales trainer, upon being told a firm never uses an outside sales trainer, might say "I understand. But tell me: If I could show you a way to get each salesperson in your organization to increase their gross sales by 10 to 25 percent or more this year, would you be interested?" When the prospect says yes, you then launch into your sales pitch.

Prospects who state that they have no immediate or future need, do not use your type of services, do not express interest in the *benefits* or results your services provide, and tell you "I'm not interested and I am just collecting brochures; leave me alone!" are probably not prime prospects for your services. They've said they are not interested, and it probably will not pay off to spend your time convincing them otherwise.

PREQUALIFYING CHARACTERISTIC 2: THE PERSON CAN AFFORD TO HIRE YOU

A prime prospect is someone who has the money to buy what you are selling. There are many people and organizations that want your service and could benefit from it but cannot afford your fee. Obviously, because you want to get paid, you must do business only with prospects who can afford you.

Ascertaining the financial status of a potential client is a bit tricky. Bring up the subject of price too soon, before you have clearly established the tremendous value of what you are selling, and you risk scaring potential buyers away. Bring up the subject of money too late, and you'll find yourself wasting many hours of your valuable time giving sales pitches to people who under no possible circumstances can afford you. That's terribly draining on any business but especially so if, for you, time spent selling means time not spent servicing clients and making money.

For instance, when I started as a freelance copywriter writing ads and brochures for corporations and ad agencies, many ad agencies would call and ask me to drop by with my portfolio. I would happily jump in the car and drive thirty or forty minutes to see them, with absolutely no prequalification whatsoever.

I'd spend another twenty minutes waiting in the lobby, then another thirty showing my work to the client. At the end, he'd say, "I love your work; what do you charge?" When I stated my rates, 90 percent of these ad agency creative directors exclaimed, "We can't afford it!" and another afternoon would be wasted. I quickly learned my lesson: Prequalify first!

My solution was to create a fee schedule that I'd mail out in advance. This way people could get a rough idea of what I charged, and if it was more than they could afford, they wouldn't waste my time or theirs in a pointless meeting. (See chapter 10 for a sample fee schedule.)

I can't tell you exactly *when* to introduce the subject of cost into your discussions with the prospect, because it depends on what's customary in your industry. However, if the prospect asks *you* about money, that's an excellent sign; the serious buyer is more likely to want to quickly get to the bottom line and find out "What's it cost?"

If a prospect never brings up money, watch out! The person who is not concerned about money is often a casual browser, not a serious buyer.

On the other hand, beware of the prospect who's *first* question is "What does it cost?" This person's key concern is not quality or service but cost. He or she is price-shopping and typically buys the lowest bid. As you're probably not the lowest-priced service around—it's a truism that someone can *always* do it a little bit cheaper—you want to avoid the price-shopper.

Here's a rule of thumb you may find helpful in prequalifying prospects regarding their ability to pay: When you're uncertain in your own mind as to whether the prospect really has money or is just wasting your time, bringing up money can quickly separate the serious from the frivolous.

For instance, if the prospect is blowing hot air about grandiose plans, but you suspect it's more to puff her own ego than to actually buy anything from you, it's perfectly okay to say "Well, I'd be happy to handle that; my fee is $250 an hour and I'll need a retainer of $3,000 to get started. Do you want to send a check out today so we can begin this work next week?"

At that point, the serious prospect will ask more questions, because now that you've stated your fee (and it's big), *she* wants to grill *you* to make sure she's getting her money's worth. The nonprospect will either balk ("That's outra-geous!") or, to prevent her ego from getting bruised, tell you sure, it's no problem, she'll send a check today. Then she quickly ends the call and you never hear from her again. Which is fine.

On the other hand, if you feel good about the prospect—you think it's a serious inquiry from a person or company with the budget to afford you—then *don't* bring up money right away. Instead, set up a time to make your full sales presentation. Remember, the key to selling serious pros-pects is to present the benefits of your service in a way that makes them desire it strongly . . . so strongly that your fee—when finally discussed—seems insignificant compared to those wonderful benefits you will deliver.

If you bluntly say "My fee is such-and-such" too early—especially if that fee is large and before the prospect has really become interested in you and your service—you risk seeming too arrogant. And that can be a turn-off to a poten-tial client.

PREQUALIFYING CHARACTERISTIC 3: THE PERSON CAN AUTHORIZE THE PURCHASE (OR OBTAIN AUTHORIZATION FOR IT) OF YOUR SERVICES

It's not enough that the prospect has a need or desire for your service and can afford it. He or she should ideally also be in a position to sign your contract and write you a check.

If you sell to consumers, for example, how many times have you thought you had the job "sold" because you con-vinced your prospect, only to find out you didn't get the job because "my husband/wife doesn't want to spend the money"?

And if you sell to the corporate market, as I do, have you ever had a prospect tell you "I'm ready to buy"—then when weeks pass and you don't hear from them, you call back and she says, "My boss thinks it's too much money" or "The committee didn't approve it"?

Unfortunately, you haven't sold your service until everyone who must approve the purchase has.

The best prospect is usually someone who can directly authorize purchase of your service. This might be the head of a household, the owner of an apartment complex, or the president of a manufacturing firm.

However, it's not always possible to deal directly with the man or woman in charge. That person may be too busy, not interested, or consider the matter too unimportant to give his or her personal attention.

If that's so, the second-best scenario is to deal with prospects who, while they cannot directly approve your contract, are in a strong position to specify or recommend your service. In a business, this might be the manager whose area of responsibility deals with your service and whose direct boss is the person who can sign your paperwork.

The worst-case scenario is to deal with some lower-level employee who has no real knowledge of what you sell, no real understanding of the problem, and no clout when it comes to specifying, recommending, or approving use of your service.

For instance, in my business, I've learned that almost all inquiries from secretaries and other assistants are worthless. If prospects don't think it's important enough to write or phone me themselves, then they don't understand the importance of what I offer and are unlikely to buy.

PREQUALIFYING CHARACTERISTIC 4: THE PROSPECT IS SOMEONE YOU CAN WORK WITH

Unlike those who sell products, we service sellers are going to be spending a lot of time with the customer after the sale is made. So it's important that we be able to get along with the prospect reasonably well.

You'll experience good personal chemistry with prime prospects and a minimal but acceptable amount of personal chemistry with marginal prospects. If you can't stand the person at the other end of the phone . . . cringe when she speaks . . . sense he'll be difficult . . . or feel the two of you just don't "click," then that person is probably not a good prospect for you.

PREQUALIFYING CHARACTERISTIC 5: THE PROSPECT WOULD SIGNIFICANTLY BENEFIT FROM RETAINING YOUR SERVICES

Product sellers—at least, the less scrupulous ones—try to sell to *everybody*. But we service sellers know that if clients can't really benefit from our services, they'll be dissatisfied no matter how well we perform. And if the clients are going to be dissatisfied, we probably should dissuade them from buying in the first place.

Why? Because unhappy clients can pose collection problems and generally aren't good for our reputation. We build our businesses by creating a large number of happy clients, not dissatisfied ones.

How do you determine whether prospects can benefit from your services? *You know better than they do.* If you've been in business for a year or more, you've gained a pretty good feel for what type of problems you can solve, what type of projects you excel at, what type of people can benefit most from your help. You also know what you don't do well and whom you can't help.

Did you ever talk to a prospect who resisted your sales pitch and think, "I've got to make this sale because I can really help this person and it would be a tragedy for both of us if he didn't use my service"? If you get the feeling that prospects will be suffering a terrible loss if they miss out on the opportunity to be helped by you, and that no one else could serve them as well as you can, they're probably prime prospects.

In other cases, you may feel that you can help prospects but so can a lot of your competitors. You know you would do a good job, but probably no better or worse than others in your field. People about whom you feel this way are good or marginal prospects, but not prime, hot prospects.

If you feel you are unqualified to help prospects, or that you are qualified but your particular services are not right for them, you should probably turn away the work unless you really need it. The best move would be to refer them to a friendly competitor, who (you hope) will reward you with a referral to a different prospect who is more up your alley.

USING YOUR "SIXTH SENSE" TO PREQUALIFY PROSPECTS OVER THE TELEPHONE

If you're an experienced service provider, you may be saying "I don't need to know these five characteristics or follow any script. I just seem to have a 'sixth sense' about prospects—after a minute or two on the phone, I pretty quickly can tell whether they're a good prospect for me or not, and whether I want to pursue them."

I believe you, because I'm the same way. After a two-minute conversation, I can quickly separate the good from the bad prospects—and what's more, I find I'm right 90 percent of the time.

But is it really a "sixth sense" that enables us to do this? No. Rather, you've discovered the five prequalifying characteristics all by yourself—without my help. And after having made hundreds of phone calls, you've permanently recorded these characteristics in your memory. So now you automatically sort all callers using these criteria to determine whether they are qualified prospects, without consciously realizing you're doing it.

Why, then, have I bothered to list the five prequalifying characteristics here? And why do I urge you to write a phone script, checklist, or questionnaire for prequalifying leads, as I have?

Because if you rely on memory or unconscious habit, you're likely to forget one or more of the five prequalifying characteristics when screening prospects, and you will probably forget to ask some important questions. For instance, you may get so excited about finding prospects who have a real need for your services that you forget to check whether they have the money and authority to retain you.

That's bad, because you'll be treating nonprospects as if they were prime prospects, wasting valuable time selling and following up with people and organizations who will never end up hiring you. Instead, study the five prequalifying characteristics and develop your own questionnaire or checklist for screening leads via short, to-the-point telephone conversations—conversations that quickly reveal whether the person has genuine interest or is "just looking."

If the person turns out to be a genuine prospect, the next step is to arrange for an in-person meeting or telephone conversation during which you do the actual selling of your service. This is covered in the remaining chapters of the book. If the prospect is a shopper or browser, or fails to meet most of the five prequalifying characteristics, you can politely end the discussion using the techniques outlined earlier.

HOW TO TURN A NO INTO A MAYBE— AND A MAYBE INTO A YES

Aside from qualifying prospects to determine which are desirable customers and warrant further follow-up and which are not good prospects and should be brushed off, another purpose of follow-up is to pursue the sale—that is, to get the good prospects to take the next step in the buying process and, ultimately, hire you.

Unfortunately, it's not only the poor prospects who give you the cold shoulder when you call. Many, many people who could really use your services and would benefit tremendously from hiring you will be negative with you. This, to me, is certainly one of the most frustrating things about being in a service business. But it's also one of the greatest challenges.

Every day I get inquiries from people who I *know* I can help and who would benefit greatly from my consultations and writing services. But most of them are not going to hire me. At least not without further prodding. There are a variety of reasons. Inertia. Lack of time. Too many other things on their mind. Concern about cost. More pressing matters. My failure to do enough marketing to establish my name in the field so that they'll hire me without question. But if I don't push and pull them toward the goal I want—a signed contract—we're not going to get to work together.

What do you do when someone says "no" or "I'm not interested" or "I haven't made my mind up yet"—someone who is a prime prospect for your services?

The goal of follow-up is to turn their *no* into a *maybe* . . . and a *maybe* into a *yes*.

Here are a few techniques for getting prospects to take action:

• *Tell prospects, in very specific terms, what the next step is*. Most prospects are unsure of the next step. They have your brochure, know where to reach you, but are not certain how to proceed. So tell them. Spell out what should be done next, when, where, how, and why. One reason why many prospects don't proceed with you is that they simply don't know what to do or say next.

• *Make an action commitment*. If you say to prospects, "Call me when you're ready to talk about it," they might—but more likely, they'll forget all about it. So if you want action, *you* identify the next step and make a commitment to clients to take it. Tell them you'll prepare an estimate . . . or send samples . . . or call on the twenty-third of the month. Then do it.

Yes, this puts the burden on your shoulders and takes more work (it's a pain, for example, to make promises to people and follow up on them). But this method forces the prospect to the next step in the buying process—which is what you want. The key is to promise to take a specific action, by a specific date, and then do what you promised.

• *Get prospects partially involved.* Even if prospects are not ready to commit to hiring you, act as if they were. For instance, if the first step is to gather some personal data about prospects, go ahead and set up a file for them and ask them the questions (or have them fill out a form). If the first step is setting a date for a presentation, pick and hold a tentative date, even if they're not firm about hiring you yet.

The reason: The more commitment prospects make, the more time and effort they invest in the "just-talking" stages, the more likely they will be to select you over your competitors when it's time to finalize things.

Think about it. If prospects spent time sending you background material, talking with you about their needs, and have set aside a date for the first meeting—and they didn't do this with your competitors—then when it comes time for them to choose a vendor, it's easier for them to choose you because you're already well into the process. And it's easier for them to reject your competitors, because prospects haven't invested any time, money, or effort with these firms, have they?

The more time and effort prospects commit earlier, the more likely they are to choose you later.

Here's an example that illustrates some of these principles.

The background: An engineering firm was interested in having me consult with them in some capacity but didn't really have an idea of what they wanted. I had mailed the prospect my package, but he never called. So I called to follow up.

ME: Hi, Bill, it's Bob Bly calling.

PROSPECT: Hi, Bob, I got your package. But we're still in the exploratory stage, and we haven't made any decision. I *think* we'd like to work with you, but I'm not sure in what capacity.

ME: Well, let me ask a question. What marketing projects are you working on right now you'd need help with?

BILL: We're developing an entire marketing campaign for a new programmable controller. But we're in the planning stages, and our budget is limited. So I don't think we can afford to have someone from the outside do the whole project for us—it would be too costly.

ME: But you would like an outside expert you could call to bounce ideas off of, ask questions, and get feedback and new ideas, right?

BILL: That would be great. But do you do that? I thought you just wrote copy and marketing plans.

ME: No, for companies with limited budgets, I can provide consultation and advice by the hour.

BILL: How much does it cost?

ME: I bill by the hour, so the total amount can be tailored to fit whatever budget you have. For example, let's say you felt you wanted to start with $500. My rate is $200 an hour, so that buys two and one half hours of time. You'll have to do most of the research and legwork putting the plan together, of course. But I can provide an awful lot of guidance and help in two and one half hours. Tell me, Bill, what's your budget: $500? $1,000? $2,000?

BILL: We can afford $500, and that sounds good. But I'm not ready to make the decision today.

ME: Fine. I have a standard form contract I use that

spells out the working arrangement. Would you like to see a copy?

BILL: Yes, please fax one.

ME: Why don't I make it out in the amount we discussed? That way, when you're ready, you can just sign and fax it back to me, and we'll get started.

BILL: That sounds good. Yes, go ahead.

At the beginning of the conversation, Bill wanted to put me off. He wasn't ready to talk business. He knew he liked what he saw but was uncertain as to how he could use my services and didn't really know what to do next. After this conversation, we had moved from a client having no intention of calling me to the final step before an actual sale—namely, a contract prepared and ready for his signature. And after another sales conversation took place over the phone, I was hired.

CHAPTER FIVE

Getting Past the Secretary

GETTING PAST SECRETARIES: THE CHALLENGE OF SELLING TO BUSINESSES

Those of you who sell to businesses have a problem that consumer service marketers do not: namely, getting past the secretary when calling to speak with the prospect. "I refer to secretaries and receptionists as 'filters' because they were hired to filter calls," says sales trainer Bill Bishop. "Some calls are to be filtered through, and some are to be filtered out."

This chapter presents proven strategies for handling secretaries so that they are not offended by your tactics—but so you also get through to the person you want to speak to.

TIMING OF PROSPECT CALLS

One way to get past the secretary is simply to call at a time when the prospect is likely to be in, but the secretary isn't. Most secretaries work standard office hours, while many hard-driving business executives and entrepreneurs put in longer hours. As a result, you can sometimes reach your prospect directly by calling during off hours. The best times to try this are: early morning—7:00 A.M. to 9:00 A.M.; lunchtime—noon to 1:00 P.M.; or late afternoon/early evening—5:00 P.M. to 7:00 P.M.

Be aware of your prospect's reaction to being "caught" answering the phone at these hours. Some like it. They feel less pressured and more relaxed after "official" business hours and may be more willing to talk. You can always develop a sense of camaraderie with a comment like "I see you're working late—like me. We seem to do that a lot in our business, don't we?" But say this only if you can be sincere. Don't say it if you feel phony.

On the other hand, if you sense the prospect has been caught off-guard and is uncomfortable with the fact that you've reached him or her, quickly explain who you are and why you are calling, ask if it's a convenient time, and if it's not, set an appointment to call back at a specific time and date. What you'll find most often, though, is that the prospect's initial shock and reluctance quickly wears off, and most will happily chat with you a few minutes.

REMIND THE SECRETARY THAT *THEY* CONTACTED *YOU* FIRST

In most cases, however, you can't avoid secretaries. They've been hired to filter calls, and many prospects rarely answer their own phones, no matter what the time. What do you do?

One powerful technique is to remind the secretary, politely but firmly and without apology, that the *prospect* contacted you first, and you're simply returning the call as requested. Your tone of voice should convey that you are a business colleague, not a telemarketer or salesperson.

Of course, for this technique to work, it must be true that

the prospect contacted you first or wanted you to call. Remember our main marketing lesson from chapters 1, 2, and 3: We want to implement sales and marketing activities that get prospects to call us rather than have us call them. Therefore, most of your calls *will* be in response to leads, inquiries, or referrals. So you can accurately claim that the prospect contacted you, and you are just returning the contact, as requested.

Use the following specific language in response to secretaries who ask why you are calling.

In response to a written inquiry generated from advertising, direct mail, or PR to prequalify a prospect before *you have mailed your brochure, package, or marketing materials:*

"Mr. Prospect had asked that I get in touch with him about our services, and I'm doing that now, as he requested."

In this situation, the secretary might tell you "Just send us a brochure." Your response should be something like "I'll gladly send more information, but we don't have a brochure. Instead, we tailor each package to the specific needs of the client. I have just a few questions to ask him to determine which materials to send him. Is now a good time?"

If the secretary absolutely refuses to put you through or set another time for a call-back, then ask *her* the questions you intended to ask her boss. Nine times out of ten, these are questions to which she does not know the answers. And rather than risk having her boss receive the wrong material, she will realize she is not qualified to talk with you about the subject and will put you through.

When following up on an inquiry or lead after *you have first sent your brochure or marketing materials:*

"Ms. Prospect had asked me to send her a package of material about our services. I'm calling just to make sure she received the information she requested and to answer any questions she may have."

When calling someone who is a referral:
"Would you please tell him that [name of person who referred you] asked me to give him a call?"

The key here is to impress upon the secretary/gatekeeper/filter that *they* (the prospects) called you first, and you are simply returning the call or getting in touch as requested—and that you did not make the initial call. A person who is returning a call is perceived as a business associate and will easily pass through the secretarial filter. A person who makes cold calls without being invited to do so is perceived as a pesty salesperson and is unlikely to be let through.

ANNOYING QUESTIONS

Most secretaries use a series of standard questions to filter calls. Only the first—"May I tell him who's calling?"—is innocent. Many of the others can be annoying.

Personally, I think businesses of all types, including yours, could create a lot of goodwill if the people who call could get through without this "grilling" procedure. As Colonel Potter of the *M*A*S*H* TV show once observed, "I like a man who answers his own phone!" I know I'm always extra-impressed when a receptionist or secretary puts me through politely and without treating me as "the enemy," or when the client answers his or her own phone.

Here are the questions you are likely to be asked by a secretary, in the order they will be asked:

"May I tell him who's calling?" That's innocent enough. Just give your name. But there are even techniques for doing that! One is the Answer/Ask or "A/A" strategy developed by Bill Bishop, which I'll cover later in the chapter.

Another technique is to answer with both your name and affiliation; for example, "Bob Bly from Bob Bly Associates." The advantage of this answer is that it eliminates the next question, which is . . .

"And what company are you with?" Again, easy enough to answer, although I personally have a problem with it, because I'm self-employed as an independent consultant. Like some of you, I don't use a company name, and so handling this question is always a bit awkward for me.

How to handle it? I simply say "No company," which probably isn't the best answer, but it's short, simple, and I say it with a sense of pride and dignity. Still, many secretaries ask me to repeat it, and it also pushes many to the harder grilling question of why, if I'm not with a company, am I calling their boss in the first place?

If you have a company name, then you simply answer with that. If you don't use a company name, instead of saying no company, you might elect to use one just for phone calls. For example, "Bob Bly and Associates" or "Bob Bly Advertising" or "Copywriting Services" are all names I've used when I didn't feel like a "no company" hassle that day.

A variation of the "What company are you with?" question is one of my favorites: "And where are you calling from?" Of course they want the company name, but sometimes I can't resist answering with "New Jersey."

You should be aware that, especially in larger corporations, a call or visit from someone who is not affiliated with a company is almost beyond secretaries' comprehension. I remember visiting a Fortune 500 client one afternoon at their headquarters. The receptionist, writing a name badge for me, asked, "And what company are you with?"

Me: No company.
[Pause].
Secretary (confused): This is a personal visit, then?
Me: No, it's business.

SECRETARY: Then what company are you with?
ME: You can be in business earning a good living without being employed by a company, you know!

My difficult nature has gotten me in trouble on more than one occasion. So please be easy to get along with, and don't follow my example. These incidents are told for your amusement only.

The next question you will hear after giving your company name is . . .

"Does he know you?" I've always found this to be an absurd question, because it requires me to be a mind-reader. Maybe the prospect and I met at a convention, or he called me on the phone to ask for my brochure, but does that mean I can say he *knows* me? Dare I even assume that he remembers who I am? That's presumptuous, yet the question demands an answer.

Whenever I am asked "Does he know you?" by a filtering secretary, my urge is to respond "I don't know," because it's usually the truth. However, a better way to answer is as directly and honestly as possible. For instance, if you met the prospect at a convention and he asked you to call him, say "He asked me to call him" or "Please tell him it's Joe Jones; we met at the Gun and Ammo Convention last week."

On the other hand, if you feel relatively certain the prospect will recognize your name, simply answer "Yes, he knows me." In fact, when calling prospects whom I know *do* know me, I avoid this question by saying, when asked my name, "This is Bob Bly; she knows me."

"And what is this in reference to?" Another difficult-to-handle question. Why? Because the business between you and the prospect may be of a complex nature. It may take several minutes to recount what led up to the call or give enough information to make your answer meaningful.

When asked this question, my immediate urge is to reply "His wife's gambling debt." I'm sure it would get me through! On occasion I have asked the secretary, "How much detail do you want?" Not to be rude, but because to answer honestly and completely would take several minutes.

But a better technique is to answer concisely but in a way that makes it sound like you are a colleague addressing an important business matter, rather than a salesperson pushing your service. For instance, don't say "We sell advertising space and I'm calling about placing an ad in *Wastewater Today Journal*." Instead, say "He asked me to make some marketing recommendations for his Uni-Flow Filter System and I'm calling with that information." The impression you want to make is that you are calling to have a business conversation, not to sell something.

This completes my list of Annoying Questions Secretaries Ask. Can you think of any more? To improve your own business image, try calling your own office and see how your phone is answered by your secretary or answering service (if you use one). By revising the script to minimize the screening questions, you'll annoy callers less and make them feel better about doing business with you.

THE ANSWER/ASK STRATEGY

The Answer/Ask, or "A/A" Strategy, was invented by sales trainer Bill Bishop and is described in his newsletter, *Master Prospector* (see the appendix under "Sales"). The technique basically involves "turning the tables" on secretaries, receptionists, and other filters by answering their questions *with a question.*

As Bill explains, "My A/A Strategy is a technique guaranteed to get you past the secretary to the decision maker. The first 'A' stands for 'answer.' This means you answer filters' question, instead of playing evasive cat-and-mouse games that tell filters you are a salesperson.

"The second 'A' stands for 'ask,' meaning you ask filters a

question in between your initial answer to their question, and before they ask you another filtering question.

"To summarize, 'A/A' means 'answer/ask.' Don't be evasive. Answer their initial filtering question, and before they can ask another, you ask *them* a question. This prevents them from asking additional filtering questions, and you'll get the decision maker on the line."

Continues Bill, "Taking the 'A/A' a step further, you can answer their question with a question." This is the way I personally use Bill's technique. Let's look at an example.

RECEPTIONIST: Good morning. Acme Widgets.
YOU: Mr. Big, please.
RECEPTIONIST: May I tell him who's calling?
YOU: Would you tell him you have Bill Bishop holding, please?

See the technique? If you simply answer "It's Bill Bishop calling," you set the secretary up for her next screening question, designed to block your call. But instead, when you answer with a question—"Would you tell him you have Bill Bishop holding, please?"—the reasonable response is for the filter to answer in the affirmative and put you through. Naturally, the secretary or receptionist will say "Yes, I'll tell him." What else is she going to say? "No, I won't tell him"?

Once in a while you'll get a tough filter who will come back with the second filtering question. Here's how the A/A strategy handles it:

RECEPTIONIST: And who are you with, Mr. Bishop?
YOU: Would you tell him my company is Bill Bishop Associates, please?

Again, if you just said "My company is Bill Bishop Associates," the likely response would be "And what is this in reference to?" or "Does he know you?" But when you say

"Would you tell him my company is Bill Bishop Associates, please?" the natural response is "Yes, I'll tell him." Can you imagine the receptionist saying "No, I won't tell him"?

Suppose you get that ultra-tough filter who bounces back with a third screening question. Here's an example:

RECEPTIONIST: And what is this in reference to?
YOU: Would you please tell him that I'm calling about [state the purpose of your call]?

The beauty of "answer/ask" questions is they can't get a no answer from the filter. Consider how awkward a filter's responses would be:

YOU: Would you please tell him I'm with Bill Bishop Associates?
RECEPTIONIST: No.

Filters generally won't answer the question negatively. Instead, they signify a yes by connecting you to the prospect.

Will answer/ask eliminate all secretarial screening? No. But it will reduce the *number* of screening questions and get you through in a certain percentage of cases where you wouldn't normally have been connected.

CALL-BACKS

Here's a frequent scenario:

YOU: Mr. Prospect, please.
SECRETARY: Mr. Prospect is in a meeting. Would you like to leave your name and number so I can ask him to call you back?

There are two ways to handle this. The first is to put the burden on the prospect's shoulders by leaving your name and number and saying "Yes, please have him call me." While this is convenient for you, there are some dangers in this, as Bill Bishop points out. Namely, here's what might happen:

1. You might not be in when the prospect calls back—and many people don't like talking to answering services, answering machines, or voice mail systems.
2. You'll be in, but on another call and will have to put the first prospect on hold while you take the second prospect's call.
3. The prospect, suspecting you're trying to sell something, probably won't return your call.
4. The prospect returns your call and you answer, "Good morning! John Doe Consulting Service!" The prospect's thoughts are confirmed that you called to *sell* and not to buy.
5. The prospect calls, isn't fazed by the way your phone is answered, and catches you by surprise. You've forgotten his name and why you called him. Imagine what he thinks!

"I must get two or three calls every day from stockbrokers who leave their name and a call-back number for me," says Bill. "The return call goes something as follows."

HIM: Hello, this is Bob Broker.
BILL BISHOP: This is Bill Bishop returning your call. . . .
HIM: Uh, well, ahh, ugh, gee . . . er, umm . . . Why did I call you, Bill?

"Well," continues Bishop, "if he doesn't know why he called, I'm sure not going to help him figure it out. The moral

is, don't leave your name and number." Instead, advises
Bishop, follow this script:

> SECRETARY: Mr. Prospect is in a meeting. Would you like
> to leave your name and number so I can ask him to call
> you back?
> YOU: I'd like to, but I'm going out shortly. When do you
> think he'll be free?
> SECRETARY: Well, let's see, it's 10:20 A.M., so I'd say he'd
> call you about 10:45 A.M.
> YOU: Gee, unfortunately I'll be gone by then. When do you
> think I should try him again?
> SECRETARY: Well, he likes to come in real early—around
> 7:15—so you could likely catch him then.
> YOU: I'll try him later today or tomorrow morning, okay?
> SECRETARY: Okay. Bye.

Notice how everything you say ends with a question (the
"answer/ask" technique in action). You learn precisely when
the prospect will be in to receive your call, all without being
sneaky or evasive.

THE FINAL FILTER

There may be times when you call prospects repeatedly and
don't get through, despite the fact that they asked you to call,
requested information, or were referred by a business associate. Let's say you've called numerous times and a prospect
so far has not returned your call. Should you call again?

That's really up to you and how far you want to pursue the
lead. Some salespeople might say "Persist until you get
through." I think there's probably a limit after which you give
up—perhaps two, three, or four call-backs, but certainly no
more.

Here's a strategy you can use with the secretary on the final call.

SECRETARY: Joe Smith's office.
YOU: This is [your name] calling again. Is he in?
SECRETARY: He's not in. Would you care to leave a message?
YOU [to the secretary]: Yes, but . . . excuse me, what is your name?
SECRETARY: Mary.
YOU: Well, Mary, maybe you can help me. Joe requested information on my [type of services you provide] service, and I've called four times and left four messages, but he hasn't returned my calls. If he's interested in my service then I still want to help him and will keep trying, but if he's not interested, I don't want to keep bothering you or waste your time. Could you do me a favor and ask him if he's still interested in the service and if so, when would be a good time to talk about his particular needs?
SECRETARY: Yes, I can do that.
YOU: Thanks, Mary, I appreciate it. Today is Monday. Would it be okay if you could ask him today or tomorrow, and I'll call you back on Wednesday or Thursday to find out where we stand?
SECRETARY: That would be okay.
YOU: Okay, Mary, I'll call you Thursday. And thanks.

If you still get the same old brush-off Thursday, forget about the lead.

But more likely, Mary will give you the information you asked for—either a time to call Joe and discuss his needs—or she will relay the message that yes, Joe got your material, but he'll call you if he needs you, and don't call him.

If that's the case, you might ask Mary if you can at least

put Joe on your mailing list. When she says yes—and she probably will—you can at least follow up in the future by mail a couple of times.

TREAT THEM RIGHT

Perhaps the best attitude to take with secretaries, receptionists, and other filters and gatekeepers is to treat them with respect and dignity, rather than view them as roadblocks to be pushed out of your way.

Many, many of your competitors treat secretaries with indifference or even as inferiors, never stopping to realize there's a human being behind that telephone headset or word processor. If you do acknowledge the secretaries' existence and treat them decently, with common courtesy, you'll be at the top of their list of favorite people.

And if you think this goodwill doesn't translate into action, you're wrong. A secretary who likes you will go out of her way to put your call through, make sure your fax gets on the boss's desk, and in general do everything to help you succeed. A secretary who dislikes you will sabotage your efforts, helping your competitors beat you out for the business.

You don't have to shower the secretary with flowers and candies to win her over. *Learning her name* and calling her by name when you telephone or visit is a nice first step; many people never bother to learn the name of the secretary or receptionist. If, after a few calls, she recognizes you and seems inclined toward making a few pleasantries over the phone, do likewise. Getting to know—and treating—the secretary like a person is the best way you can get her on your side.

CHAPTER SIX

Getting the Initial Appointment

This chapter is about getting the initial appointment with your prospect so you will have the opportunity to make your sales pitch or presentation.

Let's review where we are so far.

By now we've generated some initial interest from the prospect, typically an inquiry, using the marketing techniques described in chapters 1 and 2.

We've sent some background material on our services (chapter 3).

We have also used the telephone techniques in chapter 5 to get past secretaries (if selling to businesses) and have had the opportunity to spend a few minutes on the phone with prospects. We've prequalified prospects using the guidelines set forth in chapter 4, and we've done some initial exploring to determine the level of interest and specific need for our service, using the follow-up questions in chapter 3.

At this point, if we are still talking to prospects and still interested in pursuing their business, we know we have qualified prospects on the line. And so the next step would be to arrange a meeting during which we can make our complete sales presentation.

"ASKING FOR THE ORDER"

Sales trainers and direct-marketing experts point out that live salespeople and written marketing documents (ads, sales letters, mailers) must "ask for the order."

In other words, it's not enough to say to prospects "Here's our service, my credentials, the benefits, and why you should buy. Okay?" You must also tell prospects what the next step is, why they should take it, and give them a reason for acting now instead of later.

But "ask for the order" is actually an inaccurate term for this, as is "closing," because we don't necessarily ask for the order or close the deal when making initial sales calls.

Rather, at the end of each sales call or contact, we ask prospects to take a specific action that is *the next logical step in the buying process.* This might be to arrange the next meeting or phone call, get documents signed, or discuss terms and conditions and fees.

For instance, if you're a real estate agent, and prospects decide they want to work with you, you wouldn't "ask for the order" by asking them to buy a particular house. Rather, the next step would be "Take a look at our multiple listing services book, Mr. and Mrs. Prospect. Tell me which houses you like and I'll take you to see them." The agent needs to ask for definite action on the part of prospects to move the sale along. But to literally "ask for the order" at that point would be inappropriate, ridiculous, wrong, and ineffective.

Sales trainer John Gardner stresses that salespeople should establish the proper goal for *each* call they make. In the selling of services, the goal of the initial sales call may be one or all of the following, depending on the complexity of your service and the interest level of the product:

GOALS OF INITIAL
TELEPHONE FOLLOW-UP CALL

1. Prequalify the prospect (chapter 4).
2. Make sure prospect understands what you offer (chapter 3).
3. Probe to identify the prospect's need for your service (chapter 3).
4. Set up an appointment at which you can give the prospect your sales pitch or presentation (this chapter).

So when you first call prospects to follow up, your goal is not to ask for a contract or to get prospects to hire you. Instead, your goal is to get prospects to grant you the time required to present your services and their benefits to them.

DEFINING "APPOINTMENT"

Throughout this chapter we'll talk about getting the initial appointment. But the appointment doesn't have to be a face-to-face meeting. It can also be a telephone conference or even a written presentation prospects have promised to review and study (and then discuss with you in a follow-up call).

Whether you need to see prospects in person to sell your services depends on the nature of your business, the price, your personality, and a number of other factors. We'll discuss the issue of whether a face-to-face meeting with prospects is necessary and desirable for you, as well as how to do more of your selling by phone and mail, in chapter 7.

So for now, take "appointment" to mean the opportunity to make a presentation to prospects in person, over the phone, or in writing.

HOW MUCH TIME IS APPROPRIATE?

If you seek an appointment with prospects, how much of their time should you ask for?

In most cases, thirty minutes is ideal. Prospects perceive that they can learn what they need to know in this period without having your presentation drag on into boredom.

You may be thinking, People are busy, so I'll get more appointments by saying my presentation will take less time. But watch out! This strategy may backfire—for a couple of reasons.

First, prospects may suspect your competence and ability. If they know their problem requires some analysis, and you say you only want five minutes of their time, they may rightly conclude that you don't know what is required to understand their needs.

Second, if you ask for ten minutes when you know you need twenty, you'll end up rushing through your presentation. A professional is relaxed and dignified; rushing through a canned presentation is neither. This type of pressure situation will rob you of your confidence, and you'll come off looking stupid.

On the other hand, what if you need more than thirty minutes to make your pitch? Perhaps your services are complex, or you have a videotape or software diskette or demonstration to run through. In this case, explain to prospects *why* you need more time (because your services are complex, or because you have exciting ideas and concepts to present, or because you really want to understand the prospects' needs). If your explanation makes sense, prospects will be more inclined to give you some additional time. But one hour is usually the maximum. In some rare instances, with major service proposals to top executives at big corporations, you may be allotted two hours.

The ideal is to ask prospects for twenty to thirty minutes to make your sales presentation, with an hour maximum in most cases.

HOW TO BRING UP THE SUBJECT OF A MEETING

Professionals and tradespeople who are not, by profession, full-time salespeople become extremely uncomfortable when it's time to stop talking about their services or the prospect's project and ask the prospect to take action (or bring up any conversation that even remotely smacks of selling or pressure).

And certainly we don't pressure our prospects the way some product salespeople do. But at the same time, we can't—and shouldn't—talk forever. We must move prospects from initial interest to retaining our services, if we are to truly be of help to them (after all, we can't service or advise clients until they hire us). So there is nothing "sleazy" about going for the appointment. On the contrary, it's all part of helping prospects improve their lives or enjoy other benefits we provide.

When is the proper time to bring up the subject of "the next step"? When you've asked some questions that qualify prospects and enable you to understand their initial needs, and you feel certain they're somewhat interested and can benefit from your service, that's the time to go for the appointment.

You'll sense this with a bit of practice. Often it comes at a point where both you and the prospect are "talked out." *You've* explained briefly what you do. The *prospect* has indicated an interest and explained what is needed. There is an awkward pause and silence; nobody seems sure what to say next. At this point, you must jump in and help the prospect move to the next logical step.

MAKE APPOINTMENTS, NOT SALES CALLS

By the way, we never use the words *sales call, sales pitch,* or *sales presentation* when referring to this initial appointment, because to prospects *sales* is a negative term that implies that you are there to "sell" them (which they don't want) rather than to help them (which they want). Instead of sales call or sales pitch, we tell prospects we want to arrange an:

initial appointment
free, no-obligation consultation
free estimate
free analysis
exploratory meeting
evaluation of your needs
initial planning session

As you can see, we do not "sell"; we consult, plan, help, estimate, evaluate, analyze, measure, design, or render assistance in some other way. As service providers, we treat the initial meeting as the first step or beginning of the process of solving clients' problems. Even though they have not yet retained us, *we act, to some degree, as if they have.*

What do I mean by "to some degree"? It means we give away enough advice and know-how at the initial meeting to impress prospects and convince them we're the one to hire, without giving away so much advice and wisdom that we end up working for free or—worse—tell prospects so much that they no longer need to retain us! (More about this in chapter 8.)

Telling prospects you want to meet with them to "sell" them something lowers your status in their eyes and creates an automatic adversarial situation—after all, you want to get them to part with money, and they don't like to do that!

Telling prospects you will give them a free initial consultation or exploratory meeting to solve their problems elevates your status, making you a valuable problem-solver in prospects' eyes. It also removes their reluctance and apprehension, because you both have the mutual goal of working to solve a problem or provide a benefit.

SOME GENERAL GUIDELINES ON GETTING THE INITIAL APPOINTMENT

1. Do not ask questions that can be answered yes or no. For instance, if you ask prospects, "Do you want to meet?" their natural instinct is to say no. Instead, ask questions to which either answer is a positive answer. For instance, "Do you want to landscape your front yard only—or both the front and back?"

Another technique is to ask questions to which no (the buyer's favorite response!) is actually a yes to proceed. For instance, if you ask, "Is there any reason you wouldn't want to learn how XYZ service operates?" and prospects say no, they have told you they want to learn more about your service!

2. Ask questions that prospects must answer affirmatively. For example: "When would be the best day for us to meet—Thursday or Friday?" No is not a logical answer. The answer is either Thursday, Friday, or "Let's try for another day."

3. Sell the appointment, not your service. Don't try to get a contract over the phone. Focus your efforts on convincing prospects to grant you an appointment. That's when you'll do the actual selling of your service.

4. Be flexible. Try to accommodate prospects' needs. For instance, some prospects may want to meet with you early in the morning, before business hours, or at lunch, or after 5:00 P.M. You may resent this, feeling they are exerting their

power and superior position over you. But as freelancer Bob Schulte points out, "Remember that this is a client whom you are serving—who is paying for your service. Remember that you're there to be someone who is easy to work with—as best you can." So do what prospects want, within reason.

5. If prospects are fighting you, find out the source of the objection. Don't run away from it, but address it head on.

6. Ask for the prospects' help. Let's say a prospect says he doesn't want to meet with you because he isn't convinced your service is good. Say "I understand. Tell me, what would you have to hear me say to convince you that I can do for you what I say I can?" The prospect will literally tell you how to overcome his objection—which in many cases you'll be able to do.

7. Don't fight or argue with prospects. You cannot win.

8. Don't always assume you are right and prospects are ignorant if they don't agree with you. Treat their opinions with respect, and be open to the idea that prospects may be right. A good phrase to use when responding to a statement, opinion, or objection voiced by the prospect is "I understand."

Prospects don't like it when you argue with them. On the other hand, you can't agree with everything they say. "I understand" doesn't mean you agree or disagree with them; it just means you understand what they said and are listening attentively.

9. Don't push. After two or three attempts to get the appointment, settle into a fall-back position. Try: "I understand you're not ready to go ahead right now. May I follow up with you next month to see where we are at that time?"

10. If a prospect says "I'm not interested, stop bothering me, and don't call again" in a surly tone of voice, think about whether this is a person you want to do business with.

WHAT TO SAY TO GET THE APPOINTMENT

Here are some sample situations along with appropriate dialogue for moving prospects from indecision and uncertainty to a firm appointment for a sales call.

When the prospect asks you what to do next . . .

PROSPECT: Okay, I'm interested. What's the next step?
YOU: Let's get together to review your situation in more detail. When would be best for you—Thursday or Friday?

When the prospect doesn't seem to know what to say or do next but doesn't ask you . . .

PROSPECT: Well, your service sounds interesting. I'll definitely keep it in mind. . . .
YOU: Great. But let me ask: Are you planning [type of project you handle] in the next few months or anytime this year?
PROSPECT: We may be doing something in the summer.
YOU: Well, now would be the best time to start planning. And we have a few designs we developed for other clients you may find interesting. Is there any reason we can't get together to review them this Thursday or Friday?

When the prospect resists your suggestion to arrange an appointment for a presentation . . .
One effective strategy in this situation is to restate the prospect's need for your services or his or her desire for the specific benefit you offer:

PROSPECT: I don't think a meeting is appropriate, but I'll keep your material on file.
YOU: I understand. But may I ask you one question?

PROSPECT: Sure.

YOU: How much are you spending on graphics and typesetting per year?

PROSPECT: About $35,000.

YOU: Wow! I can bet that's eating into your bottom-line profits!

PROSPECT: It sure is!

YOU: If I could show you a way to reduce your graphics costs by 75 to 80 percent, would that be of interest to you?

PROSPECT: Well, yes . . .

YOU: Then when would be the best time to get together and review this system for reducing graphics costs—Wednesday or Thursday?

When the prospect objects to some specific aspect of your services . . .

PROSPECT: We're looking at other printers and would prefer a printer with desktop publishing capability in-house. And as you said, you don't have it.

YOU: Mr. Prospect, let me ask you a question.

PROSPECT: Sure.

YOU: If we can deliver the same product as those other printers, just as quickly, but at a lower price and with better quality, and with the same flexibility when it comes to making changes, would it really matter to you whether we owned and operated our own Macintosh computer or used an affiliated service—as we do?

PROSPECT: Well, I don't know . . . I suppose not. But if you don't own your own system, how can you respond to change requests as quickly as the printers who have Macs in-house?

YOU: We use a variety of independent Mac artists. Layouts are transmitted in seconds via fax, and electronic output is sent and received by modem. Because we have many associates to call on, we don't have the capacity limitations that printers with only one or two Mac systems in-house do. And our costs are less, because money isn't tied up in equipment we don't need to own. If I can stop by with some samples, I think you'll agree our work is what you're looking for, Mr. Prospect.

SETTLING THE DETAILS OF YOUR MEETING

If the prospect agrees to meet with you, set a definite time and date using the either/or technique presented earlier ("When would be the best day to meet—Thursday or Friday?" not "Do you want to meet this week?").

Confirm the date, time, and length of meeting. Mark it on your calendar. Then tell the prospect you're looking forward to meeting him or her on that date.

If you discussed specific designs, materials, or ideas, and you think the prospect should have them in hand before the meeting, send them out with a short cover note right away. Or fax them.

If no materials are required, then there's no need to send a letter confirming the meeting.

SHOULD YOU CALL TO CONFIRM
THE MEETING?

There are two schools of thought on whether you should call the prospect to confirm the meeting.

The first says it's a mistake to call to confirm the meeting, because this gives prospects the opportunity to change their minds and cancel the appointment. If you ask "Are we still on for Thursday?" a prospect may very well say, "No, I'm busy and have to cancel."

The second school says you should call to confirm. I'm in

agreement. Why? Because my time is valuable, and I want to make sure the prospect will be there when I show up. Prospects are forgetful. What is an important event to you— a sales call with a hot prospect—is relatively unimportant to buyers. They may have forgotten and made other appointments. Or maybe they got sick and forgot to call you.

So I always call and say, "Hi, it's Bob Bly calling. Are we still on for Thursday?" Most prospects say yes. But on occasion I have saved myself a wasted trip by calling and finding out the prospect wasn't home or in the office that day, or forgot and had other obligations.

Has a prospect ever used my confirmation call as an opportunity to back out of seeing me? No. I've never had a prospect cancel and then not reschedule. In a few cases prospects have said, "Gee, Bob, today has become rather hectic and isn't a good day to meet," but they've always rescheduled to a date that week or the next week.

And that's fine with me. I'd rather see prospects when they're comfortable and have the time to spend with me than when they're pressured and thinking of a thousand things other than my services. Wouldn't you?

PART THREE

The Initial
Client Meeting:
How to Use It to Achieve
Your Goal

CHAPTER SEVEN

Increasing
Your Selling Efficiency

THE FIRST MEETING: FEE OR FREE?

In most service-type businesses, suppliers of the service are going to give away *something* to the potential buyer in order to prove they are qualified and deserve the contract. But the question is: How *much* do you give away? Successful professionals give away a minimum of information and time before "the meter goes down"—meaning, clients who want advice and time are quickly put under an arrangement where they *pay* for this advice and time.

One of the biggest gray areas in selling services is the initial meeting. For example: A client calls you up. Asks to see samples. You mail them. The client calls back and says, "We like your work. When can you come in for a meeting?"

Most service providers are elated to hear this. But watch out. What the client may *really* be saying is "Your work looks good, but we haven't made any firm decision yet. In fact, we may be looking at three, four, or a dozen other firms for this assignment . . . but of course, we aren't telling you that.

"What we want is for you to come to our office, answer

questions, show us your work. We may also bounce some ideas off you and see if we like the way you think. You'll have the opportunity to 'sell' us on why we should hire you.

"We don't intend to pay for your time or any information or suggestions or ideas you give us, of course. After all, this is a sales opportunity for *you*. So we expect you to spend the time—probably three or four hours including travel— without compensation. In fact, we also expect you to pay for your own gas, tolls, and parking."

Do you, as a service provider, want to accept this offer? As a beginner, at first, you may have to. I certainly did. But as soon as possible, you may want to consider saying no to some or all of the prospects who ask you to come to free meetings.

MUST YOU MEET THE PROSPECT TO MAKE THE SALE?

Why would we *not* want to meet with prospects? One very good reason: time. For many of us, time spent in meetings with possible clients is time spent away from our work . . . which means time spent not making money. Obviously, the less time spent selling, the more time spent working on paying business.

Although percentages vary according to what field you work in, on average, service providers spend only half their working hours on "billable time"—that is, on project work they can bill to clients. The rest of the time is spent on marketing, selling, correspondence, paperwork, reading trade journals, administrative details, and running the business.

If you can sell clients by mail or phone without going to see them, you'll increase the percentage of time spent on billable versus nonbillable work, increasing your income. An alternative, of course, is to *charge a fee* for the initial meeting. We'll explore both options—selling by mail and phone and charging for the initial meeting—in this chapter. If you can do them, both these options can mean a dramatic increase in your business efficiency and profits.

HOW TO DETERMINE WHETHER A FACE-TO-FACE MEETING IS REQUIRED

Here are some situations in which a face-to-face meeting with prospects is either necessary or highly desirable if you hope to get the contract:

1. The job requires you to inspect or measure the client's home, office, or facility to provide an accurate cost estimate. As you're going to visit the location anyway, you may as well combine your inspection with a presentation.
2. Your service is too complex to explain over the phone and is better presented in a face-to-face situation.
3. The prospect's problem is complex and difficult to assess remotely, and you feel the need to sit down with the prospect face to face to get a sufficient understanding of his or her needs.
4. Yours is the type of service where there will be a close personal working relationship with the client involving subsequent meetings. In this case, you want an initial meeting, because you want to be able to determine whether you and the client can work well together.
5. The project is large. Generally, the higher the fee, the more mandatory a meeting. Projects with large fees in five and six figures may take several in-person meetings to close.
6. The prospect is seeking a steady, ongoing relationship rather than farming out a one-shot project.

7. You are in a type of business where service providers are expected to attend meetings and to make presentations, and to refuse to do so would be going against the standards and therefore would dramatically reduce your chances of making the sale.

8. The prospect is seeing a number of firms, and if you refused to meet with him or her, you'd probably be the only vendor who did so—thus hurting your chances for winning the business.

9. The prospect *insists* on meeting you before he or she will commit to doing business with you, despite the fact that you've repeatedly stressed that a face-to-face meeting is unnecessary.

10. The prospect is close by and doesn't understand why you would not want to meet him or her. "After all, I'm only ten minutes away!" she says when you try to sell your service by phone.

By the same token, there are a number of situations in which prospects will hire you without seeing you, making a meeting unnecessary:

1. The nature of the services you render is such that the project can be handled easily and efficiently by mail and phone, without face-to-face meetings. Your reasoning as presented to the prospect is "If you don't need to see me to work with me, then you don't have to see me to hire me, do you?"

2. Your services are fairly standard and well understood by the prospect; therefore, your presentation is straightforward and not conceptual—and can be easily communicated to the prospect in marketing documents and telephone sales calls.

3. The prospect's problem is familiar to you and can be diagnosed quickly and easily over the phone, without a face-to-face meeting or on-site inspection. There-

fore, you don't need to see the prospect or facilities to work up a fair and accurate estimate.

4. The services you or your staff render do not require a lot of close client cooperation or feedback, and therefore do not require you to meet with the prospect or his or her staff.

5. The project is small. Generally, the lower the fee, the more likely prospects are to hire you sight unseen. Prospects understand that you can't spend half a day or more of your time in a sales meeting where the job at stake is a $100 consulting assignment. Projects with fees in three and four figures are often handled by mail and phone.

6. The prospect has a one-shot project and will not have a regular need for your service. Such prospects understand that vendors prefer ongoing relationships to one-shot projects, and therefore won't spend a lot of time pitching their business. These prospects also don't feel the need to get to know you as well as they would if they were establishing an ongoing relationship, and so they don't feel as great an urge to meet you.

7. You are in a type of business where service providers regularly handle assignments by mail, phone, and fax.

8. For one reason or another, the prospect is already presold on you, so you do not have to use a great deal of persuasiveness to close the sale.

9. When you suggest to the prospect that a meeting is not necessary, he or she agrees happily and without argument.

10. The prospect is far away and recognizes that the scope of the project does not warrant your traveling there and that the work can easily be handled by overnight delivery service and telephone.

Unfortunately, for you the answer may not be so cut and dried. For instance, the project may be small, but if business is tough and there's a lot of competition, you may feel the need to visit and sell the prospect to win a relatively small job. Or perhaps the prospect is far away, but you are competing with firms local to her and you don't want to make your distance look like a disadvantage.

When will you have arrived at the point in your career when you can refuse to meet with potential clients unless you are paid a fee? Simple. It happens when you are so busy that you can afford to turn the business away.

Actually, it would be smart to try to avoid such meetings even when things are not going swimmingly, but few of us—myself included—have the nerve to walk away from a nice potential money-making assignment when we're hungry for work. I didn't start turning down work until I could afford to. But maybe you'll be different.

This advice about not going to initial meetings with prospects for free may not sound like much, but believe me, it made a major change in my career. When you run around with your sales kit, jumping in the car when any prospect, qualified or not, snaps his fingers, it creates a certain image—an image of someone who is not busy and successful but who is hungry and needs the work.

And why is this a problem? Because potential clients want to hire vendors who are busy and successful, not those who are hungry and need the work. If you look needy, you may get work—but it will be from the bottom of the barrel, from the clients who pay you least and treat you worst. The top clients, those who treat you like a professional and pay the big fees, want to deal with vendors they perceive as being at the top of the game.

Also, once you get better known, going to meetings with the prospects who call and request to see you becomes literally impossible. Remember, as a service provider, the only thing you have to sell is time. And there is a fixed amount of it available—you can't make more.

I probably get at *least* five or six calls a week from people who say they might need a copywriter and would I meet with them? I explain patiently that if I met with everyone who asked to see me, I would spend my entire week at meetings and would not be able to write copy for any of my clients— including them, if they became a client. Many people see the logic of this and accept that I cannot see them in person unless I am being paid a consulting fee.

Okay. I've given you the theory. But in reality, many prospects are going to object vehemently when you refuse their invitation to see them on a sales call or initial meeting.

You see, although I do this daily with no problem, it's still not standard practice, and so you are fighting traditional behavior, going against the grain. This is not a big problem; you just need to develop an appropriate "script" for explaining your policy.

Let's get specific. Here's how the conversation might proceed:

PROSPECTIVE CLIENT: Well, we're interested. When can we meet with you?
ME: Let me send you some detailed background information on my services. After you've had a chance to review it, we can talk again.

Explanation: When clients call, my first step is to get my "information kit" (a package of sales literature promoting my service) into their hands. So if someone calls and immediately requests a meeting, as many do, I simply sidestep the issue with the line just given. Almost no one objects to this, and most simply say "Okay, send what you've got." Then we can defer the issue of the initial meeting until later.

Sometimes, though, the prospective client will push for a

meeting. Some service providers and sales experts would view this favorably, thinking that anyone who wants to meet with you must be a prime prospect.

I hold a contrary opinion. Unless prospects are very familiar with my work or come from a strong referral, their interest is probably casual. A request for a meeting does *not*, in my opinion, indicate any strong interest or sense of commitment; many prospects will happily summon you to their home or office and waste your morning or afternoon with no solid promise of an assignment. So please don't be flattered when they push for a meeting—instead, be cautious. Here's how I handle it.

PROSPECTIVE CLIENT: Well, we're interested. When can we meet with you?

ME: Let me send you some detailed background information on my services. After you've had a chance to review it, we can talk again.

PROSPECTIVE CLIENT: Well, we really prefer to see you. When can you come in for a meeting?

ME: I'd be happy to meet with you, but let me explain my policy. I work primarily with clients by mail, phone, and fax. I am available for in-person meetings, but for this I charge a consultation fee of X dollars per hour with a Y-hour minimum.

What this means is: I charge for meetings at an hourly rate. There is a minimum charge equal to the hourly rate multiplied by the minimum number of hours. I require a check in advance, and do not bill for initial meetings.

When I say this, it typically elicits a number of questions and objections. The most common—with my answers— follow:

PROSPECTIVE CLIENT: You mean you would charge me to meet with me?

ME: Yes, that's correct. I charge a consultation fee for all out-of-office visits.

PROSPECTIVE CLIENT: But that's ridiculous. You want me to pay *you* for the opportunity to sell to me and bid on this project?

ME: I don't "sell" or "market." I have a full schedule of writing projects representing more work than I can handle, so I don't visit potential clients to bid on projects, which can just as easily be handled over the telephone. Also, I get so many inquiries about my services each week that if I went to meetings with all of these prospects, I would have no time to write copy for my clients—including you, if you become one.

PROSPECTIVE CLIENT: But other writers will come see me for free.

ME: Everyone has different business practices. But I wonder—how busy and successful can those other writers be if they have time to visit you and everyone else who calls them without charge?

PROSPECTIVE CLIENT: Your hourly fee seems high.

ME: I understand. There are others who charge much less—and some who charge more. You are the final judge as to which service offers you the best value for your dollar.

PROSPECTIVE CLIENT: If I pay you to meet with me, do you charge for your travel time?

ME: I don't charge for travel time, but there is a minimum per-meeting fee of *XXX* dollars based on my hourly rate of *X* dollars multiplied by a minimum of *Y* hours.

Note: My minimum meeting fee is usually four hours for someone within an hour's drive, eight hours for someone farther away, and twelve hours if I have to fly out of town—which I virtually never do.

PROSPECTIVE CLIENT: What do you mean by an advance retainer?

ME: It means I require a check for the full amount of the fee in advance of the meeting.

PROSPECTIVE CLIENT: Why? Don't you trust me?

ME: I do, but that's not the issue. A retainer check shows me you are serious about this project and about using my services to your best advantage. I don't like to deal with clients who are casual about their time— or mine.

Am I ever flexible about my policy of charging for meetings? On rare occasions, maybe. But the longer I'm in business, the less likely I am to bend this policy. This is because many prospects will gladly waste your time, but I have less and less time to waste.

When might I make an exception? When clients are a large Fortune 500 or "Blue Chip" account, when they are a good fit for the services I offer and the expertise I have, when there seems to be potential for a great deal of work, and when the person calling seems genuinely sincere and a "no-bull" type prospect.

However, even when going to a free meeting, you should still make clear that you *do* charge an hourly rate for all out-of-office visits and that in agreeing to see them without charge, you are making a rare exception to your usual policy. Here's how to handle it (I read this in Jeffrey Lant's *Tricks of the Trade*):

YOU: Because I am eager to help you, I will agree to meet with you on [date] without charge. My normal hourly rate is X dollars and is charged for all out-of-office visits to clients. I will come to your office and give you one hour free. If, at the end of that hour, you want to continue with me, we can do so at the regular hourly rate.

This strategy works well because it makes clear that the free meeting is the exception, not the rule, and it limits the length of the meeting to one hour.

Having said when I *would* go to a free meeting, let me now tell you when I would *not* go to a free meeting. That's when prospects are having a "cattle call," meaning instead of calling you because of some special interest or awareness of your service, they are calling *all* (or many) of the vendors in town to have them come in and make a sales pitch.

How do you know when it's a cattle call? Some sure signs:

1. They call and say, "We are so-and-so company and we are seeing/talking with [writers, printers, photographers, architects, etc.]." If they use the plural ("writers," "photographers"), it's a cattle call.
2. You get what obviously looks like a form letter.
3. You get a letter or call shortly after your name is published in some type of directory. (Some people simply like to go through directories and send request letters to everyone in the directory.)
4. One or more of your friends or colleagues in your business also get an inquiry from the company.
5. Prospects tell you there is no immediate project but that they are building a "stable" or file of vendors for future use.

If I get such a letter, I simply scribble at the bottom a short note that says "Not taking on clients right now—but thanks for your inquiry." Then I sign my name and send their letter back to them.

If it's a phone call, I simply tell them I'm booked to some future date (usually a date several months away) and thank them for their interest.

Have I ever missed out on some great job because I

refused a cattle call? Probably. Would I ever go to a cattle call if I were not busy? No—unless I was *really* in need of an assignment. And even then, maybe not.

THE INITIAL MEETING AS A STUMBLING BLOCK

How far should you push this concept of not going to free meetings? Only you can determine what's right for you. It depends on so many factors—including how busy you are, your reputation, your ability to generate new business leads, how much of your business is from referrals versus cold calling, and how vehemently potential prospects seem to object to your no-meeting policy.

On the plus side, not going to "on-spec" meetings (meetings where you go to talk with potential clients without fee and with no definite promise of getting an assignment) increases your business efficiency, reduces wasted time and effort (and the anger and frustration it can generate), and boosts your billable hours, revenue, and profits.

On the negative side, it may bring you a reputation as "difficult" if having meetings is customary in your field, and you may find yourself constantly in verbal conflict with prospects over this policy.

Here are some guidelines on when to make the initial meeting free versus when to charge for the initial meeting or try to sell without a meeting:

1. When you have more business and leads than you can handle, consider telling new prospects who call that you charge for meetings and work primarily by mail and phone. In other words, experiment with prospects when you can well afford to lose the business if they're turned off.

2. When business is scarce, go on meetings and do everything necessary to sell prospects and get jobs. This isn't the time to be experimental or difficult with your selling.

3. Think about using the no-free-meeting approach with only a *portion* of your market. For example, continue to meet with the best prospects. But try to sell less lucrative accounts by mail and phone.

4. Consider applying the initial meeting fee as a credit toward the purchase of future services if the prospect hires you. Say to the prospect, "I charge X dollars for the initial consultation. But if you decide to hire me for the project, I deduct this fee of X dollars from the total project fee." So if the prospect hires you, the meeting really is free.

This will help reduce serious prospects' resistance to the idea of paying for the initial meeting and will weed out prospects who have no intention of hiring you and just want to waste your time.

5. Charge a nominal fee for the initial meeting. If your regular fee for half a day of consultation is $400, charge only $100. And tell clients why you are doing so: "It's not that I want to make money from our initial meeting, but that I am flooded with calls from people who want a meeting. This small fee helps separate the serious from the casual prospect. And of course I'll refund your $100 or apply it against your project if you hire me, so there's really no cost to you."

6. Package the meeting as a consultation. For instance, I tell small firms that want to meet with me, "I offer an initial consultation that works as follows: You send me your materials. I review them, meet with you in your office for one or two hours to discuss your needs, then follow up with a written report outlining my recommendations. The cost is $500. You get approximately four hours of consultation, which, at my rate of $200 per hour, is worth $800. So this really is my best bargain."

7. Charge them for actual meeting time only. Say "For a one-hour meeting I'll charge you only for the hour of time we actually spend together, and I'll pick up the cost of travel time." This makes you seem willing to give something, if not everything.

8. One writer tells his prospects: "The initial meeting is free if you come to my office. If I come to you, I charge."

9. If using the no-free-meeting strategy meets with total resistance—if it offends and angers your prospects, and none of them agrees to it—then drop it. It obviously won't work in your marketplace at this time.

10. Above all, present your policies concerning meetings in a friendly, helpful, and courteous manner. Do not be difficult or high-handed about it. Even if you're so wonderful that everyone comes to you and does business the way you tell them, don't say so to your prospects. People hate braggarts and dislike dealing with conceited service providers or know-it-all advisors. Don't be that way. Develop and practice *polite* dialogue for explaining your policies and business procedures to current and potential clients.

CHAPTER EIGHT

Making the Presentation

POISED ON THE EDGE OF GREATNESS

For the person selling services, getting in to see the prospect is like an Olympic diver standing on the edge of the diving board, ready to execute a backward triple-twist dive.

Just as the diver had a long, difficult climb to get to this particular moment, so have you. You developed marketing programs designed to create interest in your service (chapters 1 and 2), prepared marketing materials to stimulate and enhance that initial interest (chapter 3), and pursued the prospect by mail and phone until he or she agreed to see you (chapters 3, 4, 5, 6, and 7).

And just like the Olympic diver, everything hinges on your performance. The diver can execute a perfect dive to win the event—or hit the water with a big belly-flop. You, too, can do and say the things that will get you the contract—or you can say and do the *wrong* things, which will fail to get you the sale and in fact turn a hot prospect stone cold.

This chapter provides guidance on how to handle the

initial sales meeting with your prospect so that you walk away with what you want: either a signed contract or a fairly firm commitment on the part of the prospect to engage your services.

Let's begin.

THE FIVE COMMANDMENTS OF PRESENTING YOUR SERVICES SUCCESSFULLY

Unlike some of the other situations you're likely to face, the sales presentation is one situation where I can't give you exact dialogue to follow. That's because everyone in business develops, over time, his or her own unique way of presenting the features and benefits of their services to potential clients.

However, there are some fundamental rules of selling that apply to every situation in which a service provider is sitting across the table—or talking on the phone—with a potential client, trying to convince that client to buy the service. Specifically, the Five Commandments of service selling that should be applied in every new-business situations are: listen, question, consult (solve, don't sell), prepare, and be flexible.

Let's take a look at each in a bit more detail.

Service-Selling Commandment 1: Listen

Most people who sell do it absolutely wrong. They go in and tell the prospect what *they* want to say, reciting a memorized list of product features and benefits. But what prospects care about, as mail-order entrepreneur Sig Rosenblum points out, are what is important to *them—their* needs, *their* problems, *their* concerns, *their* fears, *their* desires, *their* goals, *their* dreams. Successful salespeople tailor their presentations to show how the *features* of their product or service can give every client what he or she desires most or needs to solve his or her problem.

But how do you find out what prospects want or desire? First and foremost, you *listen*. Prospects who do not hear from you what they want to hear from you will tell you so. Usually these statements are in the form of objections.

You may think, I always listen to prospects and clients. But do you? Be honest. Aren't there times when the prospect is talking where you're not really listening but instead planning what *you* want to say next? And when a prospect says something that you don't agree with or don't want to hear, aren't you immediately planning your rebuttal rather than sitting back and listening to see whether the complaint or statement has merit?

Here are some tips for more effective listening:

• *Focus.* When you are listening and doing something else at the same time, you aren't really listening. When prospects speak, give them 100 percent of your concentration. If, for instance, you're talking with a prospect over the phone, don't go through your mail at the same time. Follow the advice of poet May Sarton, who said, "Do each thing with absolute concentration." Listening is an active process, not a passive one, and it requires your full attention.

• *Take notes.* Bring a pad and pen to the meeting. As the prospect talks, take notes.

There are several benefits to this. First, you can jot questions as they occur to you, so you don't forget to ask them later on.

Second, you can quickly and easily prepare a good proposal or follow-up letter based on the notes. When you take notes, your follow-up documents will be full of good, specific material prospects want to see, because you recorded their requests and preferences.

Third, the act of note taking is reassuring, visible proof to prospects that you are indeed paying attention to what is being said.

• *Bring a tape recorder.* Bring a tape recorder to the meeting and ask prospects, "Do you mind if I tape-record our conversation? I like to make sure I have an accurate record of whatever information you give me." Most people will readily agree to this. If not, put the recorder away and use a pad and pen to take notes.

I prefer the minicassette recorders because they fit easily in a jacket pocket or briefcase, and also because their smaller size seems less intimidating to prospects. Be sure to bring several extra tapes and spare batteries; I have had batteries die in the middle of a meeting! Also bring a note pad and pen as backup. (Some people like to take notes even when recording. They let the recorder capture the conversation, using the pad to jot questions and key points.)

• *Respond verbally.* Say things that indicate to prospects you are listening and have empathy for what they are saying. One simple, effective communication technique for demonstrating your understanding is simply to say "I understand":

PROSPECT: We're looking for a contractor who can handle the job from start to finish. I don't want to have to coordinate and deal with half a dozen or more different vendors. We want *one* firm to do the whole job.
YOU: I understand.

Another technique is to rephrase the prospect's statement and repeat it back:

PROSPECT: We're looking for a contractor who can handle the job from start to finish. I don't want to have to coordinate and deal with half a dozen or more different vendors. We want *one* firm to do the whole job.
YOU: So what you're saying is you want a contractor who can provide all the pieces and provide single-source re-

sponsibility for getting your system designed and installed.

PROSPECT: Yes, that's correct.

Equally effective is to rephrase the prospect's statement and repeat it back as a question to which he or she will answer affirmatively. This gets the prospect agreeing to things *you* say, which eventually leads to a close:

PROSPECT: We really need an ad campaign that will penetrate the under-thirty market for this product.

YOU: So would you be interested specifically in dealing with an ad agency with a proven track record in selling to the under-thirty market?

PROSPECT: Yes, that's what we're looking for.

Some salespeople are more aggressive, phrasing their question so that the answer indicates a tentative (if small) commitment on the part of the prospect:

PROSPECT: We would need seminars to train one hundred DP staff members no later than February 1.

YOU: So if we could train your total staff of one hundred by the first of February, you'd be interested in going ahead, wouldn't you?

• *Respond physically.* "Body language" lets prospects know you are interested and actively involved in the conversation. I like to lean forward slightly, look a prospect in the eyes directly, and nod my head slightly to indicate I am listening and understanding. If you sit back with your arms folded, or stare into space vacantly, the prospect will assume you are not being receptive or attentive.

Listening is such a broad topic that entire books and seminars have been devoted to it, and I can't repeat all that information here. The key for you is to remember that you are not in the meeting to "give a pitch," as so many salespeople and service providers mistakenly believe, but to help the prospect solve a problem or achieve an objective. You cannot help solve the problem or achieve the objective until you know what it is. And you can't find out what the problem or objective is unless you listen to the prospect.

Also be aware that if you're talking too much, you're listening too little. According to consultant Howard Shenson, when selling your services you should be speaking 40 percent of the time or less—which means you should be listening during at least 60 percent of the conversation. I am most successful in selling and consulting when I listen 80 to 90 percent of the time and talk only 10 to 20 percent.

Service-Selling Commandment 2: Question

Questions are the single most powerful technique for successfully selling your services to prospects. Questions:

- demonstrate your concern for the prospect's problems.
- put the focus where it should be—on the prospect's needs, not your services or background.
- enable you to determine the prospect's requirements so you can tailor your services to address those requirements.

"In the first meeting with the prospective client, focus on what they really need to make their problem go away," says Howard Shenson. "Don't waste the prospect's time providing a verbal résumé. If prospects need information on your skills, abilities, and experience, they will certainly ask."

Often in meetings you go into far more detail about your qualifications, company, industry, methods, or service than prospects care to hear. Many will sit politely because they think it's rude to interrupt; but they are not really listening. Instead, they are eager to get to their agenda. You want to

shift the focus to their agenda, not yours, almost immediately. Questions help you do that.

When sitting down with prospects after greetings have
been made and pleasantries exchanged, I like to get directly
to the reason I'm there. I typically open with a question or
request for information, such as "Tell me a little bit about
your situation and how I can help you," or "What problem do
you have that you'd like me to help you with?" Believe me,
this gets them talking.

Here are some other questions I find helpful in getting
prospects to open up and tell me how I can help them:

"Why did you want to get together with me today?"
"How can I help you?"
"Tell me a little bit about your current situation."
"What specifically do you need me to do for you?"
"What are you looking to accomplish in [name their spe-
    cific area of interest]?"
"That's interesting. Tell me more."

At times, prospects are unable to articulate their requirements and just go on and on without getting to the point. I
help them get back on track by interrupting and saying "I
understand. But what exactly is it that you would like me to
do for you?" This usually helps them focus on why they called
me in the first place.

If a prospect and I are having a conversation, and I decide
to interject a question, I don't jump in and immediately ask
it. I pause for a second, then say, "May I ask you a question?"
This interruption forces prospects to stop talking, prepares
them to listen, and puts them in a receptive, thoughtful
state, ensuring that they will hear my question and provide
an answer to it. It also says, "I think this is so important that
I want us to stop and question what we're talking about so we
can proceed on an accurate basis." Use "May I ask you a
question?" It works!

Of course, the point of the sales meeting is not to ask

endless questions or gather infinite information. Each question is designed to clarify and diagnose the prospect's requirements, so that you get, as quickly as possible, to the point where you can outline the prospect's project requirements, your proposed plan of action, and your fee.

Service-Selling Commandment 3: Consult

In the 1980s sales trainers and authors introduced the concept of "consultative selling." Essentially, consultative selling said "Clients and customers want you to solve problems for them, not 'sell' them. Good salespeople aren't peddlers or hucksters; they're 'sales consultants' who work closely with clients, helping them fulfill their needs."

Suddenly salespeople in all fields stopped referring to themselves as salespeople and began calling themselves consultants. People who sold financial services, for example, began putting such impressive-sounding titles as "financial planner" or "financial counselor" on their business cards. The consultative salespeople even developed a slogan— "Solve, don't sell"—to push their approach to sales.

Much of the consultative approach to selling is valid and can be applied effectively to the selling of services. However, in one respect, the consultative selling gurus and disciples went overboard: Some did so much free "consulting" before they were retained by the prospect that they ended up giving away their services for free, removing the need for the prospect to hire them.

The successful service provider today practices what I call "modified consultative selling." That is, we *selectively* consult with prospects on their problem during the initial meeting. We give enough information to convince prospects that we are experts who can help them, without giving away so much that they can solve the problem themselves and don't need our help anymore.

For instance, let's say you run a graphic design studio. A

prospect asks, "Is there any way to design a brochure that features all six products but could be easily updated if one of the products changes?" Because you know the answer, your tendency might be to dash off a sketch or fold together a dummy out of scrap paper to show how it's done. Have you sold effectively? No, because the prospect now knows the answer and can take your solution to his or her current graphic designer or staff artist—or, if the prospect is cheap, directly to a printer.

Instead, you should say "Yes, that's a requirement we've handled in the past for other clients, and when we're further into the design process, we'll present some options that would work with your particular product." This answer indicates that you are the designer who understands and can solve the problem, but makes it necessary for the prospect to hire *you* (and not someone else) to get this solution.

And that's the essence of modified consultative selling. *Consultative selling* said "Act like the problem-solving genius at the initial meeting, do everything you can for prospects, and they will hire you out of gratitude and because you're so impressive."

Modified consultative selling, on the other hand, says "Act like the knowledgeable problem solver at the initial meeting. Do and say things that convince clients that you indeed *do* know the answers, but don't give the answers away right then and there. Instead, disclose just enough information so that clients perceive that they *need to hire you* to get the solution or results they desire."

Be a consultant, by all means, but don't give away the store. Say and do things that demonstrate your abilities and create (rather than eliminate) the need for your services.

Service-Selling Commandment 4: Prepare

Why do so many service sellers stumble painfully through sales presentations? Because they haven't planned in advance what they are going to say. Planning means not only having a well-practiced presentation, but also knowing what to say in reply to prospect comments, questions, and objections.

The key to being polished and smooth is to anticipate what prospects will say and prepare, in advance, sensible answers. This way, when prospects say "But I can get it cheaper from the printer around the corner," instead of saying "Uhh . . . well . . . ummm," you launch immediately into a confident, clear explanation of why you should print the brochure even though you cost a bit more.

When you are prepared, you feel confident speaking with prospects and clients. When you are not prepared, you are nervous, because you're afraid they'll state an objection or ask a question to which you have no answer. The more prepared you are, the less likely this is to occur.

In the movie *The Verdict*, Jack Warden tells Paul Newman, "Never ask a witness a question to which you don't know the answer." The ideal in selling your services is to be so well prepared that prospects never ask you a question to which you don't know the answer.

You'll find scattered throughout this book snippets of dialogue that tell you *exactly* what to say in response to what prospects and clients say. Take these bits of dialogue, practice them, use them, adapt them to your unique selling situation—in short, make them your own. The greater your "data bank" of prepared sales talk, the more effective you'll be in meetings.

Service-Selling Commandment 5: Be Flexible

Being prepared is not a synonym for being inflexible. Yes, your presentation should be planned. But be willing and able to change course in midstream if the prospect takes the conversation in a direction in which you didn't intend to go.

Recently we had a general contractor come to our home to give an estimate on adding a family room. The contractor, a creative and talented professional, had his vision of what a family room should be. Unfortunately, it conflicted with the family room I had dreamed of having.

Mike insisted that at the rear of the room, there should be sliding glass doors leading onto a deck. I, however, do not like sliding glass doors. I don't like the temptation and easy entry they offer burglars, nor do I like the heat loss in winter.

I explained this to Mike. He countered with an explanation of what a wonderful view the doors would give me. I told him a window would do just as nicely. He countered with an explanation of how a rear door adds value to the home. After going back and forth a few times, it should have been clear to Mike that I didn't want sliding glass doors.

At that point, he should have rearranged his presentation to meet my needs. For instance, he might have suggested a fireplace or a wood-burning stove or wall-to-wall built-in bookcases for the kind of cozy family room I envisioned. But he was inflexible. He wanted to design a family room with sliding glass doors and one of his famous decks, and nothing else would do for me.

After fifteen minutes I became impatient, quickly ended the conversation, and showed Mike the door. It's possible I may still give him the job—I like him and his work—but his sales presentation actually *decreased* the probability of this happening.

And that's the risk of being inflexible. If you refuse to listen to prospects, to acknowledge their ideas and wishes, and to tailor your presentation to show that you understand and want to meet their needs—in short, if you insist on doing it your way and your way only—your sales presentation not only won't get you a go-ahead but may actually make prospects less inclined to hire you than they were before you started. Yes, an ineffective meeting with a prospect can actually *unsell* you and your services!

To make sure you are meeting the needs of the prospect, keep the Five Commandments of successful service selling in mind at all times during your meeting:

1. LISTEN to the prospect.
2. Ask QUESTIONS that uncover the prospect's real needs and concerns.
3. Act like the wise problem-solving CONSULTANT to demonstrate your expertise and create a need for your services.
4. PREPARE what you will say.
5. BE FLEXIBLE and change your presentation according to the prospect's reactions and comments.

In addition to these Five Commandments, here are some additional tips for having an effective sales meeting with prospects.

DON'T OVERPROMISE

How honest should you be about your abilities and the results you expect to achieve for the prospects? The position I advise you to take is: Present yourself and your services *in the most favorable light possible* without misrepresenting yourself.

Financial services marketing expert Denny LeBarron advises service sellers, "Don't make any commitments or claims you can't live up to." I agree. But at the same time, remember that your competitors are puffing their own abilities and making themselves look good. They stretch the truth, exaggerate. Some even just plain lie.

You should not lie, but in the face of all this hype, it doesn't pay to be overly modest either. Management consultant Gary Blake gives this advice: "Present yourself as about 10 percent better than you really are." My feeling is that you shouldn't lie or exaggerate, but you *should* present yourself as the very best you can be and have been.

As the song says, "Accentuate the positive." Tell all the good things about your service. Highlight your successes. Don't go out of your way to tell prospects about your weaknesses and failures. Your competitors will gladly do that for you. Present yourself in the most favorable light possible while maintaining complete honesty and integrity. Prospects want to hire people who are successful, not mediocre. Position yourself as such.

LIMIT THE RANGE OF OPTIONS OR CHOICES

"Don't give your client too many choices," advises direct marketing consultant Joan Harris. "This either confuses her, if she's the decision maker, or slows down the process if lots of people have to see it."

This is an old trick of clothing salespeople that can easily be applied to selling services. The clothes salesman knows that if a customer is confronted with rack after rack of ties to choose from, he or she will become overwhelmed and unable to make a decision. And so the customer does the easy thing, which is to make *no* decision and walk away.

Instead, the salesman begins narrowing the choices: "Do you want silk or polyester?" You say silk. The polyester ties are removed from the counter. "Do you want plain or patterns?" You say patterns. Solid color ties are removed from the counter. "Stripes or polka dots?" You say stripes. Polka dot ties are taken away. "Do you prefer bright colors or pastels?" This continues until two or three ties remain. Then the close: "Do you want this one, this one, this one, or will you be taking all three?"

The point is not to overwhelm prospects with lots of choices to make. Remember, they are looking to you for guidance. If they seem unsure, say "We could do it this way or this way. Which do you prefer?" By all means, give prospects choices. Prospects resent being *told* what to do and like to think it was their decision. But in reality, you control the presentation, presenting enough options to enable choice without causing confusion.

ESTABLISH CHEMISTRY

Like it or not, personal chemistry is a major factor determining whether prospects hire you. It's really quite simple: People hire people whom they like and feel comfortable with. They avoid hiring people whom they dislike, are afraid of, or who make them uncomfortable.

In certain instances, there will be a strong reaction between two personalities that cannot be avoided or controlled. One person will, for a myriad of reasons, take an instant and overwhelming liking or disliking to another person.

But in most cases, you can create good chemistry—or at least create behavior that allows good chemistry to grow and flourish. For instance, if you have a big ego, be aware that most people don't like braggarts and egomaniacs. No matter how smart, right, or good you are, many people won't hire you because they can't stand the way you behave.

Suzanne Ramos, a manager at American Express, says she occasionally sees service sellers who violate what she considers the unwritten rule that "the client is always right." They talk too much or come across as overconfident, argumentative, even mildly disdainful or arrogant. She is also alert to people who might be difficult to work with. "Life is too short," she says.

In general, people like people who:

- are friendly.
- are warm.
- are courteous.
- are polite.
- are on time.
- are respectful.
- like them.
- share their interests.
- listen to them.
- show an interest in them.
- ask them about themselves.
- treat them well.
- help them.

"I make a big effort to have prospects be comfortable with me," says freelancer Mary Beth Lareau. "Businesspeople need to be reassured that you are normal and dependable."

ESTABLISH A PEER-TO-PEER, VALUE-FOR-VALUE RELATIONSHIP

In meeting with prospects, you should not come across as superior, nor should you allow them to put you in a subservient position. The meeting should be treated as a meeting of equals. The prospect is an important person with a need to be fulfilled or a problem to be solved. You are important because you are the expert who can fill that need or solve that problem. As the Bible says. "Do you see a [person] skilled in their work? They will stand before kings. They will not stand before obscure men" (Proverbs 22:9).

You will feel most comfortable with prospects if you establish with them what Robert Ringer, author of *Looking*

Out for #1 (New York: Fawcett Crest, 1978), calls a "value-for-value relationship." That is, for a relationship to work, both parties must exchange value for value. In the selling of services, the client exchanges money for your time, expertise, labor, and the benefits or results you provide. In such a relationship, there is no superior or subordinate, merely two equals exchanging equal values.

There is no need to feel that, because they are the buyer and you are the seller, clients are the superior, you the inferior. Indeed, they need you as much as you need them. And in some cases, they need you more than you need them, such as when they have a problem no one else can solve, and you have more work than you can handle.

But don't rub that in their faces. Establish yourself as their peer, not their subordinate or superior. When this is accomplished, both parties can proceed happily and with dignity intact.

BE ENTHUSIASTIC

Enthusiasm is a key ingredient in any sales situation. You must be genuinely enthusiastic about your service and about the prospect's proposed project or assignment. If you're indifferent, disdainful, or even just plain bored, you are unlikely to get the job. And if you do get it, you'll probably do it poorly.

How do you show enthusiasm? For once, there's no technique for you to learn, because if you are enthusiastic, *it will naturally show through in your voice, attitude, manner, and presentation.* By the same token, any *lack* of enthusiasm will also become apparent to the prospect. So to be successful, provide only those services, take on only those projects, and deal only with those clients about whom you can be enthusiastic. Life is too short to do otherwise!

SELL ON A PROJECT RATHER THAN TIME AND MATERIALS BASIS

"The consultants who consistently are in the $200,000+ range in income develop whatever they're selling into a 'system,' " says Stephen J. Lanning, editor of *Consulting Opportunities Journal.* "Clients like to buy systems or 'total packages' rather than consulting time."

The same applies to most service industries. Services can be billed in two ways: by time or by the project.

In some cases, the only option is to bill by the day or by the hour—for example, freelance technical writers frequently subcontract to large corporations to work on the premises writing manuals on a weekly or monthly basis, with the fee set at so much per hour.

But whenever possible, it's best to offer a complete package price: so much for writing the manual, or so much for designing the system. There are several reasons for this.

First, clients generally prefer to buy a package or project for a fixed fee that is known in advance. They can budget for it, and there are no surprises. Billing them at a high hourly rate makes them uncomfortable, because they don't know what size bill to expect and are afraid you will "pad" the bill with extra hours to increase your revenue.

Think about it. Let's say the plumbing in your house was old and had to be replaced. Which would be more acceptable to you—the plumber saying "We'll put in an all-new copper plumbing system for $8,000" or "Our hourly rate is $50 but I have no idea of how long it will take"? Most people would opt for the security of the package price.

Second, a package makes clear to prospective clients what you will do and what they will get. Hourly service is more nebulous. As a marketing consultant, I tell prospects, "I can give you a complete marketing plan for one of your products or services for a package price of X dollars, and the

plan will include the following specific information and recommendations." Although the package price is high, this
is a fairly easy sell to those who recognize they need marketing help.

I have far more difficulty saying to prospects "My consulting fee is X dollars per hour," because their immediate
thought is "What exactly do I get when I buy 'consulting'?"
It seems less tangible, and therefore less valuable. Even
though an hour or two of time is far less than my project fee
for a full-blown marketing plan, prospects perceive it as
expensive and without a clear return on investment.

A former client of mine, Dennis Ryan, was one of the
innovators in this packaging concept. He once told me, "I
want to package my firm's DP consulting services and sell
them like products." He would give each package a name,
describe the problem it solved, and tell exactly what he
would do for the client and what it could cost. This approach
has been successful for him and many other service providers.

TEN MORE GOOD IDEAS ON MAKING
SUCCESSFUL NEW-BUSINESS PRESENTATIONS

From freelance copywriter Judy Brewton comes this list of
ten more helpful ideas on how to present yourself at the
initial client meeting so as to get the assignment or job:

1. *Silence is golden.* Nervousness or excitement can make
you babble. Instead, sit back, ask one or two short questions,
look friendly and expectant, and let prospects tell you all
about it. When you do want to speak, force yourself to speak
slowly, and be brief.

2. *Behave as if you already have the job.* Prospects often
forget they called you in (or you got yourself called in) to
have a look at your samples or résumé. As a result, you can
often sidestep the whole "audition" mode completely. You can

start right in with questions about what the prospect needs—and go home with an assignment.

3. *Once you have heard what they need, you now know what to tell them about yourself.* Make sure they hear all the bits that will identify you as just the person they want. Find low-key ways to work them into the talk.

Don't include your whole work history (and certainly not the unfortunate parts). Use only the things that relate to the prospect's business or problem.

4. *Don't show your samples, résumés, job photos, or brochures unless you're asked to.* If you bring a sample portfolio, show it only if it's asked for. Remember, you want to be out of the "job applicant" mode and into the "consultant on the job" mode as fast as possible.

5. *Don't tell the prospect your sad stories.* Don't tell about how IBM used you for eighteen years and then stopped. Stress only the positive.

6. *Prospects only want to associate with success.* Make sure you come across as a success. Hiring a difficult or inept supplier will make prospects look bad to *their* boss or client. They know that, and they won't take a chance on a blamer or complainer.

No matter how successful they look, your prospects all have their own defeats in their closets. They're looking to hook up with someone who can improve their track record— not with a war-torn fellow victim.

7. *Remember who you are: You're the expert source who helps clients.* Instead of "I recently did a big job for Pepsi-Cola," say "We recently helped one of our large clients deal with a problem similar to yours." Remember to protect past clients' anonymity if you're speaking of their problems. The fact that you're discreet might impress this prospect too.

8. *Don't be a name-dropper.* Name-dropping frequently fails to achieve its goal of impressing prospects. Many prospects are turned off or bored by it. Besides, why run the risk

of fondly dropping the name of someone they know and despise or dislike?

9. *Develop ways to end the meeting profitably.* In other words, ask for the order. If this has been an exploratory meeting about a major project, and you feel you haven't yet been able to seize the inside track, try mentioning a smallish *part* of the project. And ask to do it independently. Say "Why not let us do that for you right now? Then you'll have that taken care of, and you can see how we work firsthand."

10. *Don't hang around.* You're an enthusiastic, friendly service provider who'd love to do business with them. (Be sure to say so.) But because you're so capable, you're also busy. So don't hang around. Hanging around gives the impression that you are not busy and therefore that your time (which is what you're trying to sell to this prospect for a hefty price) is not valuable.

CHAPTER NINE

Handling Objections

TO THE SERVICE SELLER, OBJECTIONS AREN'T NECESSARILY A NEGATIVE

In selling, an *objection* is a reason given by prospects why they are not ready to buy your product or service. For example, if you sell used cars, and a potential buyer tells you, "I'm not sure whether I want a new or a used car," that's an objection. The prospect is telling you "I'm not ready to buy what you are selling, and here's why."

Many conventional sales training courses, aimed primarily at product sellers, teach you the following about objections:

- An objection is an obstacle to be overcome.
- Every objection can be answered.
- Prospects use objections to avoid making decisions or commitments, not because they really don't want or can't use the product.

In service selling, however, objections are not necessarily obstacles to overcome or arguments to be cleverly countered; often they are warning signs that the person you're talking with may not be an ideal client for your business.

Don't automatically react to objections by arguing why the objection is not valid. First, listen carefully. Listen not only to the *content* of the prospect's objection but to the *tone of voice* in which it is said. You may, based on the objection and the way it is presented, make a decision that this prospect is not for you—and that you will not pursue the sale.

For instance, let's say you offer a motivational or coaching type service to business professionals. Through experience, you discover that only those prospects who are enthusiastic and interested in your service when they call can be helped successfully, and that when the prospects are dubious or doubtful, the engagement—assuming you get the sale—is usually not successful.

On that basis, if someone calls and is negative, unpleasant, overly skeptical, and says, "I'm calling because my boss told me to, but I really don't see how your service can work," you might be better off *agreeing with him or her and ending the call* rather than pursuing a prospect who will turn into a client who fights you at every step. You could either explain that enthusiasm is part of what makes the service successful, and therefore you can't help the prospect who feels this way, or simply say you are booked up and too busy to take them on.

Many salespeople are trained to fight with prospects and use verbal arguments to counter objections and prove them invalid. Those of us who sell services must take a different tack, because the mood, attitude, and personality of the buyer determine, to a major extent, whether our engagement will be a success or a failure.

We must listen to objections, then decide into which category the objection should be placed. For the service seller, there are three basic categories of objections—warning-signal objections, legitimate objections, and sales-blocking objections.

Let's look at each in a bit more detail.

WARNING-SIGNAL OBJECTIONS

The warning-signal objection is an objection that says "Beware, service provider! Maybe this prospect is going to be trouble, and we should end the conversation now before we get into a relationship we'll only regret later."

Once voiced by the prospect, the warning-signal objection sets off the alarm within us that goes off whenever we're dealing with a difficult or unpleasant personality. Your instincts tell you to back off, but these instincts are often countered by your desire to get the job or make the sale.

Watch out! In my experience, the inner alarm set off by the warning-signal objection is accurate nine times out of ten. Whenever I've felt that I shouldn't do business with a person, then went ahead and did it anyway, I invariably regretted that decision. Trust your instincts: They're more accurate than you think.

Warning-signal objections are contained both in actual content of the statement as well as in mannerism and tone of voice. For example, I know I don't like to deal with people who are of the super-salesman, high-pressure, huckster variety. I'm extremely uncomfortable with braggarts, boasters, and others with massive egos.

A few months ago I got a phone call from an entrepreneur who began the conversation by saying "I've got a killer deal for you, Bob." Then every other sentence that followed also contained the word *killer*. My inner alarm went off, and I politely declined the assignment.

As you deal with prospects and clients on a daily basis, you'll develop a mental list of the personality traits you like and dislike in potential clients. Warning-signal objections will ring your inner alarm whenever your ears and eyes detect a trait on this negative list. Again, I say heed that inner alarm, for it will serve you well in screening out bad prospects. And that will save you the pain and aggravation of getting stuck in a relationship with a client you don't like.

LEGITIMATE OBJECTIONS

A legitimate objection is an objection prospects make based on the reality of how your services do not precisely fit their requirements. For instance, let's say you are a freelance advertising copywriter. A prospect calls and says, "I need someone who will handle the whole thing—not just the copy but also the design, photography, production, and media planning and insertions."

You say, "I'm not an agency. I write superior copy but do not do layouts, mechanicals, or media buying. However, I know people who do and can recommend them to handle that portion of the job."

"No," the prospect says, "I want someone to do the whole job."

That's an objection. The prospect is saying "I understand your business is to do writing only and that I could go to you for the copy and someone else for the layout and I could place the ads myself—*but that's not what I want*. I prefer to use someone who will provide a total service from *A* to *Z*."

Is this a legitimate objection? You could argue "No, because I'm going to write a better ad than any ad agency, and that will make the client more money by selling more of his products."

Ah, but is that really the issue? Perhaps the prospect is a busy, overworked advertising manager at a large company with an understaffed advertising department. Her need—and it's perfectly legitimate to the prospect, though you may not agree with it—is not for superior copy but simply for someone to *step in, take charge, and get the work done.* She may not have the support staff or time to serve as project coordinator or handle the design, photography, and media placement internally . . . *even though she could get a better sales result by doing so.*

The conclusion? This particular prospect's request for a single-source service such as ad agencies provide suits *her* needs at this time. Saying she doesn't want to use free-lancers is for her a *legitimate objection.*

How do you handle legitimate objections? Once you determine that the objection is legitimate, and not sales-blocking (see the next section), you must determine the *strength* of the objection. For instance, in the example given, does the advertising manager's need for administrative support and a more complete scope of service outweigh the requirement to have an ad that generates better results—the type of ad only you can write for her?

If the benefits that you can provide outweigh the disadvantages the prospect must accept by using your services versus an alternative, then the objection isn't really legitimate and should be overcome using techniques provided later in this chapter.

On the other hand, if the disadvantages the prospect will suffer by using your services outweigh the extra benefits or enhanced results your services offer, the objection is legitimate and should not be overcome. Rather, you should acknowledge the prospect's requirements as legitimate, recognize that your services don't meet her needs in this particular instance, and see instead what other help you can provide now or in the future.

SALES-BLOCKING OBJECTIONS

A sales-blocking objection is an objection that prevents you from making sales you should make, winning accounts you deserve to win, or getting hired by clients who really can benefit from your services more than they can benefit from alternative or competitive services available to them.

Prospects voice sales-blocking objections for a variety of reasons. In some cases, the objection is not the real reason for putting you off. Instead, it's merely an excuse prospects use to avoid being sold by you (which they dislike because it pressures them to make a decision or commitment).

In other instances, prospects give the sales-blocking objection because they are afraid or reluctant to tell you the real reason why they don't want to buy. For instance, the prospect will say "We don't have the budget right now," when they really mean "I'm not convinced of your abilities to handle this project."

How do you handle this situation? If you sense a prospect is not disclosing his real objection, sit up straight, look him in the eye, and say, "Bill, I understand. But tell me—what's the *real* reason for not retaining me right now?" About 50 percent of the time this will prod prospects to be more honest with you. Some prospects, however, will stick by their original statement and never reveal their honest feelings, and there's little you can do about it.

A third possibility is that prospects perceive their sales-blocking objection to be a legitimate one. For instance, they've read that desktop publishing is the "in" thing, so when you say your design studio or print shop doesn't have in-house desktop publishing, they use that as their objection or reason not to hire you. You, knowing that you can do a better job for less money than other sources and that desktop publishing is not the answer, must convince prospects that the objection is not accurate if you are to win the project.

Interestingly, circumstances change with time, and what

was once a sales-blocking objection years ago may today be a legitimate reason not to do business with you . . . and vice versa.

For instance, when fax machines first became popular, an occasional prospect would say to me, "It would be difficult to do business with you because you don't have a fax machine and that's how we communicate with our suppliers." I dismissed this as not legitimate—you didn't need a fax machine to be a good consultant—and simply didn't do business with those firms.

But today I consider it mandatory for a consultant in my field to provide clients with the option of fax communication. I also prefer to deal with artists, printers, and other vendors who have fax machines and am annoyed when freelancers or vendors tell me they don't have one. Today, having a fax machine has become standard operating procedure, and clients who tell you they are uncomfortable that you don't have one are voicing a legitimate complaint.

On the other hand, a minority of prospects won't hire me because I don't use a specific model computer in my work or write using the same word processing program they do. To me, this is a sales-blocking rather than a legitimate complaint. It's silly, and I'll either try to explain this to the prospect or simply pass on the job.

BASIC RULES FOR HANDLING SALES-BLOCKING OBJECTIONS

A sales-blocking objection, then, is a complaint that is based on prospects' perceptions and misconceptions rather than reality and is not a legitimate reason for denying themselves the benefits of your services. To sell successfully, you must effectively remove these objections. That is, you must either convince prospects that their objection is based on incorrect premises and that you are right—or, if you can't change their beliefs, at least convince them that the objection is not a sufficient reason for not retaining your services.

Here are some ground rules for handling sales-blocking objections:

1. Attitude is everything. Have a positive, friendly, helpful attitude when dealing with objections.

2. Do not convey to prospects that they are stupid or ignorant, that their objections are petty or annoying, or that they are wasting your time.

3. Treat the objection not as a rejection of you but as an uncertainty on the part of the prospect—which it is.

4. Assume this uncertainty is based on lack of data, inaccurate information, or false premises. Your job: to educate prospects so they understand the situation correctly.

5. Never say to prospects, "You're wrong." Few things make people angrier and more defensive than being told they are wrong or stupid.

6. After prospects voice an objection, repeat it back to them in their own words to acknowledge that you heard and understand. For instance, "So you're saying that you prefer a modern design in the living room, even though the rest of the first floor is done in antiques?" Prospects will immediately become *much* more comfortable when they hear their objections acknowledged and taken seriously.

7. Then say, "That's an interesting point. But have you thought about [give your own point of view]?" Then launch into an explanation of why your point of view makes sense.

8. Keep in mind that the prospect doesn't have to be wrong for you to be right. As Jerry Straus of JMW Consultants says, "Instead of 'either/or,' think 'and/also.'" Instead of "Either you are right, Mr. Prospect, or I am right," say "You are right in what you say, Mr. Prospect—and here's what else is *also* possible." Too many salespeople spend too much time in the counterproductive activity of trying to show prospects why they are wrong rather than trying to

help them find a way to solve their problems using your services.

9. Convince prospects that the advantages of hiring you far outweigh the merits of their objection. You do this not by belittling or minimizing the objection but by shifting attention away from it (which typically deals with some minor aspect or feature of your services prospects don't like) to the end result or benefit prospects are seeking (which your services can deliver better than anyone else's).

For instance, let's say a prospect says, "I don't like the green computer paper your monthly computer reports are printed on." Assuming your computer system is inflexible and you can't change the paper, you would say, "I understand. But tell me, Ms. Prospect, what's more important to you—the color of the paper used in the reports, or the information they contain that will help you manage your accounts receivables and billings so much more precisely and effectively?"

When the prospect answers, "The information, of course," you respond by repeating the key reasons why your system provides better information, thus shifting the prospect's attention away from a minor objection (green paper) and focusing it on the central issues of your service and the prospect's requirements, where it should be.

THE SEVENTEEN MOST COMMON OBJECTIONS— AND HOW TO DEAL WITH THEM

The preceding guidelines can help you in most situations. However, in the selling of trade, technical, creative, consulting, freelance, and professional services, we hear certain objections time and time again. The following are seventeen of the most common objections along with specific guidelines on how to handle them.

Objection 1: Your Price Is Too High

Of all the objections, this is the most common—and by far the most difficult to handle. The key is to make prospects understand that, unlike products, which may be virtually identical, no two services are rendered in exactly the same way, and no two service providers will achieve an identical result.

It is the differences between the way your services are rendered, the benefits they offer, and the results they achieve versus other service providers that enables you to say to prospects "The slightly higher fees I charge are a drop in the bucket compared with the quality and results you get." Of course, you must back up such an assertion with details and proof.

This objection is so vital that I have given detailed, step-by-step instructions for dealing with it in chapter 10.

Objection 2: We Don't Have the Budget

This is slightly different from objection 1. "Your fees are too high" can be taken to mean "We have the money to do this work, but we're not convinced your service is worth the price you are asking." The objection "We don't have the budget" lays the blame on the buyer, not the seller. It says "Your fee is perfectly reasonable, but it is not within our budget." Or to put it in more basic terms: "We're too poor."

How do you handle this? It depends on what the true situation is.

In some cases, they *do* have the budget, and are just hoping that by giving this objection, you'll come down in price. When you stick by your original estimate and give reasons why your service is worth the money, you'll find that prospects who said they had no budget can somehow, somewhere come up with the funds to retain you.

At other times, they may honestly not have the cash or have a budget allocated to handle your fees. You then say,

"Fine. Tell me what your budget is, and we'll see what we can do for you within that price range."

When they tell you their budget, you don't cut your price to fit that budget. Instead, you offer them a less costly alternative—a more "bare-bones" service—that's in line with what they can afford.

For instance, if a corporation wants you to do a management study for which you would bill $3,000, and their budget is only $2,500 for the job, tell the prospect, "We can still do it for $2,500, but we would eliminate one of the two on-site research days to achieve the lower figure of $2,500."

The idea is to give them the level of service tailored to their budget. If they want the top-of-the-line job, they're going to have to pay full price for it. If your hourly rate is $100, don't give your services away for $50 an hour to clients who plead poverty. Instead, if their budget is only $50, tell them they can buy a half hour of your time.

Objection 3: I Can Get It Cheaper Somewhere Else

This is similar to objections 1 and 2 but with a difference. Here prospects are not telling you they can't afford you or that you are not worth your fee. They're simply noting that your competitor across the street sells a (they think) similar service for less, and why should they pay you $1,000 when they can get the same thing from Company X for only $800?

Why is this objection so popular? Because, in reality, it's difficult for prospects to compare your service with your competitors on a feature-by-feature basis. There are so many variables, so many complexities, and so many uncertainties (after all, services are intangibles) that buyers tend to focus only on the most obvious point of comparison—the price—when deciding between service A and service B. They become confused by a myriad of features and claims, and in disgust mentally give up and say "Okay, which will cost me less?"

The key to overcoming the objection "I can get it cheaper somewhere else" is to make clear to buyers that they are *not* comparing apples and apples but rather apples versus oranges. That is, your services are *not* identical to those of your competitors—you offer many important advantages in terms of quality, credentials, service, reliability, trustworthiness, experience, and reputation—and so a strict comparison of their price versus yours is not a meaningful exercise. Further, you must convince prospects that the advantages you offer provide extra benefits that far outweigh the extra price you're asking.

Here are some additional strategies for responding to this objection:

In the movie *Tin Men*, Richard Dreyfuss walks into an automobile showroom and inquires about buying a new Cadillac. "How much will it cost?" asks Dreyfuss. "How much do you want to pay?" the salesman asks. Disgusted with the phoniness of this question, Dreyfuss replies, "I want to pay a dollar—okay?"

It's basic to human nature: We all want to get the best and pay the least. Unfortunately, the laws of supply and demand say that excellence costs. And deep down we know that the best product or service is rarely the one with the lowest price.

So remind prospects of this. They want the best, so the fact that they can get it cheaper elsewhere is really beside the point, isn't it? Remind them, in your own words, of what English critic John Ruskin said about price-shopping: "There is hardly anything in the world that some man cannot make a little worse and sell a little cheaper, and the people who consider price only are this man's lawful prey."

One way to do this without being offensive is to help prospects recall a time when they bought on price only and was later sorry they did:

PROSPECT: I am talking to someone locally who can do the job for a lot less money.

You: I understand. But let me ask: Have you ever in the past chosen someone because his price was the lowest, only to be disappointed once the job was done?

Another effective technique is to ask prospects point-blank if they are price shoppers (some people are).

PROSPECT: I am talking to someone locally who can do the job for a lot less money.
You: Let me ask . . . are you primarily concerned with price—or with [reliability, service, quality, or whatever advantage you offer]?

Most prospects will insist that they want quality, service, or some other advantage you offer. You must then offer proof that you can deliver these benefits and get prospects to agree that superior quality and service quite naturally cost a bit more (but the results are worth it).

A few prospects will tell you, "I buy primarily on price" or "It's a competitive bid situation." Unless you feel certain your price will be the lowest, don't bother pursuing such prospects. Say "I understand. Some people prefer to buy primarily on price, and my service is not for them. But do call me when you have a job that needs my special touch and you have a budget that will allow us to work together. I'm looking forward to it!"

Point out to prospects that it's cheaper to hire you now and get the job done right than to hire an inferior service, pay the fee, then pay you again to correct their mistakes.

PROSPECT: I am talking to someone locally who can do the job for a lot less money.
You: As a licensed contractor, I spend a lot of time getting paid to correct the work of local handymen who do not have the expertise or training to do this type of work correctly. Surely it would be less expensive to have the

job done right the first time, rather than pay for an inferior job from an unqualified source now, then pay me to fix it later on . . . do you agree?

Compare your credentials, track record, results achieved for clients, and other qualifications with the competing firms. If you have a strong record of proven success and a long list of satisfied clients, stress these. Clients will pay extra if they have more confidence in your ability to get the job done reliably and on time.

Objection 4: We Don't Use Outside Vendors

"We don't use freelancers." "We do it all in house." "I don't need a contractor—I'll do it myself."

There are two basic strategies for overcoming this objection. The first is to agree with prospects that they are wise to do it themselves, but then try to find something they *don't* want to do themselves and would like your help with.

For instance, in calling on large corporations, I'm often told, "We don't need a freelance copywriter because we have staff writers who do all our brochures and manuals in-house." It would be stupid for me to argue with the advertising manager and tell him to fire his staff because I'm better.

Instead, I probe to uncover hidden needs. I might say, "Do you also produce newsletters, press materials, audiovisual scripts?" One prospect recently said, "Well, we're thinking of starting a newsletter, and we wouldn't be able to handle that ourselves." Bingo! There was my opportunity. I made the sale and got the assignment. I still don't write their brochures and manuals. But I get a nice four-figure fee for writing several newsletters for them each year.

If you're unable to uncover work prospects need done on the outside, your fallback position is to say "Well, I'm available to you any time you have a project that requires my special expertise or your internal staff gets overloaded.

Please keep my material on file, so when you need me, you know who to call." Although they may not need you now, things change, and six months from now they may have too much work to handle in-house.

A second strategy is to say that yes, while you certainly can do this job yourself, Mr. Prospect, there are many advantages to using an outside expert. Then explain those advantages. Or suggest that they can do the bulk of the work themselves, while still retaining you to check their work or offer some training, guidance, or advice so they can do it better themselves.

Note: For those of you serving the consumer marketplace and providing service to homeowners, you'll frequently find that one spouse wants to hire expert help, while the other spouse wants to do it himself. Don't always assume it's the wife who wants your help; I know many couples where the wife is an ambitious do-it-yourselfer while the husband is totally inept at household tasks (this includes my wife and me).

When selling to such a couple, don't pit one against the other, or the do-it-yourselfer will fight you so strongly that you'll never get the work, even if they end up hiring someone. Instead, make your pitch as the best-qualified contractor to do the job—*if* they decide to go that way. Then sit back. Many times, the do-it-yourselfer will bungle the work, quit in the middle, or give up in disgust, whereupon the other spouse pulls your quotation out of the file and calls you to award the contract.

Objection 5: I Don't Have Time to Discuss It Right Now

This is a legitimate objection—up to a point. As I've said earlier, you should respect prospects' busy schedules. If a person says she's too busy, or hasn't had a chance to read your brochure yet, she's probably telling the truth. Ask when she'll have time to discuss the project with you. Then call back. If you're put off repeatedly by the prospect's spouse or secretary, use the telephone script given in chapter 5 for handling your final call-back.

Here's how I normally handle the I'm-too-busy objection.

PROSPECT: Bob, I just don't have time to think about this right now.

ME: I understand. I know how busy you are. I'd like to set up a time when we could spend twenty minutes on the phone discussing [name the project]. Would you like me to get back to you at the end of this week or would next week be better?

If prospects tell you they have absolutely no time to talk with you no matter when you call, and that they'll always be busy and inaccessible to you, that's probably a good indication they don't consider the project important and therefore are not really a qualified lead for your services. Also, saying "I'm too busy" may be the lie they tell you to cover up the fact that there really is no project and they are just brochure collectors.

Objection 6: We Have No Immediate Need

Here prospects are being honest with you. If prospects say "We are just collecting literature for our files and have no immediate project in mind," that's exactly what they mean.

Does this mean they're lousy prospects? No. In many service businesses, only a minority of prospects have an immediate job that has to be done right away. The rest have requested your information or estimate to keep on file for future reference so that when a project does come up, they know who to call.

If prospects don't have an immediate need, don't pester them or hard-sell them. What's the point? If they don't have a project, they're certainly not going to make one up just to keep you happy.

The best strategy is to send your information, follow up to make sure they got it and to answer any questions, then ask their permission to follow up periodically via phone and mail. The periodic follow-ups will keep your name in their mind so that when a job comes up, they think of you—and not your competitor.

About the only way to get an immediate job from people who say they have no work for you is to remind them that you handle projects in many areas, not just the specialty they called you for. The prospect who responded to your ad for stress reduction seminars says he'll keep you in mind but has no immediate need for a stress reduction seminar. You ask, "What other training does your company need?" When he mentions time management—not your specialty, but an area you do handle—you move in for the sale of that program.

Prospects often don't hire you because they don't realize you can provide a service they need but were not thinking of when they called. You can generate extra income by telling the prospect "Oh, by the way, I also do X, Y, and Z as well as A, B, and C."

Objection 7: My Boss/Committee/Spouse Has to Approve It

"It looks good to me, but of course I don't have the authority to give you the go-ahead, so I'll need to run it by my boss/committee/family for approval."

You can avoid this objection by making sure you talk only (or primarily) to decision makers, not to underlings.

Knowing who the decision maker is for your type of service helps put you in front of the right people. If you normally deal with DP managers when selling your consulting services, and you get a call from someone with the title administrative coordinator, you know you're dealing with an underling and must make an effort to present your pitch to the *real* buyer. (*Note:* As mentioned, I consider any phone or mail inquiry from an underling to be an inferior lead, on the basis that if the prospect was genuinely interested and considered the project important, he or she would have called me directly.)

If you can't force an audience with the decision maker, then your fall-back position is to seek such an audience in the guise of an offer to help the underling sell the program to her committee.

> UNDERLING: I will have to run this by our committee.
> YOU: I understand. When does the committee meet?
> UNDERLING: On the tenth.
> YOU: Great. I would be happy to attend that meeting with you and be available to answer any questions the committee may have.

Some service providers avoid this objection altogether by refusing to do business with clients who make decisions by committee. In *Confessions of an Advertising Man* (New York: Atheneum, 1980), David Ogilvy tells the story of when his advertising agency, Ogilvy and Mather, was invited to pitch for the account of a major trade association.

"Mr. Ogilvy," said the chairman, "we are interviewing several agencies. You have exactly fifteen minutes to plead your case. Then I will *ring this bell*, and the representative of the next agency, who is already waiting outside, will follow you."

Writes Ogilvy, "Before launching into my pitch, I asked the chairman how many people must okay the advertisements. Answer: the twelve members of the committee, representing twelve manufacturers.

" 'Ring the bell!' I said, and walked out."

Objection 8: We Already Use Someone Else

This is an objection that stops most service sellers cold. After all, let's say you're an ad agency. You approach a company about handling their advertising. "We already use someone else, *and we're extremely pleased with them*," says the advertising manager. What can you say? How can you respond to that perfectly logical objection?

The answer: Before you can make your sales pitch, you've got to sell this prospect on the idea that, even if the company is satisfied with the current supplier, another may do even better, and so it makes sense to at least hear you out. The gist of the argument is "When you changed suppliers in the past—from your old vendor to the firm you currently use—that paid off for you. And if change paid off then, it can pay off now too."

For example, let's say you are a four-color catalog printer—Bly Four-Color Printing. You are in a meeting with a large mail-order firm that mails millions of catalogs a year, but they currently use your largest competitor—Mean Competitor Four-Color Printing—to print their main catalog.

PROSPECT: Your capabilities are certainly impressive. But really, Mean Competitor has been printing our catalogs for years, and we're very happy with them. We're not looking to switch.

YOU: Oh, they're a good company with an excellent reputation, no doubt. But let me ask you: About how long have you been using Mean Competitor?

PROSPECT: About five years.

YOU: And were you personally involved in the process of selecting them as your primary vendor?

PROSPECT: Yes, I was involved in making that decision when we switched from Jones Color Printing to Mean Competitor.

YOU: What factors did you consider when making the switch from Jones to Mean?

PROSPECT: Oh, lots of things: equipment, color pre-

press capabilities, bindery, delivery schedules, quality controls . . . and of course, price.

YOU: So you went through a careful review process before deciding to switch from Jones to Mean?

PROSPECT: Absolutely. And I think we made the right decision; Mean has done a great job for us, and as I said, we're still very happy with them and have no plans to switch.

YOU: So let me ask a question. Five years ago, you gained considerable benefits in terms of price, delivery, quality, and service by carefully reviewing your current print buying and then making a careful, informed analysis that led to a decision to change vendors.

PROSPECT: Yes.

YOU: So why would you deny yourself the chance to again make such a review and see whether even greater improvements in service, quality, and cost-effectiveness can be achieved today?

PROSPECT: Well . . . that makes sense, I guess.

YOU: Great. Then let me walk you through our plant and show you the many unique ways in which we help our catalog clients improve profitability and sales— and how we can put this capability to work for your firm . . .

Objection 9: You Offer Only *X*, But We Also Want *Y*

Frequently the prospect wants you to provide a more complete service than you normally offer. We all face this from time to time: The printer who is asked to set type and create mechanicals; the graphic artist who is requested to not only design the brochure but handle the printing; the accountant whose client seeks investment counseling and financial planning.

There are three basic ways to handle this objection:

• *Provide the service.* If you're able to offer the extra service and are so inclined, do so. When you say "Okay, I'll also do that for you," it instantly eliminates the objection.

• *Refer the prospect to someone who can provide the service.* Often prospects really don't care whether you handle the extra tasks or someone else does it. The problem is, they don't know who to call to get those other tasks done. If you say "I don't personally handle X, but I regularly work with firms who do X, and I'd be happy to refer you to them," this is all prospects want to hear, and you've solved the problem.

For this reason, it's important to keep a database or file of experts in allied fields who can provide your clients with services they want but you don't offer. If you're not a full-service supplier, you must be able to guide clients to various vendors who can supply the missing pieces and parts you don't provide.

• *Sell your methodology.* There are arguments pro and con for using a single-source or full-service vendor who can handle the entire project versus going to individual specialists who do only a portion of the entire job.

If you're one of those specialists, know the advantages you offer, and sell these advantages to prospects. In particular:

1. As a specialist, you have greater expertise in your narrow area than a general firm trying to do what you do.
2. You have many more years of experience and have done many more projects similar to what the prospect needs.
3. You are smaller and have lower overhead, so you can charge less.
4. The prospect will have the benefit of dealing with you,

the expert, directly. No middleman. No miscommunication or interfering layers of management between the client and the person doing the actual work.

5. If the large full-service firm's experts were really any good, they'd be on their own, because independents earn so much more in your field. The fact they're on staff is indicative of a lack of skill, sharpness, and professionalism.

6. The large full-service firm may have no staff expert in your specialty. That means they're simply subcontracting to an independent and putting a large markup on the bill. Why not eliminate the middleman and deal direct?

Objection 10: You Don't Have Experience in Our Specialty

There's a trend—an unfortunate trend, in some people's opinion—toward specialization. Ten or twenty years ago, if you wanted a deck added to the back of your home, you called a carpenter. Today you call one of the many firms specializing in decks and decks only. The carpenter won't get hired because he's viewed as a generalist. And people want specialists.

As a result, a more and more common objection is "You don't have experience in the exact type of project we have in mind."

For instance, as a copywriter, I occasionally get phone calls similar to this one:

PROSPECT: This is Joe Jones, Advertising Manager of XYZ Corporation. We're looking for someone to write an eight-page, four-color brochure on silicon-coated thingamajigs. Have you written any eight-page, four-color brochures on silicon-coated thingamajigs?

ME: Well, no, Joe, but I've written a six-page, two-color brochure on plastic-coated thingamabobs—
PROSPECT: [CLICK!].

Why did Joe Jones hang up on me? Is he a narrow-minded boob? To a degree, yes. There's a range of how closely prospects expect your experience and track record of prior projects to match their current need. Some prospects cannot tolerate risk and will only buy from someone who has handled a job *exactly* like the one at hand.

So how do you handle the objection "You don't have experience in our field"? First, recognize that the prospects who make this objection are narrow-minded but certainly a minority, and therefore you can get along quite nicely without ever doing business with them. So you can simply turn them away.

But let's say you want to convince such a person to hire you. How do you get around this objection? There are two strategies.

The first is to present your background and experience so as to make it look like you do in fact have expertise either in—or closely related to—their requirement:

PROSPECT: Your client list doesn't indicate any experience with the insurance industry.
YOU: Actually, we have extensive experience with all sorts of financial services firms, including banks, financial planners, real estate, and mutual funds. And while it's true we don't have a major insurance company on our client list, we did do some work with a local insurance broker awhile back. . . .

While this first strategy works to satisfy the prospect's requirement to see your demonstrated expertise in the field, the second strategy takes the opposite approach; it seeks to show why such expertise is unimportant compared to your overall skill, reputation, performance, and so on:

PROSPECT: Your client list doesn't indicate any experience with the insurance industry.

YOU: Yes. One of the unique advantages our firm offers is our experience working with clients in 140 vertical industries. Instead of having a myopic view and taking the same approach as everyone else in the insurance marketing field, we apply proven techniques learned from other businesses to your marketing, to dramatically increase results with ideas your competitors will never even think of . . .

Essentially, you can make one of two arguments when your credentials (or lack of credentials) in the prospect's area of need are called into question. You can say:

Yes, credentials are important, and while at first blush it looks like we don't have the experience, actually, we do.

Or say:

Our being outsiders to your industry is an advantage. We're not locked into the "business as usual" approach and can bring a fresh point of view to solving your problems.

Use whichever approach works best with you.

Objection 11: We Can't Hire You Because Our Deadline Is Too Tight

In this situation, either prospects say "We can't use an outside firm because the deadline is so tight we'll have to do it ourselves," or they specify a too-tight deadline as part of the job, making it impossible for you to comply in your bid.

The funny thing about deadlines is that 90 percent of the

time they are constraints artificially imposed by the prospects with no basis in reality.

Here's how I handle it:

PROSPECT: We need it in one week.

YOU: Bill, let me ask you a question: What would happen if you got it in two weeks instead of one week?

PROSPECT: Well . . . nothing, really.

YOU: Then is there any reason we can't set the deadline as two weeks from today, instead of one?

PROSPECT: No, I guess there isn't.

You can usually get an extension on the deadline ranging from two or three days to a week or more if you just ask for it.

However, about 10 percent of the time, the deadline is genuine—that is, it's driven by a real event: The prospect is closing on a home, or moving, or has a trade show or important meeting or speech to prepare for. In such a situation, you may have to accept the tight deadline or be prepared to pass on the work. You may be able to get yourself a *little* extra time, even if only a day or so, by making sure *everyone* involved in the project shares in the rush. Tell the prospect, "I'll be happy to set other work aside and get this done for you, but let's make sure everyone on the team is pulling for you. Talk with your other suppliers, and get them to shave a few days off their schedules too. That will ensure that the job gets done on time while giving you and me the time we need to do our part effectively." Few prospects can resist the logic of this argument.

Objection 12: We've Used Your Type of Firm/Service Before and Were Not Satisfied

Most service providers do not understand the significance of this objection. Their logic is "If the prospect used someone else and was disappointed, then I'll get the sale because I'll do a better job than the other person."

Unfortunately, prospects' disappointment with their previous service provider makes them skeptical of your sales
pitch and extremely reluctant to hire others (including you)
in your field. Their attitude is "We tried one ad agency (or
accounting firm, or computer programmer) in the past and
they did a lousy job; therefore we don't believe in using ad
agencies (or accounting firms or computer programmers)."
Rather than create an opportunity for you, the previous
firm's failure—and prospects' subsequent disappointment—
has set up a formidable barrier against you.

To overcome it, ask probing questions that determine
exactly what the source of dissatisfaction was with your
predecessor. Ask "What exactly about their services didn't
meet your needs?" and "That's interesting, could you tell me
more about it?" When prospects gripe, don't badmouth your
competitor directly, but do express your empathy with the
prospects' struggle and disappointment, using such phrases
as "I understand" or "I can see why you were unhappy."

Then begin to address some of the problems caused by the
other firms. Offer a tip or two on how the problem might be
corrected, and suggest a few ways in which your company
could set things right.

Prospects will quickly see that the problem was indicative
of their *particular* service provider and not all service providers in your field, and that you seem different—helpful,
cooperative, knowledgeable, and able. Public relations expert Don Levin says that when pitching new business, he
likes to go to the meeting with ten good ideas and suggestions in mind for that particular prospect.

Finally, if prospects are still reluctant, offer to handle a
piece of their project or correct a portion of the damage
caused by your predecessor. If the prospects complain that,
in addition to doing a crummy job finishing the basement, a
replacement window leaks cold air, say "With the winter
coming up, that will cost a lot in gas bills. Would you like us to
take care of that now for you?" Once a prospect can test your

service on a small job, his or her fear of you being another wrong choice will vanish, and you'll get a bigger project.

Objection 13: What Happens If We Hire You and We're Not Satisfied with the Work You Do?

To combat this objection, offer a strong warranty, guarantee, pledge of satisfaction, or promise of performance—within the limits of reason, of course. For example, say:

> "Most of my clients are pleased and satisfied with my ad layouts when they receive them. But if you are not, I will redesign the ad according to your instructions—and at *my* expense."

> "We do not consider the job done until the client is satisfied."

> "Revisions are included in my fee provided they are assigned within thirty days of your receipt of the manuscript."

> "We offer an unconditional one-year warranty on parts and labor."

> "The landscaping is guaranteed for one year. If any plant or shrub dies, we will replace it at no cost."

If you cannot guarantee results, at least promise the prospect your best effort:

> "We have been retained by more than forty firms, and in every case, sales have gone up after the client retained us. While we cannot guarantee the same result for you, we will do our best to achieve it."

Guarantees are powerful incentives for people to do business with you. The longer the terms (ninety days versus thirty days, one year versus three months) and the fewer conditions (an unconditional money-back guarantee is most powerful), the less reluctant prospects will be to hire you.

On the other hand, we service providers must be careful with our guarantees. Those who sell products can always take the product back, refund the money, and then sell the product again to another buyer. But as service providers, time spent servicing a client can never be recovered. And the service rendered is so particular to that specific client, it cannot be resold to another client. Therefore, be careful with guarantees, lest unscrupulous buyers take advantage of you.

I offer a guarantee of *service* rather than one of *returned fee*. If a client is unhappy with the work, I will gladly revise it according to his or her wishes, but I will *not* waive the fee or refund money paid me. Most service providers in most fields use a similar guarantee of performance and avoid guarantees based on return of fee.

A good guide to structuring a successful guarantee is to study the guarantees offered by your competitors, then construct yours so that it is *slightly* better than theirs—but not dramatically so. You want enough difference so that your guarantee becomes a strong competitive selling point without locking you into promises you can't afford to make or don't want to keep later.

For instance, if your main competitor in the computer repair business offers a one-year warranty on labor and ninety days on parts, you should advertise a one-year unconditional warranty on labor *and* parts. Then stress your superior guarantee in your sales pitch.

Objection 14: Your Competitors Are Willing to Do the Initial Work on Spec, So Why Won't You?

"On spec" is short for *on speculation*. When prospects ask you to work on spec, they are saying "Do the work for us. If we like it, we'll pay for it. If we don't like it, we don't owe you anything."

In almost all selling situations for almost every service industry, even those where on-spec work is common, I am almost always against it. You are a professional, and in my opinion, a professional does not work for free—which is exactly what "on spec" means.

Spec work is bad for you because you are committing your valuable time and skills with no promise of remuneration. Think about it. Wouldn't the time be better spent pursuing clients who don't insist on spec work and instead pay the fees you ask?

Doing spec work lowers your status as a professional. Those who are successful don't have to do spec work—they are too busy servicing paying clients. Only those who are hungry and need business do work on speculation. Which image would you rather portray to your prospects?

Another problem with spec work is that it signals to your prospects that your time is not valuable. This is a bad impression to make, considering that your time (along with your ability to solve problems) is essentially what you sell.

Here is how I handle the request to do spec work:

PROSPECT: Would you be willing to do a small project on spec?

ME: I'm sorry, but I don't do spec work.

PROSPECT: Why not?

ME: I have more clients and leads than I can handle from prospects who are willing and eager to retain me at my regular rates. Since I have much more business than I can possibly handle, I don't have to do spec work to get clients.

PROSPECT: But your competitors will do spec work for me.

ME: I understand. Everyone does business differently. But tell me: How busy and successful can they be if they are so eager to work for you for free?

My experience is that if you are firm in your refusal to do spec work, you can get paid to do work your competitors are giving away for free.

Just because others in your field *tell* you "You've got to do spec work to get the business" doesn't mean it's so. Be aware that most of your peers, competitors, and colleagues in your industry are not effective marketers or skilled at selling. They base their opinions on what they've been conditioned to believe is standard, rather than on what works or is most effective.

Often by going against the established practice, your sales and marketing can get better results with less time and money spent. Just be aware when you are going against tradition, because to do so takes a little extra thought and planning.

Another problem with doing spec work is the very real possibility of getting "burned" by clients who take advantage of you. Because most of us are overly optimistic and perhaps too eager to make the sale, we tend to close our eyes to this possibility. Instead, we should proceed alertly, with our eyes wide open.

A close friend who is a management consultant tells this story: "I worked on spec once—and only once—in my career, and it was a big mistake.

"It was when I was just starting out and eager for the work. I wanted to build a reputation—and a client list—fast. So when the training manager of a big corporation resisted my sales pitch, I said, 'I tell you what—I'll come in and do the first training session on spec. If you don't like it, you don't pay for it.'

"I should have known he would be trouble when, after resisting so much, he instantly jumped on this offer. Sure enough, at the end of the first session, he came up to me and said, with a smile, 'Don't come back tomorrow . . . and don't send me a bill.' No further explanation. The explanation, of

course, was that he took me for a free seminar. This is a
mistake I will never repeat."

Avoid working on spec.

Objection 15: Your Service (or You) Are Not Exactly What We Are Looking For

If a prospect says "Your service is not exactly what we were
looking for," ask where he or she feels it falls short. The
prospect will tell you, and you can then isolate and address
these specific objections.

Objection 16: You Don't Have a Lot of Well-known Clients on Your Client List

Those of you selling to business or industry know the value
of being able to rattle off the names of four or five big
corporate clients when going through your client list. The
name recognition registers on prospects, causing them to
think that if you're good enough for Westinghouse or IBM,
you must be good enough for them too.

So what can you do if you don't have those big impressive
clients on your list?

First, when the client asks about your experience, don't
limit yourself to listing only your clients. You can include the
names of organizations you worked for as a full-time employee as well. Tell the prospect, "My experience includes
handling projects for Westinghouse and IBM." No need to
mention that IBM and Westinghouse are former employers,
not current clients.

Second, if you don't have experience working with big-
name clients, get some on your roster—even if it means
doing a small job for a small fee. When you tell prospects,
"We recently handled a project for Lever Brothers," they are
impressed. They never ask whether the project was a $50

editing job or a $50,000 annual report or a $250,000-a-year annual consulting contract. So get some experience working for some famous names as soon as you can.

A third approach is to deflect prospects' obsession with famous names by showing that such experience is relatively unimportant and not really related to their needs.

You say, "Yes, we've worked with some corporate giants. But we're proudest of our work with [name three or four local clients his size or similar]. You see, our strength is getting quick results on a limited budget for small to medium firms of your size or similar." This reminds prospects in a subtle way that they are not IBM and would in fact not want to hire a service provider who worked primarily with the IBMs of the world (and thus requires an IBM-size budget to pay the fees).

Objection 17: How Long Have You Been Doing This?

In today's youth-oriented society, prospects are not as bothered by youth and perceived inexperience in a service provider as they were ten or fifteen years ago. Still, you may from time to time be asked "How long have you been doing this?" or even "How old are you?" if you are youthful in manner or appearance.

When asked how long you've been in business, my rule of thumb is:

If you have been in business fifteen years or longer, give the actual number of years.

If you have been in business ten to fifteen years, reply "Over a decade."

If you have been in business seven to nine years, say "Almost a decade."

If you have been in business five or six years, say "Over five years."

If you have been in business less than five years, give a

figure that reflects the time spent in your own business plus the years spent working for employers. For instance, if you worked for a bank for ten years and have been a freelance financial planner for two years, say, "I have over a decade of experience in the financial industry." Do not break that down for the client unless specifically asked to do so. If asked, give the accurate figures.

If prospects, upon hearing the answer, object that you are too inexperienced, reply: "I agree experience is important. But I'm sure you've met many people who've been in this business a long time yet still don't know what they're doing, haven't you? I may not have as many gray hairs as they have, but I've handled more assignments successfully in five years than most have in a decade—and I've learned from each and every one. May I show you some of the successes recently achieved for other clients?"

Occasionally prospects will ask your age—sometimes, because they think you do not look mature enough to do the job; other times, because you look young for someone with your credentials, and they are curious.

How you answer is a personal matter. If age is indeed a private thing with you, and you do not want to reveal it, just smile and say, "I'm older than I look" (if you are young-looking) or "That's a secret even my spouse doesn't know for sure."

In my case, I was extremely baby-faced and youthful looking, and people often mistook me for someone five, ten, even fifteen years younger. (Sadly, this is no longer true. Recently a clerk at our local pharmacy thought my wife was my *daughter*.) When I was in my twenties and started my own business, I would reply in good humor "I'm older than I look" when prospects inquired about my age.

As soon as I reached my thirtieth birthday, I changed the reply to "I'm thirtysomething" . . . the name of the popular TV show.

PRACTICE YOUR OWN OBJECTION/ ANSWER SCENARIOS

There you have it: my list of the seventeen most common objections, with strategies on how to overcome them. I'm sure you'll encounter many more objections as you make sales presentations to potential clients. When you do, write them down, noting what you said to the prospect and vice versa.

Study the most common objections—the ones that you hear again and again. Write out scripts to answer them, and go over them until they're ingrained in your memory.

Try these scripts out on your next sales calls. If they work, fine. If not, rewrite and adjust until you find just the right words for overcoming the objection.

The key to overcoming objections successfully is preparation. Ideally, at a meeting you should never hear an objection to which you don't already know the answer. When you know what to say to convince prospects their objections aren't a good enough reason not to hire you, the objections won't work.

Only when you don't have a good answer can prospects use objections effectively as an excuse not to do business with you. And that's all most objections really are—excuses prospects use to avoid taking action or making a decision.

EVERY PROSPECT IS DIFFERENT

As discussed at the beginning of the chapter, not every objection should be overcome. Sales-blocking objections, yes. Legitimate objections, maybe, but only if the benefits of your total service outweigh the very real drawbacks contained in the objection.

Warning-signal objections, on the other hand, should be heeded rather than overcome. Warning-signal objections alert the service seller to situations and prospects that should be avoided.

Another reason not all objections should be overcome is that every prospect is different. A benefit that is meaningful to one buyer may be unimportant to the other. You must decide whether an objection is a warning, legitimate, or sales-blocking objection in the context of this particular prospect's background and needs.

A case in point: Several years ago I was shopping around for siding for my house. It came down to two suppliers: a large, established firm with twenty years experience, or a local one-man operation.

The local man quoted a fee of $5,000, about $3,000 less than the large firm. But the large firm backed their job not only with their reputation and stability but with a twenty-year guarantee. The local man offered only a one-year guarantee.

Whom did I choose? The larger firm, even though it cost me $3,000 extra. The reason: Several years earlier I had replaced the roof on my house. At the time I had gotten bids from this same large firm (they do roofing as well as siding) and a local roofer (not the same man bidding on the siding).

At the time, I chose the local roofer, whose bid came in at $1,800 as compared with $2,400 for the large firm. Unfortunately, when the first big rain came, I realized my mistake. The roof leaked, and when I called for service (the roof was under warranty), my calls were ignored.

Finally it took the threat of legal action to get the roofer to repair his mistake. "I'm sorry," he apologized, "but I'm just one person, and when it rains heavy like that, I'm flooded with repair calls." To me, his excuse was totally irrelevant; I had paid for a leak-free roof and was not getting it.

What's the point? Simply this. The local man who bid $5,000 for my siding could have made the logical argument, "I can do a job of equal quality and guarantee it for one year.

If there are any problems, they'll show up in the first year anyway, so there's little advantage of a longer guarantee. And besides, any repairs you would need would be inexpensive—so it's ridiculous to hire the big firm. You'd be paying $3,000 for a guarantee for service that would never cost anywhere near that much."

Now, this argument would have swayed many prospects, *but not me*—because I had been "burned" by a small contractor once and didn't want a repeat of the same bad situation. The degree to which any sales argument will convince or sway prospects is as dependent on their own perceptions, experiences, and background as the facts surrounding the actual project at hand.

This must be taken into account in every selling situation you face. And it's the reason why even when the facts support your case, you won't always get the sale. Every prospect is different. Every prospect brings different prejudices to the table. You cannot please or sell everyone. You shouldn't even try.

If you feel depressed about losing a potential job because the prospect made objections and would not be swayed by your perfectly logical arguments to the contrary, keep in mind this formula offered by sports psychologist and motivational expert Dr. Robert Gilbert:

$$SWL + SWL = SW$$

This stands for: Some Will Like (You, Your Service, Your Sales Pitch). And Some Won't Like (You, Your Service, Your Sales Pitch). So What?

Not every objection can be—or should be—overcome. You can't please all of your prospects all of the time. Concentrate on selling those prospects you feel you can please, and your sales efforts will be much more profitable.

CHAPTER TEN

Asking For—and Getting—the Fees You Deserve

One of the toughest questions beginning *and* experienced service providers wrestle with is "How much should I charge?"

You probably have a standard fee or range of fees you want to charge (or have been charging) your clients. But is it the *right* fee? The amount of money you charge—and how you *present* this fee to your potential clients—plays a big role in determining whether you make the sale and get the project.

Charge too *little*, and you diminish your prestige and importance in the eyes of your client. You also diminish the perceived value of your services and dramatically reduce your own earnings. A low fee may get you a contract you might otherwise have lost, but will you be happy doing the work for so little money?

People who sell products don't worry about this too much, because they can always make it up on volume. As comedian Jay Leno says on the corn chip commercials, "Crunch all you want—we'll make more."

But when you are selling your services, you are also

selling the finite amount of time you have available to perform these services. In fact, time is your only money-making
resource, and there's a sharply limited inventory—about
forty hours a week if you work from nine to five. So you can't
afford to give your time away too cheaply.

On the other hand, charge too *much* and you may price
yourself out of the market, losing out on jobs to other service
providers who charge less.

The purpose of this chapter is to (1) help you determine
exactly how much you can charge for your time and services
and still remain competitive in your marketplace, (2) show
you how to present your fees to potential clients over the
phone, in a sales meeting, or in writing, and (3) give you the
confidence and tools you need to negotiate successfully and
get the projects you want at the price you asked for.

Let's get started.

SETTING FEES THAT BRING YOU
MAXIMUM REVENUE

Because each industry is different, I can't go into a comparison of the hourly rates or project fees others typically charge
in your profession, how clients in your market are billed, or
give a detailed course on cost estimating for each type of
service. That's beyond the scope of this book. And if you've
been in business for any length of time, you already know
these things about your own industry.

But I *do* want to ensure that you charge your clients
competitive fees. These are fees that bring you maximum
revenue without causing you to lose those projects you want
to get. Fees, in short, that win you the sale.

Here are four important factors to consider when determining what to charge the client:

1. *Your status.* Are you a beginner or an old pro? Are you
well known in your field and highly recommended . . . or are

you still waiting to be discovered by the masses? Are you a novice, learning your craft as you go—or are you really a master at what you do? And do you just *think* you're good, or do you have the client list, testimonials, referrals, and track record to back up the big fees you want to charge?

Because of their status, experienced service providers generally can command higher fees than beginners. But ability is even more important, so a highly talented novice is worth more to clients than a hack, no matter how long the hack has been working. Still, as a rule, those who are less experienced set their fees at the lower end of the scale; old pros, at the higher end.

But be careful about underpricing yourself. Beginners have a tendency to set their fees at the absolute bottom of the scale, reasoning that they do not have the experience or credentials to justify higher rates. I used this strategy myself when starting out, and I suppose it makes sense. However, clients will probably take you more seriously if you put your fees in the range of medium to medium high. I have found that the less a client pays for a job, the less he or she respects the work and the person who produced it.

One beginner I know charged during his first year fees that it had taken me four years to get up the nerve to charge, and he had absolutely no trouble getting them—despite the fact that he was young and lacked heavy experience. So I may have lost a lot of money by charging too little for too many years. I hope you don't make that same mistake!

2. *The going rate for your type of service (what the market will bear).* Unless you are the number-one great guru of your industry, or the most in-demand contractor in your town, your rates will have to be *somewhat* reflective of what the standard rates are for your type of service. And even if you *are* the great guru, there's still an upper limit to what most clients can afford or are willing to pay you.

In some industries, pricing is fairly standard. For instance, doctors in my town in northern New Jersey charge anywhere from $35 to $50 per office visit, although some charge a premium for the initial visit. But fees above $100 for a standard visit are extremely rare. An investigative TV news team recently revealed one guru, who was charging $800 per exam, to be a phony.

Some service fields are regulated; in others professional societies or codes of behavior set fee guidelines. On the other hand, many businesses have no such standards, and their fees, as one professional puts it, "are all over the lot." For example, in my business—direct-mail copywriting—fees for writing a sales letter range from $100 to $20,000 and up.

The variation in fees in many fields is tremendous. However, by talking with a few prospects, you quickly get a sense of the upper and lower limits you can charge. You may find, for example, that some homeowners expect to pay $1,000 for landscaping, while others are willing to spend $10,000 or more. But no one expects to get it for $200, and no one is willing to go above $20,000. After a few initial conversations and meetings with potential clients, you'll get a good idea of what the market will bear.

The important thing to remember is that you are not locked into an hourly or project rate because you quoted it to one client. You can experiment with different rates until you find the right range for your services and your market.

3. *The competition.* The third factor to consider in setting fees is the competition in your local area. Call some of your competitors and ask them what they are charging.

Many will gladly tell you. If not, you still need to get this information, so it's perfectly acceptable to do so undercover. Call—or have a friend call—a few of your competitors, posing as a potential customer. Describe a typical project, and get a cost estimate. See if they have a published fee schedule or price list, and ask them to send you a copy.

Finding out the competition's fees is a real help in closing sales. You learn just where to price yourself in relation to other firms offering similar services. You'll also benefit by asking your competitors to send you their brochures and other sales materials. By reviewing these materials, you can learn much about their sales and marketing approach.

4. *Financial need*. The fourth factor is your own financial needs—how much you need the work and the income. In some situations, when cash flow is slow, you may feel financial pressure to get the work. At other times, you may not need the money, but psychologically, you need to close the deal in order to feel successful and good about yourself.

Your need to get the work shouldn't really be a consideration. But practically speaking, it is for most of us. If you've got a million bucks in the bank, or dozens of top corporations are knocking at your door, begging you to make space for their projects in your busy schedule, then obviously you don't need the work, and this helps at the bargaining table. If the job isn't right, or the prospect gives off bad vibes or haggles over your fee, you can walk away without regrets.

If, on the other hand, the rent check is three weeks overdue, and you haven't had a phone call or an assignment in the past two months, you may be willing to take on a less-than-ideal project or client—who, if he senses your neediness, may use this to his advantage in price negotiations.

Ideally, you should negotiate each project as if you don't really need or want the work. But when you're hungry and just starting out, this isn't always possible or even wise. Sometimes you need the ego boost that comes with landing a project or being busy with work. For the service provider, "psychic" wages can be as important as the green, folding kind.

PRESENTING YOUR FEES TO THE PROSPECT

Presentation of your fees to the potential client actually involves two separate issues: (1) presenting potential clients with a fee schedule or giving them some other preliminary idea of your fee range and how you charge before quoting on an actual assignment, and (2) quoting and presenting a fee for a specific job once you have discussed the specifications for the project with the prospect.

Let's take a look at how to do each of these important jobs.

PRESENTING YOUR FEE SCHEDULE, RATE CARD, OR A RANGE OF FEES

One of the key concerns prospects have when looking over your materials is "How much is this going to cost me?" Introducing the matter of fees and fee structure into the sales presentation at the right time is critical.

Bring it up too early, and you may scare off good potential clients. But if you are too evasive, prospects become suspicious and uncomfortable.

Think about how *you* react as a customer. You like to have *some* idea of what something is going to cost you before the salesperson gets too far into the sales pitch, don't you? Of course. And your prospective clients feel the same way.

If you are meeting with prospects in person, then handling the matter of fees is somewhat easier than if you are dealing by mail. In a personal meeting, you can tell, from feedback, when prospects are ready to discuss fees. Usually this will come as a direct question, such as "How much do you charge for an employee benefits review (or whatever is needed)?" Or "Can you give me an idea of how you charge?"

When prospects ask, answer directly and factually. State how you charge, what your fees are, and, if appropriate, give the reasoning behind why you charge the way you do. Do not be shy or apologetic about fees, as so many service providers are. You offer a professional service and clients expect to pay a professional fee for it.

And if prospects don't ask? You can probably tell by their

body language when the meeting has gone on too long; they will be fidgety and uncomfortable, bored and unfocused, or seem eager to be through. At this point you say, "I think we've covered all the key points concerning your project, would you agree? If that's so, let me explain a little bit about how we charge for our services." Then present your rate card, fee schedule, or explain how jobs are estimated and what the range for the prospect's job might be.

But what about a prospect who telephones?

Once I have determined that I am interested in working with the prospect, my next step is to tell him or her that I will send detailed information about my services. The material I send includes the following one-page fee schedule listing my charges and the terms under which I do business.

SCHEDULE OF ESTIMATED FEES

Print ad	$750–$1,500
Sales letter	$850–$2,000
Direct-mail package, lead generation	$1,500–$3,000
Direct-mail package, mail order	$4,000–$6,000
Self-mailer	$750–$2,000
Brochure	$500–$600/page
Catalog	$500–$600/page
Newsletter	$500–$600/page
Feature story	$1,000–$2,500+
Press release (1–2 pages)	$400–$500
Audiovisual script	$2,000–$4,000
Copy analysis	$200–$600

Terms:

Purchase order or letter of authorization required for all jobs.
Copywriting fees for initial projects are payable 50% in advance, balance upon delivery.
Copy analysis fees are payable in full, in advance.
Marketing consultation available on an hourly, daily, or project basis. Ask for rates.

All revisions must be assigned within 30 days of receipt of copy. Rewrites are made free of charge unless the revision is based on a change in the assignment made after copy is submitted.

LISTED FEES ARE GUIDELINES ONLY. CALL TODAY FOR A PROMPT PRICE QUOTATION ON YOUR SPECIFIC ASSIGNMENT: (201) 599–2277.

NOTE: This fee schedule is current as of June 1990 and valid for 60 days from date of receipt. Be sure to call for current rates when ordering copy or consulting services.

I like a fee schedule because it gives prospects what they want (an idea of what I charge) and also proves that I am an honest professional who is so open about his fees that he publishes them. In addition, the fee schedule gives me a firm position when quoting fees. For example, if I list my fee for writing brochures at $500 per page and a client needs an eight-page brochure, then she really can't argue when I tell her my fee for the brochure is $4,000.

Many, many service providers do not have published fee schedules. In one survey of seventeen top direct-mail copywriters, nine said they did not have a published fee schedule. If you do not publish your fees, you ought to give clients some rough indication of fees either over the telephone or in a letter.

For example: "For the project we discussed, my fee would be in the range of $5,000 to $7,000 plus $150 for the initial on-site inspection. I can quote an exact project fee once I review the job site in person."

The one disadvantage of a fee schedule is that it locks you into a fixed price, which may be too low for handling a particular assignment from a particular client. The solution is to list a broad *range* of fees for each item on your fee schedule rather than a single dollar figure. Then, for a specific project, you can quote a price within your fee range that reflects the difficulty of the job and the amount of work involved.

For example, I used to quote my audiovisual script rate at $200 a minute. Invariably a prospect would say, "Okay, give me a three-minute script for $600." When I explained that the fee was based on a minimum fee of $2,000, prospects felt that I was charging more than I said I would. So now I list my fee for writing scripts as "$2,000—$4,000." When clients describe the job in detail, I quote a price within that range which I feel is fair compensation for the work involved.

I think it is a mistake to give *no* indication of fee in the initial package you send out. The fee is one of the prospect's key concerns and, although they don't necessarily buy the low-priced service (indeed, the opposite is often true), most prospects want to get a feel for your fee structure fairly early on in the buying cycle.

Some service businesses—freight forwarding and word processing, for example—lend themselves to well-structured rate cards and fee schedules. Others—interior decorating, landscape architecture, computer programming—may not. But even if you can't publish your fees, the earlier you can give the client a *rough* indication, the better.

Tip: When giving a rough estimate of your fee for a given project in advance of a firm price quotation, quote a *range* of fees rather than a single number. For instance, it's better to say "$5,000 to $7,000" than "$6,000."

If you said $6,000, and you later have to revise the quotation to $6,500, clients feel you have raised the price; they feel cheated. But if you said it would cost between $5,000 and $7,000, and then quote $7,000, clients feel you have stuck to your initial estimate.

The exception to this rule is when quoting on a standard item for which you charge a set fee—for example, an attorney charging $100 for preparing a simple will. In that case, simply say to the prospect, "For preparing a simple will, my fee is $100."

WHEN TO PRESENT THE FEE

The biggest mistake beginning service providers make is feeling they *must* come up with a fixed price quotation the instant a prospect asks for it during the initial meeting or telephone conversation.

If you can give a rough range or an exact price right then and there, fine. But if you can't, it is perfectly acceptable to say "I'll need some time to prepare a price quotation. Let me review my notes of this meeting and the background material you are giving me. Then I'll get back to you with my understanding of what you want along with an estimate of what I would charge to do the job. Fair enough?" No intelligent client will find this unreasonable; indeed, most will expect you to go through this process.

ORALLY OR IN WRITING?

Should you present your fee verbally or in writing?

My preference is to call prospects and go over the quotation on the telephone. This way, they are assured that I understand their specifications completely, while I get a sense of whether my price is acceptable or, if not, why not and by how much it is not.

Also, a telephone call indicates there is flexibility and room for negotiation, while a price quotation in writing signals "Take it or leave it"—a meaning you may not be intending to convey. With a telephone call, if I have misunderstood a prospect's requirement, he or she can tell me so, and I can adjust my quote accordingly. Prospects will be less likely to work with me to correct an error in a written estimate, which they tend to view as non-negotiable.

For example, we recently got three estimates for landscaping our front yard. One was for $4,700; the second, for

$5,000; the third, for $8,700. We selected the $5,000 quote based on price and the fact that we liked the firm's initial rough design. We actually liked the design of the $8,700 firm better, but felt that that was more than we wanted to pay.

Days later, the $8,700 landscaping firm called us back to see if we were ready to proceed. When we explained that we chose someone else because of price, he complained, "But you should have called me first! I would have given you a different design that you would still have loved and that would have been within your budget."

But because his estimate had been presented as a ready-to-sign, drawn-up contract, I assumed it was firm and didn't even think it could be flexible. Your prospects will make the same assumption.

ADDING VALUE DISPROPORTIONATE TO THE FEE INVOLVED

As marketing consultant Jeffrey Lant points out, clients buy only if they perceive that the value or benefit received from engaging your services is disproportionate to the fee paid—that is, they want to get their money's worth.

Your service has to seem worth the big fee you are charging. You will sell more of your services if you present it as a valuable package at the time you quote your fee to prospects.

And how do you make your services seem more valuable? By pointing out all the things clients will get (and that you do) for the fee involved.

To take a simple example, let's say a prospect calls me and describes a sales brochure he needs written. He then asks, "What will it cost?" If I immediately answer, "Five thousand dollars," he is taken aback. After all, where did I get that figure—out of thin air? And gee, isn't that an awful lot of money for a few typed pages?

Instead, here's how I would present the fee over the phone or in writing:

The job as I understand it is to write a six- to eight-page brochure designed to sell ABC Widgets. For this fee, I will:

- read all previous brochures, ads, technical literature, and other materials ABC Company has produced on ABC Widgets.
- read articles you provide me on the widget industry.
- review the widget market research studies prepared by your ad agency.
- conduct telephone interviews with the product manager and chief engineer to learn which new features of the improved ABC Widgets should be stressed in the new brochure.
- do a random telephone survey of three to six widget users to determine what they think of ABC Widgets and what features they are most interested in reading about.
- write a comprehensive outline for the proposed brochure and submit this outline to ABC management for review and approval.
- write a first draft of the brochure copy based on the approved outline and submit this copy for review and approval.
- make any and all revisions and rewrites requested by the client (up to two complete rewrites).
- make suggestions on photos and illustrations to include in the brochure and write captions for all visuals selected for the final version.
- do a rough layout and review the artist's comps at no extra charge.

My fee for these services is $5,000.

See the difference? In the first proposal, I'm merely typing up a few pages, for which I'm asking the client to pay $5,000. In the second, I am performing an incredible list of helpful services for which $5,000 seems a reasonable fee if not a downright pittance.

Key point: Prospects find your price much more palatable when you *spell out* for them all the wonderful things they are getting for that fee.

WHAT TO DO WHEN A PROSPECT SAYS "YOUR PRICE IS TOO HIGH"

The most common objection service sellers hear is "Your price is too high." There are two ways to handle this objection.

The Wrong Approach (what you are probably now doing): You quote a fee of $2,000 for the project. The prospect says: "Your fee is too high." You, scared of losing the assignment, immediately say one of two things. Either, "Okay, well, for you I can do it for $1,000." Or you say, "Well, I'm flexible, tell me what your budget is." The prospect tells you the budget is $1,000 and you say, "Okay, I can do it for that."

What's wrong with this approach? Several things. First and foremost, you didn't get the fee you wanted—the fee you thought you deserved.

Second, when you immediately offer to do the job at a lower price after the prospect objects to your initial fee, he or she can only conclude—quite rightly—that when you quote a fee, it doesn't really mean much; it's only a starting point from which you can always be bargained down, probably because you are desperate and need the work.

Let's say I'm your prospective client with a $2,000 budget. When I asked you what your fee was, and you said $2,000, I would probably say "too much"—because I want to get your service for as little as possible, and I know your initial quote is meaningless and you can always be bargained down.

The Right Approach: You quote your fee for the project as $2,000. The prospect says, "That's too high." *You* say: "I understand. Of course, I can't do the job as outlined for a lower price, but if you tell me your budget, I'll tell you what I can do for you at that price."

How does this work? Let's say the project is to design a small annual report. Your fee is $5,000. The client says the budget is $3,000. You say, "I can't do the layout and mechanicals for less than $5,000, but for $3,000, I *can* do just the layout and design. That's the creative part—the part you want. You can then take my layout and get it typeset less expensively elsewhere. So, Mr. Prospect, I can do the job for $3,000—if you handle the mechanical aspects in house."

To break this strategy down into steps:

1. You find out what a prospect's budget is.
2. You do not back down from your initial fee. In fact, you explain that naturally, your fees are fixed and you cannot offer something that costs $X for even a penny less.
3. But you tell the prospect how much you *can* do within his or her budget. In essence, you give the prospect a lower level of service to match the limited budget.

Why is this strategy so effective? First, prospects respect your honesty. They see that your fees are fair and have meaning—if you say it's $2,000, then you really mean $2,000.

Second, instead of blowing them off, you are trying to help them by working within their budget. Of course, they understand that they can't buy a Cadillac on a Volkswagen budget . . . and so reasonable prospects will at least try to find out how much you *can* give them within their budget constraints.

This strategy works when you decide to stick to your guns and not back down . . . but you still want the job and are willing to work with the prospect to find a way the two of you can get together on this. However, there is another approach, equally as valid.

The Second Right Approach: The prospect says, "Your fee is too high." You pause a second, then say, "I understand. I do hope we can work together on another project where my rates fit in better with your budget."

Most prospects automatically expect the service provider to back down and agree to whatever figure they say. This strategy is your way of stating "I am already busy and successful with many projects contracted at my full fees, so there is no reason for me to do any work at a lower fee, and if you want me, you'll have to pay the full fee as do all my other clients."

Use this second approach when you feel you can afford to easily walk away from the job unless you get the total project price you quoted, or when you don't feel like doing just part of the job, as often happens with the first approach.

One other thing about fees. A tactic some prospects use to get the service provider to lower prices or back down from a quotation is to be silent when the fee is quoted. The service provider says, "The fee is $2,000." The prospect is silent for a long time, while the service provider fidgets on the other end of the phone line.

Finally, unable to contain his suspense, shaking with fright that the fee will be rejected, the service provider utters that deadly phrase, *"But of course, I'm flexible and I'll work within your budget."* The prospect immediately knows he is dealing with another dime-a-dozen hack who can be bought for peanuts.

Once you quote your fee to a prospect, shut up. The next person to talk loses the negotiation.

WHEN PROSPECTS STILL WON'T BUY...

In some cases, prospects will still feel your fee is too high. If you need the work, either for financial or psychological reasons, you are certainly free at that point to "give in" and agree to do the job for the price that was offered. Lord knows, I've certainly estimated low and reduced my fee many times to make sure I could pay my mortgage and feed my family. But I always hated doing it.

Now that I am in a position of having much more work than I can possibly handle, I simply tell people, "This is my fee. If you cannot afford it right now, I certainly understand. There are others who charge less than I do; I'm sure one of them can handle this job for you, and I'd be happy to give you the names of some good people you can call." Prospects are grateful that instead of snubbing them, you are helping them by connecting them with another service provider who can solve their problem.

Now, many of the prospects who you turn away in such a manner will never hire you. But you would be amazed at the number of people who *do* come back to retain your services. Some prospects expect service providers to be frightened and bend to their every whim, and are impressed when you do not.

The lesson? If you charge a fair price for a fair day's work, stick by your guns. You are entitled to your fee and should not work for less than what is fair. You are in business to offer a professional service and get paid a professional fee for it. Don't let fear get in the way.

ANOTHER WAY TO OVERCOME THE OBJECTION "YOUR PRICE IS TOO HIGH"

What do prospects really mean when they say "Your price is too high"?

It can mean one of three things.

First, it can mean that your price isn't really too high, but the prospect is a haggler who wants to see if you can be bargained with. The techniques I've just showed you will work with this prospect.

Second, the prospect truly may not be able to afford your services. Prospects without the money to buy what you are selling really aren't prospects; they're just nice people who can't afford to do business with you right now. You can't sell these people—and you shouldn't try. You should just walk away.

By the way, you should always turn down cash-poor prospects *politely*. Don't snub them—they'll remember it, and some day, when they're in a position to retain your services, they won't—because of the way you treated them. Always be nice to everyone who calls you—even those who are not genuine prospects.

Third, prospects may have the money to afford what you are selling but aren't convinced of its value. Either they don't think the service itself is worth the fees being charged, or they don't think *you* are special enough to warrant your high fees.

You handle these prospects by showing them that the benefit, value, or results they will get from your service far outweigh the money they must pay for it. Here's how I handle it in my freelance copywriting business. You can adapt the dialogue to fit your own situation.

PROSPECT: How much do you charge to write a two-page sales letter?

ME: Two thousand dollars.

PROSPECT: Two thousand dollars! That's a lot of money!

ME: Mr. Prospect, if you think of it as $2,000 for a couple of hundred words on a page, then you're right—it's a lot of money. But may I ask you a question?

PROSPECT: Sure.

ME: For each new account my sales letter brings in, how much profit will you make?

PROSPECT: About $1,500 per sale.

ME: So, if my letter does just marginally better than your letter—and brings in, say, ten more new customers than a less persuasively written letter—you will make $15,000 in profits, right?

PROSPECT: Yes.

ME: Tell me—would you normally be willing to spend $2,000 to make a minimum of $15,000?

PROSPECT: Of course!

ME: So my fee is really only a drop in the bucket compared to the potential for increased sales and profits for your business, isn't that right?

PROSPECT: Yes, I guess it is.

The essence of this technique is to make your fee seem insignificant in proportion to the potential benefit prospects will receive in terms of money made, money saved, time saved, or happiness gained.

A variation of this technique is to make your fee seem small in terms of the project as a whole. For the sales letter just described, this would go as follows:

ME: How many letters are you planning to mail?

PROSPECT: About ten thousand.

ME: Then the cost of my fee comes to only 20 cents per letter. Do you think 20 cents is a lot to pay to put a more powerful, persuasive sales message in front of your best prospects? After all, you spend hundreds of dollars to send salespeople to call on prospects. Isn't 20 cents per letter a fair price for a better shot at closing the sale?

PROSPECT: Yes, it is.

This is similar to the TV commercials that ask you to pay for something in three installments of $19.95 each. The price is really $59.85, but the viewer finds $19.95 much easier to swallow. The same technique can work in making your price seem less of an obstacle to the prospect contemplating purchase of your services.

You might also warn prospects of what it will cost them if they *don't* buy your services today. For example, if you sell accounting services, tell prospects about the costly mistakes other businesses were making in tax filing before they hired you.

BEING FLEXIBLE

As we discussed earlier, you are not going to back down from your quoted fee. Instead, you are going to quote accurately and fairly, and then stick by your price. Remember, if you immediately back down after quoting a fee, then prospects feel your first price was meaningless.

This can backfire on you. I remember visiting a well-known health club with my wife; we were thinking of joining. The salesperson, an obnoxious high-pressure type, just about kept us prisoners in her office in an attempt to get us to sign up. When we objected that the $1,200 membership fee was too high, she said, "Okay, how about $700?"

Instead of taking the bait, I was outraged. "You mean," I said, "that if I had been interested initially, I would have paid $500 more than your *real* price to me?" The first price given should be the final price.

Magazine publishers have learned this through experience. In sending renewal notices, the first notice gives the best deal the publisher can offer, and subsequent notices just repeat the offer. Circulation directors know it's a mistake to save a big money-off or free-gift offer until the last notice. You might think that would work, but it doesn't: If consumers know that the price is going to get lower, they won't reorder right away. Instead, they will simply wait until the last mailing and the best offer.

So quote an honest price right off the bat and then stick
to it.

Where you *can* offer some flexibility is in terms and
conditions. For instance, if a corporate client says they cannot meet your net thirty-day payment terms and asks for net
sixty days, give it to them. You are not really losing anything. Most corporations take sixty days to pay anyway and
never even ask whether that's okay with you—they just do it.

Or let's say you quote a fee to paint the interior of someone's house. Your fee is $3,000 for the walls and ceilings in all
rooms but the bathroom. The prospect says, "For that fee I
want you to paint the bathroom ceiling too." It's a small
bathroom. It will take your helper another twenty minutes
to paint it. Do you stand by your original quote and throw
away the job? No. You say okay and paint the bathroom
ceiling. On the other hand, if the prospect wanted his six-
room guest house painted as well for the same fee, obviously
you wouldn't do it.

One other area where I offer flexibility is in the advance
retainer payment I require. For instance, many prospects
would prefer not to pay half my fee up front. And that's
okay—having half rather than a different amount is not the
key point; what's important for me is getting some money
up front to signal the client's serious commitment to the
project.

When a prospect says, "I would rather not pay half up
front," I *don't* say "How much would you like to pay up
front?" because this gives them the opportunity to answer
"nothing!" Instead I say, "I understand. What would be
better for you as a retainer—one-third or one-quarter of my
fee?" One or the other will be chosen, and either is fine
with me.

Here is a final tip: When stating your fees and terms,
don't present it like a challenge, or in an aggressive or whin-
ing or begging tone of voice, or as if you expect the prospect
to object or yell and scream. Just state the facts casually, as if

this is the standard routine and you do this every day. If prospects believe that a fee or term is standard or routine, they are much more likely to accept it than if they think the price or policy has been specially formulated for their particular contract.

PART FOUR

Getting
the Project:
Closing the Sale;
Contracts, Proposals, and
Letters of Agreement

CHAPTER ELEVEN

Closing the Sale

Let's look at where we stand with our prospect.

We have made our sales presentation (chapter 8), answered questions and objections (chapter 9), and have presented our fee or rough estimate of what the job will cost (chapter 10). The next step is to close.

"Closing" means getting the prospect to agree to retain you, or at least make a tentative commitment contingent upon final approval of your fee and contract.

Most professionals and skilled workers selling their own services don't enjoy pressuring prospects and would prefer that potential clients close themselves by saying "Okay, let's go, I'm ready to buy."

Unfortunately, fewer and fewer clients close themselves these days. Consumers are more hesitant to spend money and more likely to examine each purchasing decision more carefully than they did ten years ago. As a result, *you* are going to have to bring up and negotiate the final details of the deal if you want to get the assignment.

CLOSING IS NOT UNPROFESSIONAL

Closing requires that you come right out and say to the prospect, "I would like to have you as a client. May we get started?" This makes many professionals uncomfortable. Many of us were taught that asking for the order is inappropriate. While that may have been true years ago, it is not today.

Closing is necessary because it overcomes prospect resistance, inertia, and ignorance.

Prospects are *resistant* because, like most people, they hate to part with money. They suffer from *inertia*—the natural tendency of all objects, animate and inanimate, to resist action and movement. Worse, they are also, to a degree, *ignorant*, in that even if they want to hire you, they're not quite sure how to go about it. Do they sign a contract? Write you a letter? Phone? Pay some money up front?

When people are unsure of what to do next, their choice is to do *nothing*. By closing, you provide prospects with welcome guidance on what the next step is—and how to take it.

So if you want the prospect's business, you've got to step forward and ask for it. Clearly. Forcefully. Directly. And persuasively. We'll explore techniques for doing so in this chapter.

SEVEN PROVEN CLOSING TECHNIQUES FOR SERVICE SELLERS

Here are seven proven techniques for closing. These techniques apply specifically to selling services and may not be applicable to selling products (a warning to those of you who sell both services and products).

1. *Get prospects to invest time and effort in your relationship.* The more time and effort prospects invest in making

the decision whether to hire you, the more likely you are to close the sale.

This doesn't mean you should waste prospects' time or make it deliberately difficult for them to communicate with you. Far from it.

But it does mean that if you can get prospects to invest their time and effort in a relationship with you before you are officially retained to perform services on a paid basis, you are more likely to get the assignment than someone with whom prospects have not invested a lot of time and effort.

Consider this scenario. You have been talking with a prospect on and off for the past six months. She's visited your office two or three times, and you've exchanged lots of letters and information. Now she's ready to hire a consultant to handle her firm's outplacement. Who will she be more likely to hire—you, a person with whom she is already familiar and comfortable, or your competitor, who called her for the first time last week? Unless your competitor offers some tremendous advantage or proprietary method you don't have, you stand the better chance of getting the business.

For this reason, it pays to try to get prospects involved with you at an early stage, even before any money is exchanged or any contracts are signed.

If you're a professional speaker, for example, send a demo tape or invite prospects to your next talk. That hour or so prospects invest in going to see you or listening to your tape is an investment for which they won't get any return *unless they ultimately hire you.* If they go to your speech or show-case presentation and don't use you, they've wasted their time, and they know it. So prospects naturally tend to want to hire the service provider they have already invested time and effort learning about, investigating, or speaking with.

In my business, instead of just sending prospects my brochure, I'll also ask certain ones to mail to *me* extensive background material on their company. I tell prospects I need this material to better understand their marketing problems and how I can help them (all true).

This helps me close the sale. For two reasons. First, it impresses prospects that I care enough about them to want to read and learn about their company. But second, it requires prospects to spend some time deciding what to send me, making the selection, writing a covering letter, and preparing the package for the post office or Federal Express.

I believe that when making a decision about whether to hire me, many prospects say to themselves, "Well, I already spent all that time sending him our background material, and he's already up to speed on our situation, so the easiest thing is to go with Bly." They pass over my competitor because that person isn't ready to start the job, and because they haven't invested any time briefing him.

In keeping with this strategy, many service providers offer a free initial meeting or consultation, even though their hourly rates may be substantial. Now, in such cases prospects aren't motivated to hire you because they feel guilty about wasting your time. No. Rather, they consider such an initial meeting an investment of *their* time, and that's what they are afraid of wasting—their time, not yours.

Think about how you can involve your prospects early. Do you survey their employees? Give them a demonstration? Get them to attend your free seminar? Have them watch a videotape? The more time prospects invest, the more eager they will be to make sure that the relationship moves forward on a productive (and for you, a paid) basis.

2. *Incremental closes.* In sales lingo, closes are categorized as "major" or "minor." A *major close* is clients saying "Yes, you're hired." Before that occurs, there will typically be a series of minor or incremental closes. These "incremental closes" involve getting prospects to agree to different ideas, concepts, and suggestions you propose as you talk your way to the close of the sale.

Basically, this technique involves getting prospects to say yes to a number of miniproposals you present orally. Each miniproposal covers one of the items or conditions of the sale. Taken together, they are the total package of services you want to sell the prospect.

After getting prospects to say yes to each miniproposal, you then sum up the total package, noting that they have agreed to each point. Finally, you restate your proposition in its entirety and get prospects to finalize the agreement.

For instance, here's how I used this technique recently with a prospect who wanted me to write a mailing piece promoting his graphic design studio:

ME: So Mr. Gates, I understand you are looking for a direct-mail piece to generate sales leads that will result in new clients for your design studio.
PROSPECT: Yes.
ME: As we've discussed, the best format would be a sales letter with an illustrated brochure and reply card.
PROSPECT: Yes.
ME: And you would prefer that it be mailed in a personally addressed, standard-size business envelope. . . .
PROSPECT: Yes, that's correct.
ME: We've gone over my fee schedule and you understand that it's $1,500 to write the brochure, $950 for a one-page letter, and $150 for the reply card. . . .
PROSPECT: Fine. I have no problem with that.
ME: And you would like to have a first draft of the copy in two weeks or sooner, is that right?
PROSPECT: Yes.
ME: And because you're a design firm, you'll handle all the graphics and design of the piece yourself.
PROSPECT: Yes.
ME: Okay. So let me prepare an agreement that spells out I'll be writing for you a lead-generating direct-mail pack-

age, with letter, brochure, and reply card, for a fee of $2,600 total, and it's due two weeks from today.

PROSPECT: Fine.

See the technique? First I get clients to agree to each point concerning the deal we are making. Once they've done that, how can they say no to my final proposition, as it merely sums up a number of points they've already said yes to?

A series of small or incremental closes in which you get prospects to say yes step by step to the deal as you've structured it makes it easy to go for the final close, where it is almost impossible for prospects to refuse you.

Of course, if prospects say no to one of your intermediate closes, then it becomes an objection, and you either must overcome that objection (see chapter 9) or remove that particular element from the agreement you are trying to finalize.

3. *Act as if you already have the job.* This doesn't mean you pour the foundation, write the report, conduct the seminar, do the survey, or start the work. That would be premature and foolish. When I say "act as if you already have the job," I mean your tone, mannerisms, and posture should exude confidence. Without being obvious or high-handed, you should behave as if getting the project is a foregone conclusion, with fee negotiations, contracts, and purchase orders a mere formality standing in the way of you getting started. As Judy Brewerton observes, you want to get out of the "audition" mode and into a working-relationship mode as soon as possible.

Most service providers handle the closing phase of the sales process awkwardly. They act as if they don't know what to do, are ashamed and embarrassed to be closing the sale, and want to give prospects sufficient time to contemplate this major decision.

Successful service sellers are confident and decisive. They feel sure enough about their abilities to say to prospects "We are best qualified. Our service can solve your problem—and do it well. What are you waiting for? Sign on the dotted line and we'll get started."

Prospects want to hire people who appear to know what they're doing. This means being a man or woman of action. It's time for prospects to move forward, but inertia, laziness, or uncertainty prevents them from doing so. They look to you for guidance. You must take prospects by the hand and gently but forcefully get them to commit to action.

False modesty (or maybe genuine lack of confidence) prevents many of us from acting confidently. Our attitude is "Gee, Mr. Prospect, I don't blame you for not wanting to make a decision. There are lots of people who can do what I do, and besides, it's a lot of money and I don't want you to make a rash decision. Take your time; we're in no hurry." Unfortunately, this attitude only feeds prospects' natural inertia. It will not get you the sale you want, which means prospects will not benefit from the services you provide.

Act as if you already have the job, project, or order. Your attitude should be "Mr. Prospect, I'm happy you called me here today, because I've handled many clients with needs like yours, and I know I can help you immensely. The fee is X dollars payable in these installments. Here's a pen and a contract; please sign on the dotted line so we can get to work. I'm so thrilled and delighted to be working with you!"

This attitude will subtly alter the texture of the conversation between you and prospects. Instead of being in a *selling* mode, you'll be in a *working partnership* mode. Your comments will be directed toward understanding clients' requirements or helping to find the best solution for their problems, not desperately thinking of what you can say to persuade them to give you a retainer check or sign a contract.

And when this happens, you'll perform better and close more sales. Why? Because prospects like to deal with service providers who are genuinely helpful and interested in

them; they don't like to deal with ones who are pushy and
only seem interested in getting their money.

When you act as if you're already on the job, you will
behave as if you're in the former category, not the latter. So
prospects will like you better. And you'll close more sales.

Always act as if you already have the job—not as if you're
auditioning or begging for it.

4. *Avoid time-limited, high-pressure face-to-face closing.* In direct mail, having a time-limited offer is an extremely effective technique. Phrases like "Offer expires
December 15," "Supplies are limited—order today!" and
"This is a limited offer, and once it expires, it may never be
repeated again" give indifferent readers a genuine reason to
respond now instead of later, which dramatically increases
response rates.

But, while most people are understanding and responsive
to such time-limited offers in direct-mail situations, they
resent such pressure in a face-to-face selling situation.

For instance, when buying a car, I resent it when the salesman tells me, "This price is good today only—if you walk out
the showroom it'll be more costly if you come back later."

My response is to walk out and buy the car across the
street. True, some prospects will be scared into buying the
car on the spot. But this tactic makes them unhappy and
resentful. While the car salesman can afford to make the
prospect uncomfortable with pressure selling—he'll probably never see the customer again, anyway—you cannot. You
will be dealing with prospects on a daily or weekly basis if
they become clients, so you don't want to start the relationship off on a negative note. And that's exactly what pressure
selling does.

Here are a few of my "don'ts" concerning pressure selling:

- *Don't* tell prospects "I can give you this price, but only
  if you commit today." This makes you look sleazy and
  makes prospects extremely uncomfortable.

- *Don't* tell prospects "I'm getting extremely busy, and unless you sign up with me today, I may not be able to handle your job"—unless it's the absolute truth. (If it's true, then you're doing prospects a favor by indicating to them what they must do to ensure they can get you for this project.)
- *Don't* lie or say things that prospects will not believe. If business is scarce for service providers throughout your industry right now, and you're desperate for a job, don't try to pressure prospects by saying "We're very busy and we only have one slot open on our schedule, so you need to sign up this week or we won't be able to take you on." Prospects will know you are lying.
- *Don't* use two-tier pricing—that is, a low price if prospects buy today versus a higher price if prospects want to think about it and get back to you. While this works effectively in direct-mail selling, it does not work in selling services and will only cause people to dislike and distrust you.

5. *Remove the risk*. The fastest route to overcoming buyer resistance when attempting to close a sale is take the burden of risk off prospects' shoulders and place the risk on the shoulders of you, the seller.

For instance, if prospects resist your closing, stress the fact that they can hire you risk-free . . . that you will make any changes or revisions they request at no charge . . . that you guarantee your service for thirty days, or ninety days, or better still, for one year . . . that you will warrant the job against defects in materials and labor . . . that you stand behind clients 100 percent . . . that you will give more service at no cost or refund all or part of the money if you don't perform as promised.

Obviously, in selling services, we can't make our guarantee *too* good, or we leave ourselves open to unscrupulous buyers who would take advantage of us.

The trick is to appeal to sincere prospects with an offer
that makes it as painless, easy, and risk-free as possible for
them to try our services.

You can do this either with some sort of guarantee, warranty, or promise of performance . . . or by allowing prospects to sample a small portion of your services before
committing to a larger contract.

In my consulting business, for example, I charge $200 an
hour, as do many consultants in my field (direct marketing).
But most of the others have minimums of $2,000 or $3,000 or
more. I, on the other hand, will take on a job for as little as
$500. I tell prospects, "This allows you to try my service and
see if you like it for a minimal investment." This puts prospects at ease; many are uncomfortable committing thousands of dollars to someone they don't really know or haven't
worked with before.

How do you work this into your closing technique? Let's
say a prospect resists having you do her ad campaign because she's not sure if the firm really want to switch ad
agencies (despite her claim they *were* ready to switch when
they called you in). You could ask, "Do you have any one ad
that needs to be done right away?" Then offer to do the single
ad on a project basis.

You'll probably close, because it's much less of a commitment for a company to hire you to do one ad than to switch
their entire account to your agency. Interestingly, in the advertising business, most ad agencies I know would refuse to
do this. Their attitude is "We want the whole account or nothing at all." Competitors who are more flexible and willing to
allow the prospect to "sample" their services with a trial project can succeed against them in winning new business.

6. *AFTO.* Marketing and sales expert Ray Jutkins says
the key to success in marketing and selling is AFTO, which
stands for "Ask for the order." This means if you want a
signed contract, you must present a contract ready for
signature—and preferably, place the pen in the prospect's

hand and put his hand over the blank space provided for him to sign. If you want a check, tell the client, "Make out a retainer check for X dollars, and we'll get started."

You have to ask for the order, the assignment, the project, the contract, the agreement, the paperwork, the go-ahead, the check, the purchase order, the job. If you don't, you won't get it.

At a meeting of the Wednesday Club, a group of independent PR firms based in and around New York City, owners of small PR agencies were discussing how they closed sales and got clients to put them on retainer. I asked one experienced PR man, "What do you do when the client is ready to go and wants to know what the next step is?" The man reached into his briefcase and pulled out a poster board. On the poster was a pasted-up copy of his agency agreement, with a big arrow and the words "SIGN HERE" (drawn in huge lettering) indicating a blank space at the bottom. "The next step," said this successful service seller, "is to get them to sign on the bottom line."

7. *Act fast.* When prospects indicate they are ready to buy, act fast. Immediately write up a quotation, prepare the contract, or send an agreement. Have it in the prospect's hands within forty-eight hours. You can send it by first-class mail, Federal Express, or, if it's just a page or two, via fax.

Why is prompt response important? Two reasons. First, it makes sense to get prospects to commit right away. If they've too much time to think about it, they may find additional reasons for delaying or deferring. The delay may also give your competitor time to move in.

Second, prospects judge you on first impressions and form their opinion of you largely based on how you perform in the initial phases of any engagement or relationship. If you're tardy or indifferent about preparing the quotation or contract, or getting started on the assignment, this gives prospects cause to think you'll be even less motivated and caring later on. And that's not what they want.

CONSTANTLY CLOSING

When, exactly, can you consider the sale "closed"? When prospects call and say they're tentatively interested? When clients say, "Yes, go ahead"? When the contract is signed? When you get your advance check? Or is it when that check clears in the bank?

Actually, in the service business, the sale is never truly closed. In product selling, once the contract is signed, the goods delivered, the check deposited, and the money-back guarantee period has expired, the deal is truly closed: The client owns the product and is "stuck" with it. The seller has the money in his or her pocket—money that is his or hers and will not have to be returned.

In service industries, on the other hand, we are constantly closing—that is, we're always striving to make sure clients are satisfied and pleased with us. We can't really consider the sale closed when we get the signed contract or purchase order, because clients can always cancel, and it may be difficult to collect all or even a portion of your fee if that happens.

One service provider confided in me, "I consider the sale made when the client's check clears in my bank account." But even that isn't the end of it. You've got to perform as promised, or the client might sue for return of fee based on nonperformance.

Plus, with most of us, the one-shot client is the least profitable. The real money is made with clients who retain us on a periodic or, even better, an ongoing basis. The repeat business is where the profits are made. To get these repeat assignments, our performance on the initial job must be superior.

In a sense, everything we do or say in the course of our relationship with the client determines whether we close that next sale. We are constantly closing this sale and the next. Selling does not end with the signed contract but is ongoing throughout the life of the vendor/client relationship.

LET PROSPECTS HELP YOU CLOSE

According to veteran salesman Tim Connor, as reported in *In Business* magazine, your prospects will tell you what you need to say to them in order to close the sale. This means you have to ask questions, get them talking, and listen to what they really want from you.

For instance, I was trying to get a prospect to retain me as a consultant to help him start up a mail order business for an exciting new product. Although the prospect had been enthusiastic when he called me, and he maintained his enthusiasm for me throughout the meeting, I couldn't quite get him to commit to the next step (a signed contract retaining me for eight hours of service at my rate of $200 per hour).

Finally I said, "What's holding you back?"

The prospect said, almost reluctantly, "I believe you know what you're talking about, but all of this is new to me. I'm afraid that other vendors I need—the designer, manufacturer, printer, mail house, and list broker—will sense my novice status and take advantage of me."

Based on his statement, I understood that the cause of his reluctance was that I was a "hands-off" consultant and would not assist him with the nitty-gritty details. When I assured him I could act as project manager (for a small additional fee), overseeing the details and coordinating with his vendors, his anxiety disappeared and I won the contract.

Listen to your prospects. Frequently they will tell you, word for word, what they want to hear from you—indeed, what they *need* to hear from you—before they will hire you. A technique that works well is to ask prospects what they want, then repeat it back to them in your own words. When prospects hears their requirements spoken by you, they will be confident that you truly understand what they need. Example:

> PROSPECT: I need someone who can meet with our production people next week.
> YOU: So if we could prepare an initial briefing for your production team to be presented next week, I take it you'd be interested in proceeding with this project?
> PROSPECT: Yes.

MATCH CLOSING TACTICS TO BUYER MOOD

Another piece of good advice Tim Connor gives is that you must sell to prospects in the way they are comfortable buying, not the way you are comfortable selling. And this especially goes for the closing, which is the situation in which the prospect, faced with finally having to make a real decision, has the greatest level of fear and anxiety.

We've all been in situations where we haven't bought a product or service because the salesperson made us uncomfortable. To increase your chances of closing the sale, be in sync with the mood and personality of your prospects, and adjust your presentation accordingly.

For instance, telemarketers speak at an average rate of 150 words per minute or so. But they will speed up when calling New York City and slow down when calling Tennessee or Georgia, because they sell more effectively when the pace of their chatter matches that of the person they're calling.

In the same way, training seminars on selling overseas advise international businesspeople to follow the local business customers of the client's country. After all, most people would rather buy from people who are like them rather than people who are strange and different.

Now, this doesn't mean you should be a chameleon, totally changing your stripes and colors to match whatever personality you think would be ideal for selling a particular prospect. This would be phony, and people can spot a phony.

However, it does pay to be sensitive to the prospect's personality and mood and to adjust your style—within reason—to match.

For example, if prospects seem pressed for time, compress your sales pitch to accommodate their busy schedule and get to the close quickly.

On the other hand, if prospects seem relaxed, with plenty of time on their hands, you can slow down and have a more leisurely chat.

I have one client who is a real gabber. She loves to talk and talk and talk. While I can't afford to let her go on indefinitely, and sometimes must ask her to get to the point, when I get a call from Shirley I generally settle in for a five- or ten-minute chat. Why not? I genuinely like Shirley. She's interesting and has a lot to say. And with the huge fees she pays me, I can afford to indulge her a bit—something I might not do with a smaller client.

Another client, Randy, is a brisk, no-nonsense, to-the-point guy. Many people are turned off by Randy's brusqueness and consider him rude. Not I. We get along great—mainly, because my personality is close to his.

Leo, on the other hand, was a child of the sixties and is into touchy-feely interpersonal relationships. He frequently tells me how beautiful I am and that he loves me. I'm not fully able to respond to Leo in the same way, because I'm not like that, and we both know it. But that's okay with us, and I am more personal and warmer with Leo than I am with Randy.

Adjust your presentation and style to the prospect's mood and personality, especially during the sensitive closing period, and you will improve your sales results and client relationships.

BECOME COMFORTABLE WITH CLOSING

You may hate closing now. And although many service providers come to love the selling and marketing aspects of their business, some never do. But most people I talk to tell me they become more at ease with selling, more comfortable with the idea of asking for the order, over time.

Here are a few suggestions for putting yourself more at ease with the concept of closing:

1. Remember, the worst the prospect can do is say no. And that's really not so terrible. There are plenty of other prospects and jobs out there for you. There's always tomorrow.
2. The situation need not be awkward or unpleasant if you maintain professional, cool, detached behavior at all times. If the prospect says no, it doesn't mean loss of dignity or face for you. Your inner mental attitude should be: "I'd like to help you, Mr. Prospect, but if you refuse to see the wisdom of engaging me, the loss is primarily yours, not mine."
3. Most service providers take the position that any client who hires them is doing them a favor. They aren't. Think of the transaction as (in the words of *Looking Out for #1* author Robert J. Ringer) a "value-for-value" exchange of services for money. Realize that they need you as much as you need them.

THE NEXT STEP

After the prospect has agreed to hire you, the next step is to get a signed contract, agreement, or purchase order and a check for any deposit or initial fee you require. This is covered in the next chapter.

CHAPTER TWELVE

The Written Agreement

PUT IT IN WRITING

Once you agree to a fee, put the terms of your agreement in writing. This written agreement should include:

- the name and description of the project, including estimated size and scope.
- the schedule and deadline for completion.
- the fee and schedule of payments (how much money are you charging and when will you get it?).
- terms and conditions, such as what happens when the client doesn't like your work, changes the assignment halfway through the job, or you run into an unexpected obstacle (like finding rotted timbers when adding a dormer to a home).
- a description of materials, processes, and methodologies to be used in completion of the work (for example, if you're a roofer, specify the material and color of shingles).
- disclaimers, such as limits of liability or conditions un-

der which you are not responsible for problems and delays (for instance, a home inspector might put in that he is not liable for damages beyond the cost of his inspection fee).

GET THE PAPERWORK SIGNED BEFORE YOU START THE WORK

Make sure you receive a written agreement, signed by your client, before you begin the assignment. Explain that you cannot begin the work until you get the go-ahead in writing. Otherwise, the client could decide not to proceed with a project after you've already done substantial work on it.

If you work with consumers, you will probably bring a contract or proposal to clients' homes and have them sign it on the spot. Or clients can review it at their leisure, then mail it back to you. Always provide an extra copy for clients' files plus a self-addressed stamped envelope they can use to send you the signed contract and deposit check. Having the envelope on hand exerts subtle pressure on clients to read the thing and get it off their desks.

If you work with businesses, you can handle most contracts by mail or even by fax. Fax is handy when speed is of the essence.

Often service providers send out contracts and do not get it back from prospects. When they call to follow up, prospects say something like "Oh, don't worry about it. I still want to go ahead; but I just haven't signed the contract yet. But please get started on the work and I'll mail it out in a day or so." Don't fall for this line. Politely but firmly explain that a signed contract (and retainer check, if you require it) will give you the go-ahead you need to get started on their work.

At this point, some prospects play the rush deadline

game. They say, "Well, I'll get the contract to you—trust me. But hey, you've got to get started right away or we'll miss my deadline!" Again, don't fall for it. With Federal Express, you can prepare and send a contract Monday to clients, who will receive it on Tuesday morning. It can be signed and returned to you by Wednesday morning. If the job is more of a rush, a contract prepared Monday at 10:00 A.M. can be received by the client, read, signed, and returned to you by 10:05 A.M. on the same day if both parties use a fax machine. So "the job is a rush; don't wait for the contract" is no longer a valid request. Insist on getting the paperwork before you start.

If you require an advance check, you can fax the contract to clients today, then have them Federal Express a signed copy and check to you by tomorrow morning. Or you can say, "Fax the signed contract back to me now and I'll get started today, but Federal Express the retainer check so I have it tomorrow."

If a client objects to your insistence on a contract (and possibly a check) in hand as a prerequisite to starting the job, simply say "It's my policy." As entrepreneur Joan Harris points out, "Few people will argue with something that's a 'policy.'" Clients will be much more likely to comply with these requirements if they believe it's your "standard operating procedure."

MAKING THE CONTRACT SIMPLE
AND UNINTIMIDATING

Some clients do not like to sign contracts, and no one likes to sign something that looks confusing, incomplete, or is hard to understand. Here are some tips for creating contracts that will get signed and get you the sale.

Have a standard form contract. When you hand clients a

CONTRACT FOR COPYWRITING SERVICES

From Bob Bly
174 Holland Avenue
New Milford, NJ 07646

Phone: (201) 599–2277
Fax: (201) 599–2276

Date:

Client:

Job:

Fee:

Advance retainer required:

Balance due upon completion:

Notes:

Your signature below authorizes me to write copy for the project described above, for the fee listed. Revisions are included if assigned within 30 days of your receipt of copy and are not based on a change in the assignment made after copy is submitted. Payment due net 30 days upon receipt of invoice.

Signed _____

Title _____ **Date** _____

Please sign and return this form with your check for the amount listed under "Advance retainer required." This will give me the go-ahead I need to proceed with the assignment.

NOTE: If no retainer is required, you can save time by signing above and faxing the form back to me at fax #(201) 599–2276.

standard form contract, it signals that you are professional and that this is a standard procedure you do all the time.

A copy of my standard contract is on page 268.

Note: I'm not a lawyer, and I can't give you legal advice. The sample agreement and contract in this book are shown as examples; they're not meant to be copied and used by you, nor do I warrant that they're legally binding documents.

You need to write your own contract or agreement and show it to your lawyer for an opinion. He or she may add or change language to make the document more legally binding. You must make the final decision on language, striking a balance between being thorough and comprehensive versus clear, understandable, and unintimidating.

A print shop, typesetter, or desktop publishing service can inexpensively create a contract form for you. The desktop publishing service I use and can recommend is Martin Unlimited, Two Marineview Plaza, Box 5E, Hoboken, NJ 07030, (201) 798–0298. Stationery and office supply stores also sell standard proposal, quotation, agreement, and contract forms, which can be imprinted with your name and logo.

If the word *contract* makes you uncomfortable, and you think it'll scare your customers, call it an "agreement" or "quotation."

LETTERS OF AGREEMENT

Some service providers prefer customized letters of agreement instead of form contracts. They keep the basic text of the letter on computer, then revise it to produce individual letters of agreement for each client.

Here is a typical letter of agreement.

date

Mr. Joe Jones
President
Big Corporation
Anytown, USA

Dear Mr. Jones:

Thanks for choosing XYZ Ad Agency to handle your Job #3333.

Job 3333 is a series of three capability brochures. I will write these brochures for you and provide such marketing and editorial consulting services as may be required to implement the project.

My base fee for the services I described above is $10,000. That fee estimate is based on 100 hours of working time at my hourly rate of $100, and includes time for copywriting, editing, teleconferencing, meeting, consulting, travel, and research.

Copy revisions are included in my base fee, provided that at such time as the total time devoted by me shall exceed 100 hours, I shall bill you for additional working time at the rate of $100 per hour.

Out-of-pocket expenses, such as toll telephone calls, photocopies and computer printouts, fax charges, messengers, local and out of town travel incurred in connection with the project will be billed to you in an itemized fashion.

Payment of the base fee will be made as follows: One-third of the above-mentioned base fee is due upon my commencement of work; one-third upon delivery of first-draft copy; one-third is due upon completion. Payment for expenses will be made within ten days following receipt of invoice.

Sincerely,

John Jones

ACCEPTED AND AGREED:

by: _____

Do not use handwritten letters of agreement or write quotations on the backs of business cards. This signals that you are an amateur.

KEEP IT SIMPLE

Make the contract or letter of agreement short and simple. Try to cover major points of concern, and add any legal language necessary, but don't overdo it or try to cover every last contingency.

For example, one desktop publisher I know has a three-page contract packed with densely laden prose. An attorney would applaud him for being thorough and covering all bases.

But as a marketer, I question the wisdom of this practice. Many prospects would be afraid to sign such a complicated document without detailed legal review, and rather than spend the time, I suspect they would just choose another service without such a demanding requirement. (This publisher told me that one prospect had a lawyer on the phone discussing the contract with the publisher for over an hour. I am certain the publisher was not compensated for this time.)

Your contract should not intimidate prospects nor "cost" them an inordinate amount of time to read and approve. Keep it to one page, if possible. People are most comfortable with one-page agreements.

Avoid small type, if possible. Put all contract text, even the traditional fine print, in ordinary size type. People become suspicious when they see type smaller than eight point. It signals that you are trying to pull a fast one.

Avoid forms that have the bulk of the contractual language in fine print on the back. Put everything up front in regular type.

Make it easy for clients to return the contract to you. Offer to pick it up, send a messenger, provide a reply envelope, or transmit it via fax. One service provider I know provides prospects with a self-addressed, prepaid Federal Express label for speedy return of applications and contracts.

IS A CONTRACT ALWAYS NECESSARY?

With existing clients, many service providers do routine work based on oral agreements. If you had an ad agency on retainer, for instance, it would be a pain to have a signed contract for every job. Yet other service providers tell me they get it in writing for *every* project, even with regular longtime clients they know well and trust.

If you do make an oral agreement, at least send a letter of confirmation specifying what was said, what the project is, and what you are to be paid. And keep a copy on file.

When in doubt, put it in writing. And get clients to sign.

GETTING MONEY IN ADVANCE

Getting all or part of your fee in advance is generally a wise idea, especially when dealing with a new client. Many service providers require an advance retainer check from clients before beginning the work. Typical amounts for this retainer are one-half, one-third, and one-quarter of the fee, with the balance to be paid either in installments or in one lump sum upon completion of the work.

When you get the initial payment from a new client, photocopy the check and keep the photocopy on file. This gives you the client's bank and bank account number, which may be helpful in collecting your bill if there are payment problems later on. With such information, you can generally collect on court judgments against the client. Without it, any judgment is likely to go unpaid.

Once you've been working with a client on a regular basis, you may decide to reduce or even eliminate the advance payment on future assignments. Or you might prefer to continue getting advances.

WHAT IF THE CLIENT OBJECTS TO PAYING AN ADVANCE?

Clients should not object to paying an advance unless the amount you are asking is way out of line with what is normal for your industry or profession. If an objection is raised, explain why you need an advance. It may be to cover the cost of materials or services you are purchasing on clients' behalfs. Or you can simply say, "It's my standard policy."

The fastest way to separate serious prospects from those who are just puffing their egos or entertaining themselves by calling you is to mention that you get part of your fee in advance. People who are not serious prospects will quickly end the discussion when you ask them to "put up or shut up."

Any individual or firm that can afford you and is serious about using you will not be put off by a request for partial payment in advance. It is an accepted way of doing business.

Do I wait for the check to clear in the bank before starting work? No. But then again, I deal mainly with medium-size and large established corporations. However, I don't think it's necessary to wait for checks to clear even if dealing with consumers. But you have to decide that for yourself.

Some service providers, to avoid being stiffed, require the client to pay the fee with a certified bank or cashier's check. This may work, but I know I resent firms that will not

accept my personal check and want me to waste my valuable
time going to the bank because they don't trust me.

ARE ORAL CONTRACTS BINDING?

Many service providers call me and say, "I'm already working on a project with a client, and we didn't sign any papers.
But isn't an oral agreement good enough?"

My understanding is that an oral agreement or contract is
valid and legally binding upon the parties who made it. The
problem, however, is that if there's a dispute, it's your word
against theirs. You might think you agreed to one thing, but
they claim you agreed to something else. In some instances,
clients may be lying to get out of paying you. More likely,
they genuinely have a different understanding or memory of
the oral agreement.

This is another reason why you should get it in writing.
Making sure clients have a clear understanding of what they
are getting for their money (and what they aren't) should be
a standard component of the service provided by every service seller.

PART FIVE

Continuous Selling: How to Keep Clients "Sold" After the Sale Is Made

CHAPTER THIRTEEN

Increasing Your Sales with Client Satisfaction

THE IMPORTANCE OF REPEAT BUSINESS AND REFERRALS

As anyone who has been selling services for a few years or longer can tell you, *repeat business and referrals* can mean the difference between a business that is profitable versus one that is just getting by.

Repeat business—ongoing assignments from existing clients—can fill your schedule with lucrative projects even if you decide not to take on any new accounts for a while. The repeat business is much easier to get, because it eliminates the process of having to "sell" a company or person on using your services; the repeat client already knows you and is predisposed to buying from you. And repeat business is more *profitable*: You don't have to spend time marketing, selling, or familiarizing yourself with clients, because you already know them, and they already know you.

Next to repeat assignments from existing clients, referrals from these clients to their friends, family, and colleagues are the second-best source of business. People who are re-

ferred to you with a good recommendation from a user of
your service are *far* more likely to buy your service—and far
less likely to resist your sales pitch—than people who know
you only from a mailing piece or newspaper ad, simply because they trust that other person.

To get maximum sales and profits, then, we must generate repeat business and referral business.

TO GENERATE REPEAT AND REFERRAL
BUSINESS, KEEP YOUR CLIENTS SATISFIED

How do we get repeat and referral business? It's simple and
obvious. Clients who are satisfied with our service and
pleased with us will give us more business and refer us to
others. Those who are not pleased and satisfied with our
service will not. As Jonas Salk, inventor of the polio vaccine,
has observed, "The reward for work well done is the chance
to do more work."

Client satisfaction, then, is the key to generating a
steady stream of profitable referrals and repeat assignments. It follows, then, that the way in which you render
your service is in itself a sales tool. In fact, it's probably the
single most important factor in your sales effort. If you do a
lousy job for people, word gets around and no one wants to
hire you. But render a superior service that clients love,
they'll not only tell all their friends but keep coming back for
more of that same good service themselves.

KEEPING CLIENTS SATISFIED

There are basically three things you can do to keep your
clients satisfied:

1. Always do the best job you can.
2. Never miss a deadline.
3. Give clients more than they expect.

These three rules are really very simple to follow.

Do the best job you can. For those of us who charge by the project, the faster we work, and the sooner we complete the project, the more profit we make per hour. However, you should never rush a job or spend less time on it than is needed simply to increase your profit on that job. If you do, you will be the loser in the long run.

If a job is taking many more hours than originally anticipated, my advice is to keep on working and spend as much time as it takes to do a superior job. Don't worry about your profit. Clients are concerned with the quality of your work, not your profit or loss.

Never provide work that is less than your best. You cannot defend such work if clients don't like it. You have a professional obligation to give every client your best effort—even if you could "get away" with less. Doing second-rate work is the fastest way to lose your current clients and get a poor reputation in the business.

By the same token, doing superior work is the quickest way to build your reputation, get referrals, and generate repeat business. Isn't it true in your neighborhood that certain service providers are more in demand than others? That there are some people whose reputations are so good, they don't need to sell, because their happy customers do all their selling *for* them?

If you do great work, your clients will not only be happy to refer you to their friends and relatives; they will be *eager* to refer you . . . and will do so without your prodding. People enjoy sharing a good thing and letting a friend in on something they know about.

So always do your best.

Never miss a deadline. Next to price and the quality of your work, your reliability when it comes to deadlines is what clients are most concerned with.

In most service businesses, deadlines are critical. The client who needs your report on January 3 will miss a critical deadline date if you are late. The client who gives you a November 14 deadline for brochure copy may have no literature to hand out at an important trade show if you don't print the brochures until November 21.

Here are some tips for not missing deadlines:

- Don't take on a project if you can't meet the deadline. It is better to refuse the assignment and explain why than take on the assignment and miss the deadline.
- Don't take on more projects than you can comfortably handle. Never risk a missed deadline or do a second-rate job because you wanted to book more work.
- Negotiate with the client if proposed deadlines are too short. In most cases the client can—and will—give you more time. *Take it!*
- If there is research involved, start collecting your research materials as soon as you get the assignment. Failure to acquire key research materials early could hold you up later on.
- Work evenings and weekends if you have to.
- Hire someone to do some of the routine work such as typing drafts, proofreading, collecting research materials, ordering supplies, or getting permits or paperwork approved.
- Never load your schedule to its maximum capacity. Always leave some extra time open so you can handle clients who call at the last minute with additional assignments, rush work, or revisions on current projects.
- Keep a list of your current projects and their due dates posted on the wall near your desk or some other location where you will be sure to see it every day.

- Jot down all project deadlines in your appointment book or any other calendar you consult on a daily basis.
- Try to schedule deadline dates so they fall on a Monday or Tuesday. This gives you the weekend to work on the project if you fall behind.
- Use one-day delivery services (Federal Express, Express Mail) or messengers to deliver drawings, outlines, renderings, and so forth to your clients. Use the fax machine to communicate with business clients.

Give clients more than they expect. "Don't cheat or take advantage of your customer, you'll be the loser," advises publisher and author Russ von Hoelscher. "Instead, win success by giving your customers their money's worth. And if you really want great success, give your customers more than their money's worth."

This doesn't mean you should give away your talent and hard work for free. Far from it. But giving a little extra shows clients that you genuinely care about their business success and want to help them.

For example, I was asked to write a brochure on a new software product—so new that it had not been named yet. Although the client didn't ask for it, I submitted a list of names along with my manuscript.

They didn't use my names. But they were appreciative, and the next assignment was even bigger. And I knew I earned a lot of goodwill—not a bad investment for twenty minutes spent writing a few suggestions on a sheet of paper.

In another situation, I met with a consulting firm that was thinking of producing a brochure. By asking questions, I learned that they planned to mail the brochure to people they called cold over the phone. By suggesting that a sales letter would be a better way of generating interest in their consulting services, I won a $2,500 brochure assignment plus an additional $500 assignment to write the sales letter. I was successful with this client because I was viewed as a *marketing consultant,* not just a "writer."

"Be everywhere, do everything, and never fail to astonish the customer," says Margaret Getchell of Macy's.

Good advice.

DON'T PUSH A BILL ON THE CLIENT

This is a minor point, but, as they say, it's the little things that make a difference.

I feel you should not be too quick to push a bill on a client.

A lot of people would say this is poor business, that the goal is to get the bill out and paid promptly to maximize cash flow. But it's my belief that clients—although they would rarely say it—resent it when you bill too quickly. I know I do.

For instance, we recently hired a contractor to remove some asbestos from pipes in our basement. He explained his terms were half up front, with a check for the balance upon completion. Fine. But, during the next few days, every time we spoke to his secretary, the first words out of her mouth were "Don't forget—have a check ready for us when we get there." Eventually it became annoying. Obviously they were more interested in getting the check than in doing the job right.

The day of the job, the workmen made a mistake and left some asbestos. When I called to tell the secretary, she said, "Well, I'll ask the boss and get back to you, but don't forget they get paid before they leave."

I replied that they would get the check *if* and *when* they finished the job and did it properly and to my satisfaction . . . and they still had a way to go before that would happen. "Worry about getting the job done right," I told her boss angrily when he called, "not about getting paid."

Needless to say, I would never use him or recommend him to anyone.

I think we all feel this way—about lawyers, doctors, plumbers—and dislike it when they shove a bill into our hands or when we find it in our mailbox bright and early the next day.

And do you think your clients feel any differently about bills from *you*?

When is the right time to bill? I generally wait a week or two after the work is done. This gives clients time to "live with it" and be comfortable with it. If clients want revisions, I make the changes, mail the revised work, give clients another week to review it, and *then* send the bill. This way, clients perceive that I am more concerned about getting it right than with getting paid.

And if your "deliverable" is a report, drawing, or other document, never, *never* mail your invoice with this material, as some service providers do. The invoice should not be included with the "product." Getting your report is (you hope) a pleasing experience for clients; getting a big bill is not.

You don't want to dampen the clients' pleasure at reading your great work by putting a big invoice in with it. And if clients *don't* like what you've done for any reason, they will be extremely annoyed to see a bill for a job they don't consider finished.

Always send the invoice in a separate envelope and at least several days after the last of the work has been delivered to clients.

And what about tradespeople—roofers, contractors, and such? I know you folks have a tendency to hand the client the bill on the last day of the job and wait around for the check. Don't do it. I know you're afraid of getting stiffed, but people resent being treated like suspected felons. I especially hate it when contractors hang around without specifically saying why they are doing so, when I know they are hoping to get a check from me.

Far better is to mail the bill when you get back to your

office at the end of the day, so customers receive your invoice in the mail a day or two *after* you've left the job site. This shows them that you are more concerned that they are pleased and happy with their new roof, porch, deck, or whatever than with getting your bill paid.

FOUR ADDITIONAL SUGGESTIONS FOR KEEPING YOUR CLIENTS SATISFIED

1. Don't overpromise. Don't tell clients you can do more than you actually can do. Don't exaggerate the results your service is likely to achieve. Don't overstate your expertise, experience, or credentials. Says stockbroker Andrew Lanyi, "The more you tell the client you are not a witch doctor, a rainmaker, the more credibility you get."

2. If for any reason you foresee exceeding the estimate you've given the client or missing the deadline date, let the client know as far in advance as possible—not after the fact.

3. Keep detailed records on all discussions, decisions, drawings, correspondence, and other aspects of the job. In case there is a question or uncertainty, clients will look to you for information on what was discussed or decided.

4. When presenting preliminary outlines, concepts, drawings, or ideas, be polite, flexible, and easy to work with. "If the client wants a totally different approach or extensive changes, acquiesce pleasantly," advises Cam Foote, publisher of *Creative Business* newsletter. "Just as your first obligation to the client was to recommend, your obligation now is to follow direction. After all, it is the client's money you are spending."

CHAPTER FOURTEEN

Coping
with Difficult Clients

Everyone who is a consultant, self-employed professional, or service provider in *any* field has problems with clients, sooner or later. Any service provider who says to you "I never have any problems" is either not telling the truth or is doing so little business that problems haven't come up.

Why will you eventually have conflict with your clients?

1. They will not like your work, and this will offend you. Although you may have in theory met the contract specifications, if clients do not like the finished job for any reason—or for no reason—they will not be happy with you.

2. A client will behave in a rude or offensive manner.

3. You will do something that is not to the clients' liking, and they will complain about it or vent their unhappiness in other ways.

For instance, even if you cancel an appointment for a valid reason (for example, you are having a heart attack and need to be rushed to the emergency room), there are some unreasonable people out there who will still be annoyed that you didn't show up. Amazing, but true.

4. You are both human beings, and human beings—even the nicest ones—sometimes have trouble getting along.

5. One or both of you will say or do something under pressure or in the heat of the moment that the other resents.

6. You will have a miscommunication that results in misunderstanding, and the client will blame you.

7. Either you or your client will change fees, payment terms, or other ways of doing business, and this will upset the other party.

8. You find that, after being hired by the client, you have to deal with other people—usually family (if you sell to consumers) or staff (if you sell to business), and one or more of these people are unpleasant, rude, uncooperative, or obnoxious. When you report this to clients, they become annoyed by this situation, and a portion of this annoyance is reflected at you.

9. Or one of any of a dozen other reasons why people argue, fight, or get angry.

There is nothing wrong with a little conflict now and then, so long as it blows over quickly, is resolved pleasantly by you, and doesn't prevent normal friendly business relations between you and your client. If you are getting into blow-ups with clients all the time, perhaps you do not select your clients carefully enough, or else you are too short-tempered and need to be more in control. Or, maybe there is something in the way you perform and deliver your service that does not meet the wants and desires of clients.

The following are some of the most common problems you will encounter in handling clients, along with some guidelines on how to resolve them. The goal is to prevent small problems from becoming big ones, so that your clients continue to give you lucrative, ongoing assignments.

PROBLEM 1: YOU AND THE CLIENT HAVE FUNDAMENTAL DISAGREEMENTS ON HOW TO DO THE PROJECT AT HAND

A problem inherent in the majority of service businesses is that you are delivering an intangible. Those who sell products don't have this problem. If you order a twenty-nine-inch color TV with remote control from me, and I deliver a unit in good working condition, then I have clearly fulfilled our contract and you will be satisfied. But if you ask me to clean your house, and I do the most thorough job possible, my job might still fail your "white glove" test if you are fussy, unreasonable, difficult, or expect perfection beyond what you are willing to pay for or should reasonably expect from a service of this kind.

Client satisfaction is based on subjective judgment applied to a review of the final job or service performed. And whenever subjective judgment is involved, there exists the possibility of dispute.

You know, for example, that if you go into a hundred different shoe stores and ask for a pair of size 9 Florsheim black loafers with laces, you will get one hundred pairs of identical shoes. But if you hire a hundred different ad agencies to design your next ad campaign, you will get a hundred wildly diverse and *different* ads.

In fact, the chances of any two service providers in a creative field (such as advertising, design, or communication) handling the same job in exactly the same way are about a billion to one—on a par with the earth colliding with the sun.

By the same token, if you show an architect's design for a new corporate headquarters to a hundred executives in the client company and ask them to make comments, you'll get back sketches with a hundred completely different opinions on it, from "I love it!" to "It stinks!"—and everything in between.

So you can see that it can be a major headache when you and the client disagree about how the project should be handled, what constitutes an acceptable quality or approach, or what the final result should be.

The secret to handling this problem is to prevent it from happening in the first place. This is done by carefully pre-screening prospects and selecting only those clients whose creative philosophy, style, and business approach are similar to your own.

If clients have a certain ingrained style of working, they are not going to change it to accommodate a service firm they hire to do one job. Rather, they are looking for someone to execute the project along the basic lines they are comfortable with. They may want you to *improve* on what they've done in the past, but they don't want you to fundamentally, radically alter it.

Only a top-level consultant (such as a big management consulting firm or law firm) working with them on a long-term strategic basis has any hope of changing these clients' basic way of thinking—and even then with great difficulty. But a small or medium-size service provider (you) isn't going to waltz in and revolutionize their philosophy and style overnight.

For this reason, clients should choose service providers— and service providers should work with clients—who have a similar style, philosophy, and tone.

For instance, even if you are Manhattan's "in" interior decorator this year, you're going to have problems if you try to force your art deco look onto a homeowner who wants a light, airy early American colonial look.

You may *think* clients will bow to your superior taste or expertise. And they may actually seem to defer to you in the early stages of the engagement. But rest assured that the first time you do something they don't like or don't agree with, *their* preference will prevail over yours.

Remember, the majority of service providers are advisors. It is *clients'* money we are spending—and thus clients are the final decision makers. If there's an argument, the best you can hope to do is *persuade* them to see your point of view. However, you cannot force them to agree with you. Forget this and clients will quickly remind you of it.

If you are uncertain as to whether you should work with particular clients because you are uncomfortable with their tastes and preferences, then have them look at your samples or photos of your work—and make them understand this is the type of look, job, or result they will be getting from you. At the same time, look at what they've had done in the past . . . and make sure you are comfortable with it.

If you don't like their style, or they don't like yours, pass on the project. They are not the right clients for you. You may indeed convince them to hire you, but you will be at odds with them from the moment you sign the contract. It's much better to work for clients who like and are looking for your style. This ensures compatibility and eliminates the risk of basic disagreements in execution and style.

PROBLEM 2: YOU AND THE CLIENT HAVE FUNDAMENTAL DISAGREEMENTS ON YOUR WORKING ARRANGEMENT AND THE TERMS OF YOUR RELATIONSHIP

This is similar to problem 1, except here the conflict is not on creative philosophy, taste, or style, but on working arrangements. For example, some clients love meetings, endless meetings. I detest meetings. Therefore, a client who wants to get together and "brainstorm" three times a week is probably not a good client for me.

To make sure you don't have a conflict in working style, discuss your working preferences up front and at the same time try to learn any preferences clients may have. This can be done through questioning, such as "Do you feel we need to

meet, or can we handle the assignment by phone and mail?"
Or "Do you need progress reports, or would you prefer that I
simply submit my report when it is ready?"

This way you can gauge the clients' expectations and
preferences and see whether they fit your working style.
This helps you make a decision about whether to accept or
pass on the assignment.

As service providers, the sales we make today dramatically affect the quality and style of our lives tomorrow. We
don't want to work with clients who will force us to do things
we don't want to do.

For example, I know one man who sells software. He is
one of the top two sellers of software, seminars, and consulting services in his field.

His competitor flies all over the country wooing, wining,
and dining potential clients. My friend won't—even if refusing to do so costs him some sales. "Hopping on planes, being
away from home—that's not for me," says Jack. He is successful, making good money while maintaining the closeness
with his family that's so important to him. He simply sells
only to those clients who don't require him to jet around the
country for (to him) unnecessary meetings.

PROBLEM 3: THE CLIENT DOESN'T LIKE YOUR SERVICE OR THE FINISHED JOB

You need to distinguish between clients' asking for changes
or refinements, which is normal, and clients fundamentally
disliking your service or the finished job.

Although some do not, most clients will ask for minor
touchups or changes. This is normal, as long as the changes
do not fundamentally destroy the design or concept of the
finished job, or call for substantial reworking beyond what
you believe your contract calls for.

The problem arises when clients have no respect for the work you have done, don't like it, and want the whole thing changed. Or when a client simply says, "I don't like it, I think it stinks, and I'm not going to pay your invoice."

How do you handle this? First, stay calm. Maybe the client has not hired a service provider before, didn't know what to expect, and panics when the job is not 100 percent exactly as he thinks it should be. Try to find out what the client liked, what he didn't like, what he wants changed, and why. Often, after such a session, the client calms down and discovers the job is much better than he thought, and only a few things were "off the mark."

Sometimes buyers just have to live with the service or the job a few days or weeks before they decide they like it. At first, the newness of it frightens them. And so they say, "I don't like it." If you say, "Give it time," 90 percent of the time the problem will disappear.

But what if a client still isn't satisfied . . . and wants the walls repainted or the job redone, at your expense?

This depends on what your working agreement calls for, as spelled out in your contract, purchase order, or letter of agreement with the client.

Ideally, you've constructed these documents so they give clients the right to request a reasonable amount of changes, while protecting you against unreasonable clients who, for no reason, decide they simply don't like the job they originally asked for.

Let's say a client asks for revisions that are substantial but to which she is clearly entitled to under your agreement.

When faced with a major reworking of the job, politely but firmly force the client to be as specific as possible in her criticisms. Don't allow general comments to pass unclarified; instead, insist that the client specify exactly what she doesn't like—and what substitution or change she desires.

Explain that without this specific commentary, you are

unable to proceed further with the job. You might even build such a statement into your sales literature and client contract.

In rare instances, the client may be an irrational person who is not interested in getting a good job but simply delights in torturing service firms, contractors, craftspeople, and other outside vendors. The best way to handle this client is politely but distantly.

Grit your teeth, put up with the client long enough to do a satisfactory revision, then send your bill and move on to the next client. Refuse to work for this client again despite any promises for an easier next assignment; it will never happen.

Do not allow any client to treat you in a rude, abrasive, or undignified manner. Tell him or her that you will not tolerate it. If it continues one second longer, get up, walk away, send your bill, and pursue collection until it is paid.

And what about clients who request a reworking or redoing of the job that clearly falls *outside* of the contract?

Politely but firmly remind these clients of the terms of your agreement. Explain that you would be happy, even delighted, to help get the desired result they want. But, as they have now changed their minds and are specifying a different job from the one originally contracted for, naturally there will be an additional fee involved.

Reasonable clients will recognize the truth of this (perhaps grudgingly, but they will recognize it) and will be willing to sit down with you and work out a new arrangement mutually agreeable to both of you.

When writing this new contract, remember that clients are displeased, could have decided to stiff you but didn't, and are being—at least in their minds—accommodating. In return for this consideration, you should be accommodating also. Don't say, "The client is changing the job in the middle, so I can really hit him with a big fee, because he has no choice and really can't get another person to take over at this point." This is a greedy attitude. While clients may feel pressured enough to agree to this arrangement, they'll know you're taking advantage of them. They'll resent it. And they'll tell others what you did. The extra fee you gain on this one job isn't worth all that negative publicity.

On the other hand, what if a client says, "No, I don't agree that a new contract is called for. You did a lousy job, I don't like it, and I don't care what the contract says, I'm not going to pay you. Redo the job or you will never see a cent from me!"?

At this point, the amount of money you have collected determines whether you can negotiate from a position of weakness or strength. If you've collected half the fee and done only a third of the work, you can take a strong position. Tell the client that the changes are not covered by the original contract, show where and why, and if he or she doesn't relent, refuse to do more work. You can do this comfortably since you've already been paid in full for all work done to date.

On the other hand, if you didn't get money up front, but you did half the job, you may rightfully be worrying at this point about whether you will ever get paid. Only you can judge whether the client is sincere and this is merely a dispute over perceived quality of the work—or if the client is a deadbeat intent on cheating you.

One solution might be to agree to do the changes at no cost, providing the client makes a progress payment for work done to date. If such a progress bill goes unpaid, you have a good reason not to proceed with the job, and instead begin the collection process.

PROBLEM 4: THE CLIENT IS LATE PAYING YOUR BILL

This does not mean that clients don't intend to pay you, although that is a possibility. More likely, they either forgot or just are slow payers. Many Fortune 500 firms routinely pay invoices in sixty or ninety days, despite the fact that you wrote "net ten days" or "net thirty days" on your bill. It's just a fact of life you'll have to live with.

And it's the same if you sell your services to the general public. Many people buy things they cannot afford to pay for at time of purchase, hoping to make payment later. A few buy things they never intend to pay for at all.

What happens when a reasonable time has passed and you still have not received payment? Then you begin your collection cycle.

This is a series of letters and phone calls designed to remind clients that the bill is still unpaid and to get them to pay it. The first contact is a letter. In this first letter, never get angry or accuse clients of deliberately cheating you. It should be written as a reminder, with the assumption that clients *meant* to pay you but simply forgot. This prods them to pay without making them feel guilty.

Your goal is *not* to put clients in a compromising position, or to prove that you are right and they are wrong, but simply to get the check they owe you.

For example:

date

Mr. Bill Smith
Anytown, USA

Dear Mr. Smith:

Just a reminder . . .
. . . that payment for the Ajax Security System we installed in your home on March 4, 1991 (see copy of invoice attached) is now past due.
Would you please send a check today? A self-addressed stamped reply envelope is enclosed for your convenience.
Regards,

John Smith, President
Ajax Security, Inc.

Another way to get bills paid faster is to either give a small discount for prompt payment (for example, "deduct $X if paid within ten days") or charge the current legal interest rate for overdue bills (for example, "2½ percent service charge for bills thirty days or more past due"). If you intend to charge interest on late payments, you must state that intention in your contract or agreement with clients.

Should you *not* press hard to collect an unpaid invoice, on the theory that you don't want to anger or offend clients who can potentially give you a lot more work? No. As collections expert Milt Pierce points out, "The client who owes you money will not give you more work." The only way to get further business from these clients is to get them current on their account. Only when they no longer owe you will they feel comfortable enough to pick up the phone and call you again.

For more information on collecting bills from clients, contact Milt Pierce, President, The Collection Institute of America, 162 W. 54th Street, Dept. SS, New York, NY 10019, (212) 246-2325.

PROBLEM 5: THE CLIENT REFUSES TO PAY THE BILL—OR CAN'T PAY THE BILL

After an intensive collection effort, you still haven't been paid. This means that clients either can't or don't intend to pay your bill.

Now is the time to write a strong letter saying that if you do not receive payment within two weeks, you will have no choice but to take legal action to collect the bill. This means court.

Send this letter certified mail, return receipt requested, to prove that clients received it. If you don't hear back, wait the two weeks, then send a second letter stating the same thing.

If you still don't hear from the clients, hire a collection agency or attorney or take the clients to court. The more paperwork you have—a signed contract, a purchase order—the better your chances of collection.

Remember, always make a photocopy of the first check you receive from any client. This ensures that you have a record of their business bank account on file, making it easier to collect any judgment you obtain against them. Getting a retainer up front from any new client ensures that you always have such a check on file.

PROBLEM 6: THE CLIENT PRESENTS YOU WITH AN UNREASONABLE DEADLINE

First, what is a reasonable deadline? From your point of view, it is enough time to do the job properly without being rushed. This means doing the job at your normal pace without working overtime or putting off other work to accommodate the client.

Clients often do not understand that they are not your only client or that you have other work. They will often give a deadline regardless of your schedule and act as if it's a given that you will accept it.

The key to solving this problem is *client education*. I begin early, addressing this point in my sales literature, explaining that (1) my normal turnaround time is two to three weeks, but (2) sometimes if I am busy the waiting period may be four to eight weeks or longer, and (3) if I *do* take on their job, I promise to get it done by the deadline date we agree to.

However, I make it a point *not* to promise that I will always be able to do a project no matter what the deadline.

The definition of a "rush" job varies with the service provider—and the client. For me, in my copywriting business, two to three weeks is an acceptable deadline, although I will try to push for three to four weeks on difficult or complex assignments. I *rarely* promise anything in less than two weeks, and a one-week turnaround is an extreme rush.

Yet I know of others in my business who consider one week or less standard. One service provider even advertises twenty-four-hour turnaround. I guess the firm is just not terribly busy and so quick turnaround is the advantage they sell and advertise.

Obviously the typical deadline figures vary from business to business.

Cam Foote, who presents seminars on selling creative services, points out that service providers usually choose to stress one of three advantages in selling and marketing their services: price, speed, or quality.

As for myself, I sell quality, expertise, and the ability to write copy that generates results. I do not emphasize low price or fast turnaround, because I offer neither.

Okay. Let's say you get a phone call, and it is a client or prospect with an assignment. Only it's a rush assignment. How do you handle it?

If you are not terribly busy, then you might agree to handle the job, either at your normal fee or with an added charge for rush service.

But make sure clients understand you are bending over backward to accommodate them. Don't let them know you are sitting around doing nothing. Clients want to hire service providers who are busy and successful, and you must project such an image.

If you are too busy to take on the project, and the call is from a *prospect* (someone who has not hired you yet) rather than a regular client, simply say "It sounds interesting and I'd like to handle it. However, I am booked solid for the next eight weeks [or however long it is until you could do the job].

If you can wait until then, great. If not, I'll have to pass."
Then try to schedule the job for some future date, if the
person is willing to wait.

Whether clients will be willing to wait or will go to someone else to get the job done right away depends on what
business you are in.

General contractors, home remodelers, and carpenters,
for example, find they can schedule most jobs many months
in advance. After all, adding a porch, deck, or family room is
usually not an emergency. Plumbers, on the other hand, find
that most jobs involve servicing the client on an as-soon-as-
possible basis.

However, just because it's standard in your field for clients to demand immediate service doesn't mean they won't
make an exception for you if they perceive you are worth the
wait. For example, most freelance copywriters would agree
that when clients call, they want the ad or brochure written
right away.

But my friend Richard Armstrong, who has developed a
reputation as one of the top political and fund-raising direct-
mail writers in the country, regularly tells clients he is too
busy to write their sales letters now but would be happy to
schedule them later.

"About half go somewhere else," says Richard. "But
amazingly, half agree to it, and these days I am usually
booked three to four months in advance."

A more serious problem is getting a call from an ongoing
client (rather than a new prospect) who asks you to handle a
rush job when you are already overloaded with work. Obviously, you want to maintain the client's goodwill, and clients
do not like it when you turn them down. Yet you should not—
you cannot—take on more work than you can realistically
handle.

In this case, the first step is to see whether the deadline is
real (that is, it exists because of an actual event, such as a
sales meeting or trade show date) or artificial (the date was

picked arbitrarily or because the client wants the job done "as soon as possible").

To ascertain this, ask the client, "You say you absolutely must have the report from me in one week, is that right? Well, let me ask a question. What happens if you have it in two weeks instead of one week?"

The client pauses, thinks about it, realizes that it makes no difference, and so you get a one-week deadline extension.

Or you compromise and agree to a ten-day deadline.

Only about 10 percent of the time will the deadline be real and inflexible. And if that's the situation, you have a difficult decision.

If you fear the client will react negatively if you refuse, and if you can do the job even though it means working nights and weekends, you may decide for the sake of the relationship to go ahead and do it. However, you can compensate for this by charging a higher fee, and also by pointing out (without making too big a deal of it) that this is an exception to your policy and that you are doing the client a favor. Let the client know that only for *him* or *her* would you agree to such a deadline, and that if anyone else called you would have said no.

PROBLEM 7: THE CLIENT WON'T SIGN YOUR CONTRACT

As I discuss in chapter 12, you should always have a contract, proposal, letter of agreement, purchase order, or other piece of paper that serves as a written record of your agreement with clients. And it should always be returned to you with a client's signature (and preferably an advance check) before you begin the job.

In a recent seminar, a freelance graphic artist complained to me, "The idea of a contract is all well and good, but most of my work is rush. By the time I write the letter, send

it to the client, have them sign it, and get them to mail it
back, the deadline for the job has passed."

This is a psychological weapon clients use. The argument
is "Yes, I will sign your contract. But the job is a rush, and I
don't expect you to hold me up on formalities. So begin
without your contract and I'll get it to you—trust me."

One partial solution to this problem is simply not to take on
rush jobs, as explained above under problem 6. Don't do jobs
in two to three days—do them in two to three weeks—so
there is plenty of time to get the paperwork before you begin.

Another solution is to have a standard contract form you
can fill out and mail to clients immediately. This is less time-
consuming than drawing up a new letter of agreement for
each client.

One more good idea: If most of your clients are businesses, buy a fax machine. Having a fax machine virtually
eliminates any client excuses.

Nowadays my response to a client who says there isn't
time to sign a contract is: "As we agreed, I need the signed
contract before we can begin. So give me your fax number. I
will fax you a contract in a few minutes. Sign it and fax it
back to me, and I'll have what I need to begin today." If I
need an advance check, I tell the client to send the check
overnight Federal Express or Express Mail. With the fax
machine, there is no reason on earth why clients can't receive, sign, and return to you the signed contract within
minutes after your phone call.

PROBLEM 8: THE CLIENT'S SPOUSE— OR PEOPLE ON THE CLIENT'S STAFF— ARE UNCOOPERATIVE

As a service provider, you cannot operate in a vacuum. Often
you must work with clients and others in their organization
or their family to get the job done.

What do you do when people on the client's staff or members of the client's family are uncooperative?

First, don't lose your cool. Even though the person may not be directly involved with the project, a complaint about you could create problems in the relationship.

You see, that person is a part of the family or company team, while you are just an outsider. If someone has to take a fall, a manager will find it easier to blame or dismiss an outside consultant rather than an employee. A husband will defend his wife if there is a dispute with the decorator, even if the wife is wrong.

So, treat everyone in the client's family or business organization with politeness and respect—even if they don't deserve it. If someone gives you a hard time, displaying anger is not the solution.

If someone gives me a hard time, my rule is to treat them with cool, detached professionalism. Have minimal contact with them—only as much as is needed to get the job done. The rest of the time, simply ignore them.

When dealing with business clients, I've found that the fax machine is a great tool for dealing with people I can't stand to speak with in person or over the phone. Instead of having to put up with their obnoxious personalities, I simply fax my communication and let them do the same. Dealing with them is easier if I don't have to hear their voice.

Finally, if someone is a total roadblock, you have no choice but to let your client know this. Don't do it emotionally; simply inform the client that Joe or John or Mary is not being cooperative. Suggest alternatives, such as another person you can work with or another way to proceed. Often the client knows John or Mary is a troublemaker, appreciates your saying so, and is all too happy to get John or Mary out of the picture.

PROBLEM 9: THE CLIENT CANCELS THE
JOB MIDWAY

Does your contract have a clause that says what happens if
clients decide to cancel the project? If not, you might want to
add one. A standard cancellation clause reads as follows:

> XYZ Company will have the right to terminate this
> agreement at any time upon notice to me. In such an
> event, you will compensate me for the hours actually
> worked on the project through the date and time of can-
> cellation, plus any out-of-pocket expenses incurred up to
> that time.

This means that if clients cancel on Tuesday at 9:00 A.M.,
you have the right to bill them for all labor and materials up
to that instant. To be fair, you should, in exchange, turn over
to clients any and all work completed to date.

But if clients call to cancel, ask why. Often clients can
blow a frustration or misunderstanding concerning one
small aspect of the job out of proportion, and in their panic
they simply decide to cancel the job before things get worse.

I was recently hired by a client to write a 1,000-word
research report on a specific topic. The contract specified
that I would base the report on ten to twelve articles the
client would provide me.

After I did an outline on the topic based on these articles,
the client called to cancel the job. When I asked why, she
replied that the information did not seem interesting or
timely enough. I pointed out that instead of canceling, she
could retain me to research the topic further, and that the
research fee would be only an additional $300. She was de-
lighted to hear this—apparently she didn't realize I could do
such research—and immediately decided to go forward with
the project.

In many instances, the reason for the cancellation is some

minor item that you can quickly and easily correct. If you patiently and courteously explain this to clients, and promise to give your immediate attention to this matter, they will typically breathe a sigh of relief . . . and rescind their order to cancel the job.

PROBLEM 10: THE PROJECT IS MUCH MORE WORK THAN YOU ANTICIPATED

This happens a lot: In your eagerness to clinch the assignment, you underestimate the amount of work involved in order to quote clients a lower fee. Then, once you start work, you discover the project is much *more* involved than you anticipated, and you are not making much money on it.

What to do? Again, this is one of those problems best solved by preventing it from happening in the first place. So when you do estimates and quote fees, make sure you are being realistic.

If anything, make your quotation a little *high* to protect yourself from unexpected complications and snags.

Your only hope for raising your fee after you've signed the contract and begun the work is when you can legitimately claim that clients have increased or changed the scope of the project.

For example, you agreed to write a single sales letter for $1,000, and during the job a client decides he needs a second version aimed at a different market. You certainly are entitled to charge an additional fee for creating the second version.

Or, if in finishing a roof, you find rotting beams that should be replaced. Obviously replacing them will cost extra.

You should then send a separate contract or "change order" amending your original agreement to the client for signature. Have the signed copy on file before you proceed with this new work.

As always—get it in writing!

PROBLEM 11: THE CLIENT PESTERS YOU

Most of us who are self-employed or own our own small firms choose this life-style because we work best without supervision. It's difficult for many of us to deal with clients who want to keep a tight rein on us, demand constant progress reports, and phone or visit us far more than is necessary.

Freelancer Marybeth Lareau tells of one situation where a client who hired her to do a big and important project called her an average of fifteen times a day, with the calls starting at 8:00 A.M. and continuing until 11:00 PM. "Needless to say, it was impossible to concentrate on the work," she reports.

Finally, after three weeks of constant calls, Lareau laid down boundaries by telling the client what hours she would take calls—and when she would not (something she had never done before). She also explained that both parties would save time if they were on the phone less. She said that while she was not always available to answer calls, she would return them as promptly as possible.

The result? After about a week, the situation improved dramatically, and the project was completed on schedule. The lesson? "Put down boundaries quickly with clients whose demands are unreasonable," says Lareau. "It makes them respect you."

ALWAYS PART ON GOOD TERMS

While you can solve these problems most of the time, occasionally you will reach a point where you, the client, or both of you decide to end the relationship.

Donald Dell, author of *Minding Other People's Business* (New York: Villard Books, 1989), advises service providers to always end any client relationship on good terms. "Contact the client, tell him or her you're sorry it didn't work out, wish him or her good luck, and say that your door is always open for the client in the future," writes Dell. He notes that a bitter or disgruntled former client who badmouths you can offset ten people who may say great things about you.

Also, some clients who end relationships may in fact want to hire you again months or years from now. They might change jobs or companies and need your service. Or maybe after trying other people, they realize how good you really were. You can get their business again, but only if you parted amiably. If you were rude and "burned your bridges" by insulting or arguing with the client, then you are not likely get his or her business back again.

And above all, when a client leaves you and you lose the business, try not to take it so hard. "It is not what happens to you," writes numerologist Kathy Bury, "what counts is how you handle it."

CHAPTER FIFTEEN

The Key to Successful Service Selling

Let's take a look at some of the things you can do to "go that extra mile" to make your clients happy and satisfied.

BUILDING THE CLIENT RELATIONSHIP

Your goal should be to win clients, not assignments. Although it's always good to get an assignment, your income will grow larger when you build a "stable" of regular clients who keep coming back to you again and again.

Here are some things you can do to encourage this type of ongoing relationship:

1. Seek out clients who can provide a steady flow of assignments rather than just an occasional project.
2. Go out of your way to please these clients and do a good job for them.
3. Build a personal relationship. Visit with the client now and then. An occasional cup of coffee or lunch out wouldn't hurt.

4. Participate in client activities. Accept any invitations you receive to attend Christmas parties or similar events. Make sure you say hello to the client at conferences and other industry events. Drop by clients' booths if they're exhibiting at a local trade show.
5. Send clients copies of pertinent articles, news clippings, and competitors' ads. Keep in touch by mail.
6. Pick up the phone and say hello every now and then. Just say hello—don't beg for new business.
7. Cultivate relationships with as many people in the client organization as you can. Even people you think are unimportant can have a major say over whether you get hired.
8. Be especially considerate of secretaries, assistants, and receptionists. They wield a lot of influence over who gets through to the boss—and who doesn't. And one day they might be promoted and become your client.
9. Never be rude or lose your temper. Always be patient, courteous, and friendly.
10. Remember that clients have all the power. Clients can choose not to continue working with you at any time, for any reason . . . or for no reason.

BE HELPFUL

No matter how great you are, how busy you are, how successful, or how much money you make, always come across as someone who wants to be helpful, not someone who is a snob and full of himself. This applies to all facets of your business.

Let me tell you two stories that illustrate how a particular situation can be handled—the right way and the wrong way.

A friend of mine who is one of the country's most in-demand direct-mail writers received a call one day from a prospect. He was interested in my friend's service and requested the writer's information package to be sent.

The prospect had an immediate job and mentioned that he wanted to get the information as soon as possible.

My friend has a full-time secretary, but she was out that day. He told the prospect, "Well, I'll be happy to send it, but it will take a few days, as my secretary is out."

The prospect, obviously annoyed, said, "Let me make a suggestion . . . *why don't you do it yourself?*"

"He was right, of course," my friend said. "I was trying to emphasize what a big shot I was. I even told him that with my time billing at $400 per hour, I didn't do that type of menial work.

"This just turned him off, and rightly so. I was acting like a snob, not like someone you'd want to do business with. If this were to happen again today, I'd promise to send the package right away—and do it myself."

Contrast this with the following story. I had requested information from a company on its services. The owner called me to follow up and ask a few questions, so he could send me the proper materials. I asked him how long it would take to get, as I was eager to buy.

"I'll put together that material right now and it will be in the mail in twenty minutes, Mr. Bly," he replied cheerily.

This was years ago, but I never forgot the way he phrased it. By saying "I" instead of "we" or "my secretary," he took personal responsibility for servicing my needs. And I was struck by the mention of "twenty minutes"—this phrase put a powerful visual image in my mind of this man preparing with care a customized package for me, rushing it down to the post office, and mailing it himself—even though that's probably not what happened.

But the point is to always make the customer or client think you care—something most easily accomplished by actually caring and then behaving or acting as if you do.

And sending out your package quickly is a good example.

Let me stress this—inquiries should always be followed up quickly. Phone calls should be returned the same day—within a few hours, if possible. Brochures or information kits should be mailed the same day you get the request, or at the latest, the next day. And a client who needs an estimate, proposal, or price quotation should receive it within twenty-four to forty-eight hours . . . the sooner, the better.

One year, over the Christmas vacation, my assistant took the week off. I received one inquiry, which I thought wouldn't result in business, and so I let it sit until she returned.

We finally mailed the package, but it went out a week after the inquiry was received—which is about a week later than I normally send it. When I called the prospect, he told me, "Bob, yours was the best package. You are obviously the most expert of the copywriters whose information I requested, and I sure wish I could have hired you for this project, but it took a long time to get your material—in fact, yours was the last package I received—and so I hired someone else for the job."

The job turned out to be a $4,500 assignment to write three sales letters. Ouch! It hurt losing a job I would have gotten over my competitors if I hadn't been too lazy to put a few sheets together and take them to the post office.

That's a bitter lesson to learn after eight years in the freelance writing business—but believe me, I learned it. Now I treat all inquiries seriously and fulfill them immediately. That's the way to do it.

CONFLICTS

Most clients will prefer to work with you on a by-the-project basis. Some, however, will seek to establish a closer working relationship—they'll want something longer-term, more permanent sounding than project by project, but they won't have any idea of what this is and will turn to you for guidance.

I tell these prospects, "It isn't necessary to lock into a monthly retainer, an annual contract, or anything of that nature. You don't have to make me any promises or pay me extra fees to get the best service and attention from me— that's what you get anyway, on each and every project I handle for you. And since I value your business, I will always give your work top priority."

This seems to satisfy most business prospects. However, a few may raise the issue of *conflicts*—that is, they don't want you to work with firms they consider competitors, firms in their same line of business.

Let common sense be your guide here. Obviously if General Motors asks you to give a one-day seminar to six of their employees, you can't agree not to accept a lucrative five-figure training assignment from Amtrak on the theory that they are both in the transportation business.

On the other hand, if your town has two local banks, and you do all the advertising for one of the banks, it would probably be wrong for you to accept work from the other bank while you are still working for the first one—even though you may not have a formal contract. It would, however, be okay to work for the second if the first bank clearly no longer intended to use you anymore.

A few clients have asked me to sign agreements saying I wouldn't work for their competitors for a specified period of time—usually one or two years—after doing their assignment. This is acceptable as long as the language in the contract defines the competitor in a narrow sense.

For example, one client who asked me to do this sells expensive PC software used by bankers and investors for financial analysis of real estate deals involving the purchase of large apartment buildings, shopping centers, and office complexes. Obviously I could not sign an agreement saying I would not work for any other firm selling PC software. I do a lot of work in that area and would not sign anything preventing me from working in such a broad field.

I *did* sign an agreement saying I would not work, for one year, for any other firm selling PC software for financial analysis of real estate deals involving multiple partners buying office complexes or apartment buildings.

As there were only two other companies selling such software, and I don't rush out to a client's competition offering to do work for them after working for the client, I was more than comfortable with signing this agreement.

DO WHAT YOU WANT TO DO (WITHIN REASON)

Every couple of weeks I get a call from a service provider who says "My small firm specializes in doing X and Y, but the client wants me to handle A, B, C, and D also. Must I do it?"

The answer is no.

One of the main reasons to become an independent service provider is to do work you enjoy and avoid things you don't like or aren't comfortable doing.

As an advertising manager, I enjoyed planning advertising campaigns and writing the copy. And so these are the services I offer to my clients. I hated getting brochures produced, placing ad space, proofreading mechanicals, or supervising print production. So I simply refuse to do these things.

Will this create difficulties for you? No. As a one-person business, you offer those services you want to offer. If a particular prospect wants something different, let him or her go elsewhere. There are more than enough clients out there who want exactly what you offer and are happy to handle the rest themselves or get help elsewhere.

I do, however, find I can increase my value to the client if I can assist them in finding competent people to handle all the

related and ancillary tasks that I don't do. For this reason, I
have assembled a network of other freelancers and vendors
who handle things that I cannot do. Whenever something
comes along that I don't do, I refer the client or prospect to
one of the people in the network.

I benefit because I have helped clients instead of turning
them away, and they will remember me favorably for that.
And clients benefit and feel comfortable hiring me to do just
the portion I want to handle, because I have instantly solved
their problem of getting the rest of the job done.

I do not charge a fee for these referrals and accept no
money from the people I give referrals to (or from clients
for making the referral). I also do not pay other people to
refer prospects to me—instead, I reward referrals with
referrals back to them. Some people want to pay or receive a fee for accepting or giving a referral. To me this
only makes life complicated, and I don't get involved in it
as a rule.

I do, however, always send a thank-you note promptly to
anyone who gives me a referral. And people who give me
good or frequent referrals also receive a thoughtful but inexpensive gift—usually an autographed copy of one of my
books, or perhaps a basket of fruit.

GIVE CREDIT WHERE CREDIT IS DUE

Many service providers have big egos. They love to come in,
do the job, and take all the credit for work well done.

But do you *deserve* all the praise?

What about your client, the corporate executive who is
stuck with all the unglamorous details of getting the thing
approved and produced?

Or the assistant, who runs around the company gathering
information you request?

Or the company's chief engineer, who took time out of his or her busy schedule to explain how widgets work so you could design an attractive widget package for them?

Or the secretary, who was always cordial and got you coffee when you wanted it?

Make sure you thank these people and treat them well. And try to give them credit whenever possible.

For instance, when the advertising manager compliments you on the ad campaign your agency designed to promote their new word processing program, say "Thanks, but Bill (the software programmer) made it easy with that great demo he gave me."

When the company president says how pleased she is with the new redesigned lobby, remind her that it was your client, the president's assistant, who suggested the initial design concept and even picked out the wallpaper.

In short, always thank people for their help, praise them when they deserve praise, and make them look good to their colleagues and superiors. Don't hog the glory all for yourself. Give credit where credit is due. Even if they weren't that helpful, don't criticize what they did wrong, but go out of your way to praise them for what they did *right*. This is not only fair but it also ensures gratitude and a long, profitable relationship with clients.

THANK YOU'S AND BUSINESS GIFTS

When someone does you a favor, always send a thank-you note. A brief one- or two-sentence letter on your letterhead is best. Because so few people in business bother to send thank-you notes today, the other person will notice your letter and remember your courtesy.

I spend five to ten minutes a day writing thank-you and "keep-in-touch" notes to clients, prospects, colleagues, and friends in business. This activity has always paid off in improved client relations and superior goodwill.

If the person getting your thank-you note did something out of the ordinary and really fantastic for you, you might consider sending an inexpensive but fun gift. I keep several mail-order catalogs in a file specifically for this purpose. These mail-order firms wrap and send the gift with a card for you, eliminating the need to go to a store, pick out a gift, take it home, wrap it, and mail it.

Gourmet foods, such as Wolferman's English muffins and jams, or Harry and David's fruits or cakes, or a cheese package, are usually appreciated—almost everyone likes to receive these things.

As to timing, your gift will have the least impact at Christmas because everyone else is also sending the client a gift at Christmas. It will be much more appreciated and noticed if you send it at a nonholiday time, such as the client's birthday or as a thank you or just a gesture of goodwill.

Also, a gift sent at "random" is viewed as something special and clients won't expect it to become a regular thing. But once clients get one Christmas gift from you, they'll expect one every year . . . and that can be costly.

DEVELOP YOUR "PEOPLE SKILLS"

What has hurt me more than anything else in my service business is my lack of patience and tolerance in dealing with people, a problem it took me many, many years to remedy. (And even today I'm far from where I should be!)

I used to think that if I did great work that pleased clients and sold their products and programs, then the rest didn't matter. Boy, was I wrong! The client service aspects of this business—how you deal with and treat people (clients, prospects, employees of client and prospect firms, and other vendors dealing with clients)—is at least as important in keeping clients satisfied as the quality of your work—and may be more important.

Put yourself in the clients' shoes. They are busy. They have a lot of responsibility. They need to hire people—freelancers, consultants, ad agencies, printers, and other vendors—who make their life *easier*, not more difficult.

Let me give you an example. A client once called at 5:00 P.M. and said, "Bob, the copy you sent me is fine, but I'm going into a meeting with our production manager and the copy needs to be retyped in a forty-character width. It would take us too long to retype it here; can you just reformat it on your computer and fax it to me? I know it's extra work, but I would really appreciate it."

Should I have done it? Technically, no. I'm hired to write and think; I'm not a typist. Did I do it? Yes. I decided that my client really needed me to be flexible here and that by helping him in a tight spot, I was showing him that I really valued him and was not just there to squeeze all the money I could out of his ad agency.

It took me about twenty minutes to do what he asked. Did I bill him? No. In fact, he later said, "Send a bill." I said, "It's on the house." At the time, I was charging $120 an hour, so twenty minutes work would have cost him $40. Believe me, I bought a lot more than $40 worth of goodwill that day.

If you have ever been on the other side of the desk, working as a *client* hiring service providers, you know that every word I'm telling you is true. There are times when clients truly need you to cooperate and not argue with them and just do as they ask, even though it's not exactly in your job description.

At those times, pitch in and be the helpful, caring friend.

It will pay you back many times over in goodwill and new assignments.

To give you another example: Fred Ellis, a client of mine, runs his own small ad agency. Years ago he had a project that I was not qualified to handle. I recommended a freelancer I knew of who had the credentials to do it.

To make a long story short, the freelancer did some concept work, but the agency lost the account and was never paid by the client. Fred, one of the most honest and forthright people you will ever meet in this business, promised to pay the freelancer's big bill but asked for a little extra time, suggesting payments spread over a few months.

The freelancer exploded in anger. He demanded his payment instantly, and from then on constantly called and sent letters, even though he was getting regular payments from my friend.

Needless to say, Fred would never hire that freelancer again. And although he understood the freelancer's concerns about payment, he resented the way he was treated. Years later, that freelancer's name came up again as someone to handle work for a certain client sitting at my table at an advertising luncheon.

"Oh, no, we would never use him," said the client. "Did you hear about the way he behaved with Fred Ellis?" Although Fred had not gone about deliberately badmouthing the freelancer, Fred was well known and people sought his opinion. When they asked about the freelancer, Fred could only relate what happened. And the freelancer lost a lot of business.

I guess the golden rule applies as much or more to business as it does to anything else: "Do unto your clients and prospects as you would have your clients and prospects do unto you."

Put yourself in the clients' shoes. Treat them as you would like to be treated if you were the client. If you do, things will go well most of the time.

DO NOT DISCRIMINATE AGAINST SMALL CLIENTS OR ACCOUNTS

While it makes sense to give your biggest clients and most lucrative accounts extraordinary service and attention, it doesn't make sense to neglect your smaller accounts or to treat these less important clients with contempt or indifference.

Small accounts expect to be treated every bit as well as your biggest account. And they should be. They are paying good money for your services—perhaps (to them) a lot of money. They don't deserve to be treated as second-class citizens.

Recently a small client I had written only a few short pieces of copy for called *months* after the last job had been done. The firm was finally ready to go to press with the brochure and had a question about how to hyphenate a word.

Now, having been paid months ago and being under tremendous pressure when she called, I could have put her off. I was busy with a rush job for my largest account and didn't have much time to spare. And I almost told her so.

But instead, I took the time to look up the grammatical rule in a reference book.

When I gave her the answer, however, I could tell she wasn't satisfied that it was accurate. So, after she hung up, I photocopied the appropriate pages from the book and faxed them to her.

She called back immediately. As I suspected, she hadn't been convinced of my answer at first. But now she was. She thanked me for taking the trouble to fax the pages so she could have them as "backup" in case someone questioned her decision—and added, "This is such a good grammar book. Do you know where I could get a copy?"

I couldn't help being a bit self-satisfied when I answered, "Well, Jan, the name of the book is *Technical Writing: Struc-*

ture, Standards, and Style. It's published by McGraw-Hill, and *I am the author of the book!*"

"How marvelous!" she exclaimed. "Can I buy one from you?"

"Jan," I replied, "I will be happy to send an autographed hardcover copy in today's mail, and for you there is no charge. Enjoy!"

The book costs $12 and I get them from the publisher for $6 at the author's discount price. I think $6 is a reasonable sum to spend to help ensure that a client will remember me favorably for the next $2,400 assignment. Do you agree?

One other story about giving excellent client service, and then I'll move on. Years ago another small ad agency client had me accompany him to a client meeting in the Midwest. He was to do most of the talking, I was there primarily so the client could "meet the writer" and so I could get a thorough briefing (yes, I was paid to be there).

As the client struggled with his luggage and bags, I grabbed the slide projector and a suitcase. "No, you don't have to do that," he protested. "Let me help you," I insisted.

I worked for that client for years until he sold his agency to another, larger agency in the South. At the end of our relationship, he told me, "You gave us great copy and ideas for many years and helped us with a lot of clients, but the thing I always remembered was your willingness to pitch in and help with something as mundane as carrying equipment. That's something you don't see from copywriters, art directors, and consultants too much."

A simple gesture, but one that made a big impression in his mind—and put a lot of extra dollars in my pocket. Especially knowing he was one of the smaller accounts on my client roster.

And this reminds me of something sales trainer Tom Winninger tells his audiences: "Be good—not great."

What he means is: Clients want to hire people who are cooperative, helpful, who make life easy for them, and who help them do their jobs better and look like heroes to their employers.

Some service providers want to be recognized as great craftspeople or creative geniuses, and seek a standing ovation every time they complete a project.

Genius is fine, but what clients want is a service provider who is *consistently* good—one who delivers, reliably and on time, on project after project.

Don't worry about being great. Instead, focus on being consistently good.

GETTING NEW BUSINESS FROM OLD CLIENTS

Chapter 2 presented you with many techniques for getting sales leads. But don't concentrate all your sales effort on getting new clients. Too many service providers neglect another profitable source of income: getting new assignments from *existing* clients.

How do you get your clients to turn over more of their work to you?

1. *Make your services available to many people within the client company.*

Typically, a service provider is hired by—and works for—one individual at a corporation. But the company may have many managers, each with his or her own requirement for your type of service. If you can find out who these people are, and let them know about your services, they might hire you. You would have an advantage over other vendors in that the client company is already a satisfied user of your services.

One of my clients, the advertising manager for a large industrial equipment manufacturer, hires me to write ads and sales brochures. While sitting in the lobby of their building, I noticed a slick color magazine aimed at the company's employees and customers. I had never seen it before.

When I inquired, the ad manager said he had nothing to do with it; the magazine was produced by the public relations manager. Would it be okay if I sent my information kit to the public relations manager? Not only was it okay, but the ad manager took me to the PR manager's office right then and made introductions. I soon got an assignment to contribute to the magazine. "I would have introduced you sooner," said the ad manager later, "but I didn't realize you did articles as well as ads and brochures."

Don't be shy about asking clients who else in their companies might be able to use your services.

2. *Let the client know what you can do.*

Some clients may have need for a broad range of services yet hire you for one specific type of assignment. Perhaps they have other resources that handle these other types of tasks.

At the beginning, you should concentrate on what clients hire you to do. Do a great job on every project. Dazzle clients with your ability. Then, once you are established in their minds as the service provider who gets the job done, you can bring up the subject of helping in other areas and talk about your experience. Many times a client will say, "Oh, I didn't know you did filmscripts. It just so happens I have to produce a film on our new product. Would you be interested in writing it for us?" And another assignment is yours.

3. *Send samples.*

You don't want to appear too high pressure or badger clients about giving you other types of assignments. A good way of letting clients know what you can do in other areas is to send samples or photos of jobs completed for other clients (as long as the material is not proprietary and showing it does not violate a client confidence).

You can attach a short cover note that just says hi or gives a brief description of the project. For example: "Bill: Here's a feature article I ghosted for Sumitomo Electronics. Published in September's *Electronic News*. Has generated 500 responses—so far. Can I do the same for you? Regards, Frank."

You can also send letters of testimonial from one manager within the client company to other managers who could also use your services.

CHAPTER SIXTEEN

Selling Your Services in a Recession

No matter how successful you become at this business of selling services, don't get too big an ego. If you do, you'll only fall that much harder—sooner or later. That's what happened to me in early 1990.

Sure, I had heard the reports of a softening economy. And many of my clients, colleagues, and friends were complaining that business was slow. But things had been going swimmingly for me for a number of years . . . and so I didn't pay too much attention to the rumors and forecasts of recession and depression.

Then it happened. Or rather, *they* happened: a series of events with a devastating impact on my business:

1. The economy did indeed soften. If 1990 was not in fact a recession, it was certainly the phase *preceding* recession.

2. The advertising/promotion business was especially hard hit. Service firms nationwide reported a dramatic business slowdown. And—slowly—I began to feel the effect.

3. My two biggest clients stopped giving me business. One—an ad agency—had no work to farm out. The second—the advertising manager of an electronics firm—quit his job. And he had personally been responsible for giving me $20,000 in assignments in the past four months alone.
4. After several years of steady publication, a monthly column I wrote for *Direct Marketing* magazine was canceled by the publisher during a revamping of the magazine's format. This had been a major source of new business leads for me.

After these events, things changed for me—dramatically:

- The quantity of new business leads I received each month declined by 75 percent.
- The *quality* of the leads I was getting was terrible. Most of the firms calling me were small companies that were not the type of firms I handled and that certainly could not afford my services.
- Of the decent leads I did get, I was not able to close the sales. At one point I lost seven jobs in a row! In each case I lost the job because the fee I quoted—fees I had been getting months earlier with no problem—were considered too high.
- Clients were doing fewer projects . . . smaller projects . . . and budget was becoming more and more a concern. Instead of doing $5,000 jobs, I was getting $500 and $1,000 jobs—when I was getting them at all.

The lessons I learned?

First, don't get cocky. No matter how successful and busy you are, your business can take a downturn. Quickly. And quite unexpectedly. Take it from me.

Second, ongoing marketing and selling efforts are vi-

tal to your continued business success. I had neglected my
marketing . . . hadn't done mailings in *years*, in fact . . .
so when existing sources of leads dried up, I had no
other mechanisms in place for producing new business in a
hurry and avoiding a lull. Don't you make this same
mistake.

Third, I learned not to give in to despair. Things can get
bad—but the wonderful thing about being in your own business is that you have the power to turn them around. If you
take appropriate actions—the right action aimed at the right
people at the right time with the right message—you *can*
turn them around and begin to generate sales leads and land
contracts again.

What actions should you take? That's the subject of this
chapter—to tell you the exact steps you can take to generate
more leads, close more sales, get new clients to hire you, and
get old clients to give you new projects—to overcome slow
periods or soft economies and make your business a success,
even when times are tough for others. I'll tell you how to do
all this in twelve easy-to-master steps.

RECESSION-FIGHTING STRATEGY 1:
REACTIVATE DORMANT ACCOUNTS

To reactivate a dormant account, you must contact past
clients—people you worked for at one time, but are not
actively working for now—and get them to do business
with you.

The quickest and easiest way to do this is to sit down with
your list of past clients, call them, say hello, and see what's
going on.

Don't make this a hard-sell call. Tell them, "Hi, it's Bob.
I'm calling just to check in and see how you're doing, since it's
been a few months since we last spoke." Ask them what's new

... how they're doing ... what's going on with their business, their home, or whatever portion of their life your service relates to.

You don't have to ask for work directly, but when you end the conversation, you might say something like "Well, it's been good talking with you. Keep in touch, and if there's anything I can ever help you with, don't hesitate to give me a call."

This lets them know you are interested in working with them again—*without* putting the pressure on them to give you an assignment right then and there.

If you are uncomfortable phoning, you can send a letter. As an "excuse" for writing, you can enclose a recent article you wrote, a sample of your work, or a photograph of your latest project. This accomplishes essentially the same goal—to recontact clients and remind them of your existence, services, and availability.

What kind of results will you get? It depends on whether you catch people with an immediate or upcoming project with which they need help. I'd say you could expect one project for every ten calls you make.

Warning: Don't call up and say "I'm not busy and need work right now; do you have any assignments?" This is a terrible approach—for two reasons.

First, clients feel pressure, feel they have to come up with an "excuse" why they haven't given you any work lately. This is uncomfortable—and awkward—for both of you.

Second, it makes you seem desperate, and you do *not* want to seem hungry or needy.

In fact, a key principle of all of these twelve strategies is always to make it seem that the purpose of your call is to serve clients better and more efficiently, not fill a gap in your slow work schedule. Always say you are calling to help *them* ... and not, as is really the case, because you are desperate and need the work.

RECESSION-FIGHTING STRATEGY 2:
REACTIVATE OLD LEADS

If you're like me, here's how you handle inquiries.

Someone calls. You send information. You call to follow up. The person doesn't respond. You call again. After that, you give up and forget about the lead.

But believe it or not, many of those leads you simply gave up on can be turned into profitable business for you . . . with just a little extra sales effort.

In fact, a study by Thomas Publishing Company reveals that most salespeople, regardless of the industry, give up too early. According to the study, 80 percent of sales to business are made on the fifth sales call, but only 10 percent of salespeople call more than three times.

So you have probably not followed up on leads diligently enough (for example, I almost never call more than twice), and the new business you need may already be right in your prospect files.

The best way to reactivate these old sales leads is to call them. Below is a script from an actual conversation I had with such a prospect:

ME: Dan, this is Bob Bly calling. About six months ago you had requested information on my direct-mail copywriting services.

PROSPECT: [disinterested] Yes, okay. I think I remember.

ME: Well, Dan, are you still using direct mail to sell your software packages by mail? [*Note*: I have asked him a question to which I know he will answer yes and that calls attention to his need for my service.]

PROSPECT: Yes, we are.

ME: Would you like me to send you some helpful article reprints that tell how to increase response to your direct-mail packages? [Again, I ask a question to which I know the prospect will answer yes, thus giving me permission to send him my sales materials.]

PROSPECT: That sounds interesting. Please send it. And could you also send me some samples of your work?

ME: Of course. Just one other question—are you planning a mailing now or in the next several months I might be able to help you with?

PROSPECT: Well, we're doing mailings all the time. We normally do all of them in house. We've been thinking of using an outside writer like you to create a mailing for us, but we haven't been able to come to a decision about it.

ME: I see. What information do you need from me to help you make that decision?

PROSPECT: Sending the samples and the articles will be enough.

ME: And what's the best way for me to follow up on this with you—would you prefer me to follow up by mail or by phone? [*Key Point*: I *don't* ask *if* I can follow up, because he might say he doesn't want me to. Instead, I ask *how* I should follow up; his only answer can be "mail" or "phone."]

PROSPECT: Give me a week or so to read your material, then call me.

ME: Great. Then I'll make a note to call you in two weeks.

You can use this script, modified to fit the circumstances, to reactivate old leads. I think it can be profitably used on prospects who have inquired within the last year or two. The best prospects, however, would probably be those who contacted you within the past six months.

I find that 25 to 50 percent of the prospects will encourage you to send information, and perhaps one or two out of ten will come through with an assignment.

RECESSION-FIGHTING STRATEGY 3:
HELP EXISTING CLIENTS CREATE NEW
ASSIGNMENTS FOR YOU

Normally, my clients come to me with assignments they want me to handle for them.

That's probably the way you get most of your business too, isn't it?

But if my existing clients *don't* come to me with projects, and I need work, I will call them up and suggest marketing ideas they can use—ideas that, if they go ahead with them, they will of course need me to implement for them.

Now, normally I encourage you not to give away your advice for free and to charge for this kind of consulting service. But if business is slow, there's nothing wrong with tossing out a few quick ideas—things that may be obvious to you and you didn't spend any time coming up with, but that will be extremely valuable to the client.

For instance, when one of my clients introduced a new service, I immediately suggested a marketing idea he liked, which resulted in a $2,500 copywriting assignment on the spot—a $2,500 assignment he would never have come up with on his own.

So when things are slow, and the clients aren't calling, you can call them and help them come up with assignments for you.

Key Point: Obviously, your approach is "Here is an idea that can help you, Mr. Client (and by the way, I'd be happy to handle it for you)."

Successful service providers give their clients good ideas from time to time, but they never beg for work.

RECESSION-FIGHTING STRATEGY 4:
GIVE A SUPERIOR LEVEL OF SERVICE
TO YOUR EXISTING CLIENTS

In a recession, or during other times when business is slow, you want to do everything you can to hold onto your existing clients—your "bread-and-butter" accounts.

The best way to hold onto your clients is to please them. As discussed, the best way to please clients is to give them not their money's worth, but *more* than their money's worth.

Now more than ever is the time to go the extra mile, give that little bit of extra service that can mean the difference between dazzling clients and just satisfying them.

The best protection against a downturn in new business is a client roster full of happy, satisfied clients—clients who give you a steady stream of continuing assignments that pay the rent and feed the family.

Cultivate your current clients. Nurture them. Serve them well.

RECESSION-FIGHTING STRATEGY 5:
QUOTE REASONABLE, AFFORDABLE FEES
IN BID SITUATIONS

If times are tough for you, they may be tough for other service providers, consultants, and entrepreneurs. Clients know this and may seek to take advantage by sending jobs out for multiple bids, where previously they might have come to you only.

And if there's a recession, cost of services will become more of a factor than it normally is, and clients and prospects will be unusually price-sensitive.

The solution is to bid competitively, but reasonably. If you are high priced to begin with, and you insist on getting top dollar, be prepared to lose out in some bidding situations—as I did in early 1990.

How should you price your services during a slow period or a down economy?

Don't instantly lower your prices to rock bottom. You may never be able to raise them again.

Also, you don't necessarily have to reduce your published fees . . . especially if your fee schedule presents a range.

You should, however, bid toward the middle or lower end of your published fee schedule range, rather than at the maximum.

For example, if you list $5,000 to $8,000 for an assignment, quote a price of $5,000 or $6,000, not $8,000—to make sure you are not charging way more than other service providers bidding on the job.

As a rule, during a recession you probably want to adjust your bids so they are 15 to 20 percent lower than what you would normally charge in a healthy economy. This gives the clients the break they are looking for, shows fairness on your part, but does not cost you much in the long run.

Note: Do *not* tell clients that the fee is a special reduced fee. Simply present it as your bid on the project. If clients and prospects sense you are cutting fees because you are losing jobs, they will take advantage and try to force your prices even lower. So keep your pricing tactics secret, and simply present the price as you normally would.

RECESSION-FIGHTING STRATEGY 6:
USE LOW-COST "ADD-ONS" TO GENERATE ADDITIONAL REVENUE

One way to generate some extra profitable business is to encourage clients to add on or expand existing assignments.

For instance, if a client is putting a new roof on her home, chances are she could use new gutters also. Offer to do both for a package price. For instance, if your fee for the roof is $2,000, tell the client, "As long as you are putting on a new roof, you should also replace the gutters, which are shot. I normally charge $600 for gutters. But if I can do them at the same time I am here doing the roof, I can do the whole job for $2,400."

Frequently the client will accept your suggestion, and you get an assignment that is $2,400 instead of $2,000. And it's easy to do the small add-on project, because a big cost factor in doing the job in the first place is getting to and from the job site. By doing both at once, you save time, get a larger overall fee, and the client gets a better value.

This is an easy income-booster. Using this technique, you can increase the average dollar value of each project 10 to 30 percent or more with virtually no extra sales effort.

I *always* look for ways to tack extra ancillary assignments onto the major assignment when I am not as busy as I could be and need the extra work and income. Try it. It works!

RECESSION-FIGHTING STRATEGY 7: AVOID BEING A PRIMA DONNA

Let's face it. When you're busy and in demand, and have much more work than you can handle, it's a heady feeling. The tendency is to get a swelled head. My advice is: Don't. And why not? Because when things become slow, as they probably will at least once more before you retire, it will come back to haunt you.

Nobody likes a prima donna. You don't. And neither do your clients.

Now, your clients *may* put up with a carpenter, contractor, consultant, doctor, or freelancer who's a prima donna,

simply because they feel you are the best at what you do . . .
and they know you're so in demand that *they* need you more
than *you* need them.

But that doesn't mean they enjoy your boorish behavior.
In fact, they *don't* like it—they resent it—and they'll always
be on the lookout for another supplier or professional to
replace you.

They may even switch to someone who is not as competent
as you if that person has a better personality.

So when a recession hits or the economy slows, and things
are slow for you, clients realize that the tables are turned:
Now you need them, but they don't need you. They'll take
revenge and you'll be out.

The solution? Always, *always* act like a pro—like a helpful friend and consultant to your clients. Be useful, courteous, and accessible. Don't be a snob or act high-handed.

If you give your clients genuine reason to like you, and
you are always helpful to them, they'll stick with you . . . and
that can make a big difference in your life when things
get slow.

Remember, in a depressed economy, continuous business
from *ongoing, current clients* is what keeps you afloat. In a
recession, service providers need work more than ever . . .
but clients have less work to give . . . and there is less work
to go around overall.

Make sure you have that business when you need it tomorrow by acting professionally and properly today.

RECESSION-FIGHTING STRATEGY 8: POSTPONE ANY PLANNED FEE INCREASE

A recession, depression, business downturn, or soft economy is not the appropriate time for you to increase your
fees—even if you feel you deserve it and that a raise is long
overdue.

During such a period, you should *defer* any planned fee increase announcements until later, and instead keep your fees at their current levels.

Note: Don't announce to your clients and prospects that you are "holding the line" on prices due to the recession and your desire to help them through it. Remember, even though you are feeling the effects of a soft economy, they may not be going through similar difficulties in their business. Thus, your announcement would clue them into the fact that you are in trouble . . . and some might take advantage of your perceived need of business by haggling over prices with you.

So leave your fee schedule as is and continue with business as usual.

RECESSION-FIGHTING STRATEGY 9: SLIGHTLY DOWNGRADE YOUR ACCEPTABLE CLIENT/ASSIGNMENT PROFILE

You have a set of written or mental guidelines that determine which clients and assignments are desirable to you and which are not. During a depressed economy or personal business downturn, you may want to be more flexible in this area than you usually are.

For instance, if you normally do business with Fortune 500 companies only, you may want to consider taking on assignments from smaller local firms . . . provided the pay is decent and their credit rating is good.

Or, if you normally work only on major annual reports, you might consider knocking out some small quarterly statements to generate needed revenue.

This doesn't mean you throw your standards out the window and work for any idiot who calls you. Far from it. Instead, you are simply readjusting your acceptable client/assignment criteria during this temporary lull to accommodate a wider range of prospects and projects.

How far should you take this? It's up to you. If, for example, you normally have a minimum project fee of $1,000, you might accept $500 assignments, but you probably should stick by your guns and not take on $50 assignments.

RECESSION-FIGHTING STRATEGY 10: PLAN AN AGGRESSIVE NEW BUSINESS MARKETING CAMPAIGN

This strategy has two parts to it.

The first part, which seems obvious, is that when things are slow, you increase the percentage of your time spent on marketing and prospecting for new business.

If you usually spend 10 percent of your week in marketing and sales when things are fairly busy, you might increase this to 25 percent—for instance, a day or more per week devoted entirely to marketing and selling. During a lull in business, you need to make this extra effort to attract clients, follow up on leads, and close sales.

The second part of the strategy may not be so obvious. It's this: To prevent a lull in business from ever happening in the first place, you should market consistently and aggressively all year long, whether you need the business at the time or not. Regular and ongoing marketing ensures a steady stream of new business leads. Marketing done today begins a selling cycle that may result in a project assignment six months from now.

This means that if you don't market when you are busy, you will not have prospects primed and ready to hire you when your current assignments run out weeks or months from today.

Send sales letters. Keep in touch with clients. Make phone calls. Write articles for the local newspaper. But be sure to do some marketing at all times. This is the surest way to prevent lulls in business from ever happening in the first place.

RECESSION-FIGHTING STRATEGY 11:
REPACKAGE YOUR SERVICES TO ACCOMMODATE SMALLER CLIENTS AND REDUCED BUDGETS

When you're busy, there's a whole group of prospects you probably turn away without a second thought—companies too small (read: too underbudgeted) to afford your costly services, or consumers too poor to afford what you offer.

But when things are slow, it pays to look for ways to generate revenue from this normally overlooked market segment.

This is best done by repackaging your services to accommodate smaller clients and reduced budgets.

For instance, clients who cannot afford to pay you $3,000 to write their direct-mail package *can* afford to pay you $200 to critique a package they write themselves.

They can also afford to pay you $100 an hour for your consultation services—take your direct-mail course for $200—or buy your book for $25.

Service providers can repackage their expertise and services in a variety of formats, including hourly consultations ... audiotapes ... instruction manuals ... reports ... books ... courses ... seminars ... and so on. You get the idea.

For instance, a person who cannot afford to buy a bigger home right now is a prospect for a home remodeling service.

A homeowner who can't afford to have you build on another room is a potential client for your basement-refinishing service.

A small business that cannot afford to buy a same-day, twenty-four-hour service contract for its equipment may be able to purchase a contract specifying a lesser level of service.

All of these alternatives do not provide as complete and customized a solution as having you render your premium service. But they give smaller clients the help they need at the price they can afford.

When the big companies and affluent clients are not giving you the big projects at the big fees, selling these alternative services to the less affluent segment of the market can put lots of extra dollars in your pocket.

RECESSION-FIGHTING STRATEGY 12:
KEEP BUSY WITH ANCILLARY ASSIGNMENTS

A slow period in your service business is a good time to busy yourself with other projects, such as cleaning out your files . . . or putting your client and prospect list into a computer database . . . or organizing your office . . . or getting more involved with your local chamber of commerce . . . or updating your sales brochure . . . or coming up with ideas for new services you can sell to your customers.

Or any of a hundred things that need doing but you never seem to have time for.

Now you have the time. So do.

Don't waste the extra time available, but instead put it to good use.

Having something to do will make you feel better. And your positive mood will be communicated to prospects and clients, which will in turn help you close more sales.

BE POSITIVE

During a slow period, it is very important not to be depressed. If you are depressed, prospects can sense your desperation and fear, and it has a negative effect in your dealings with them.

Remember that everybody in business has slow times; those who say they never do are liars. You are talented and successful; the lull is temporary; and people will call you and hire you again.

Don't despair, and don't give up too soon. It is possible to have two, three, even four or more slow months. But if you follow the twelve strategies outlined in this chapter, then things will improve. I know it.

As for me, my story also has a happy ending. While the first couple of months of 1990 were the worst I had had in many years, by following the strategies outlined here, I managed to turn it around, and by March I was busy again. The end result was earnings of well over $50,000 by the end of April . . . not a record, but not bad for my "worst year"!

I am positive you can achieve similar results if you carefully study and apply the tested strategies outlined in this chapter.

APPENDIX:
SOURCES AND RESOURCES

Below I list newsletters, seminars, books, special reports, and other information resources of interest to service sellers and providers.

FOR CONSULTANTS

Consulting Opportunities Journal. Monthly practice-building newsletter for the independent consultant. For information contact: J. Stephen Lanning, CRNC, 27-A Big Spring Road, P.O. Box 430, Clear Spring, MD 21772, (301) 791-9332.

Howard Shenson, 20750 Ventura Blvd., Woodland Hills, CA 91364, (818) 703-1415. Newsletter, special reports, books, cassette programs, and consulting advice for independent consultants. Call or write for details.

DESKTOP PUBLISHING

Martin Unlimited, Inc., 2 Marine View Plaza, Box 5F, Hoboken, NJ 07030, (201) 798-0298. Affordable service for desktop publishing of proposals, reports, brochures, and other marketing documents. Call or write for details.

FOR DOCTORS

The Practice Builder. Monthly newsletter and seminars on how to build and market your medical practice. For information contact: Alan L. Bernstein, The Practice Builder, 2755 Bristol, Suite 100, Costa Mesa, CA 92626–5985, (800) 333–3969 or (714) 545–8900.

FOR ENTREPRENEURS

James Evers. Books, manuals, seminars, and consulting services in business writing, problem solving, and other basic business skills. Call or write: James L. Evers Associates, 10 Rockland Ave., Nanuet, NY 10954, (914) 623–7129.

MARKETING ADVICE

The Direct Response Specialist. Monthly newsletter on selling via direct-response advertising and direct mail. For information contact: Galen Stilson, Stilson & Stilson, P.O. Box 1075, Tarpon Springs, FL 34688, (813) 786–1411.

The Marketing Communications Report. Short, concise, lively monthly newsletter providing marketing tips and ideas. For information contact: Pete Silver, 4300 N.W. 23rd Avenue, Suite 528, Gainesville, FL 32606, (904) 371–2083.

Sure-Fire Business Success Catalog. Quarterly sixteen-page catalog containing more than 120 recommendations on small-business marketing and management. For free one-year subscription contact: Dr. Jeffrey Lant, JLA Publications, 50 Follen Street, Suite 507, Cambridge, MA 02138, (617) 547–6372.

MOTIVATION

Dr. Rob Gilbert, The Center for Sports Success, 91 Belleville Avenue, Suite 7, Bloomfield, NJ 07003, (201) 743–4428. Offers motivational books and tapes plus a personal counseling service available by telephone. If you're in a slump and need a shot of enthusiasm, Dr. Gilbert can help! Call or write for details.

PUBLIC RELATIONS

The Levin Report. Newsletter presenting practical, proven public relations tips and techniques that work. For subscription information contact: Don Levin, Levin Public Relations, 30 Glenn Street, White Plains, NY 10603–3213, (914) 993–0900.

PR Hotline. Public relations advice and counsel available by phone. Charge it to your credit card! For details contact: Alan Caruba, PR Counselor, The Caruba Organization, Box 40, Maplewood, NJ 07040, (201) 763–6392.

SALES

Bill Bishop & Associates, 834 Gran Paseo Drive, Orlando, FL 32825, (800) 445–3237 or (407) 275–7355. In-house seminars, audiotapes, videotapes, and a newsletter on prospecting, selling, and closing techniques. Call or write for information.

FOR SEMINAR MARKETERS

Howard Shenson, 20750 Ventura Blvd., Woodland Hills, CA 91364, (818) 703–1415. Newsletter, special reports, books, cassette programs, and consulting advice for those who market and promote their own seminars. Call or write for details.

FOR SPEAKERS

Sharing Ideas. Newsletter, special reports, seminars, and consulting service providing marketing and selling advice for professional speakers. For information contact: Dottie Walters, Royal Publishing, P.O. Box 1120, Glendora, CA 91740, (818) 335–8069.

FOR WRITERS

TOWERS Club U.S.A. Newsletter and networking organization of writers who want to make money self-publishing and selling their books, special reports, and other how-to information by mail. For information contact: Pam Powers, TOWERS Club U.S.A., P.O. Box 2038, Vancouver, WA 98668, (206) 574–3084.

Joe Vitale, P.O. Box 300792, Houston, TX 77230, (713) 434–2845. Books and audiocassette programs for writers.

Writer's Profit Catalog. Resource guide containing over thirty recommendations on how to make $100,000 a year or more as a freelance writer. For free copy, write: Writer's Profit Catalog, 174 Holland Avenue, New Milford, NJ 07646.

FOR MORE INFORMATION ON BOOKS, TAPES, AND OTHER PUBLICATIONS WRITTEN BY BOB BLY

Write for a free copy of our Resource Guide: Bob Bly, 174 Holland Avenue, Dept. SS, New Milford, NJ 07646.

Index

ABOUT THE AUTHOR

In his work as an independent marketing consultant, copywriter, and seminar leader, Bob Bly has helped dozens of companies and hundreds of individuals sell more of their professional and consulting services through his articles, lectures, and training sessions.

Dubbed "Sales Trainer to America's Service Industries,"™ Bob presents the popular seminar, "Selling Your Services—Successfully," to corporations, trade associations, and professional groups nationwide. He also offers private consultations for small networking groups, small businesses, and individuals.

In addition, Mr. Bly has written sales letters, direct-response ads, brochures, and other marketing documents that have generated millions of dollars in sales for clients in a wide range of service and service-related businesses, including telephone companies, computer repair firms, freight forwarders, banks, software vendors, and consulting firms—to name just a few.

Bob Bly is the author of eighteen books, including *How to Promote Your Own Business* (New American Library), *Create the Perfect Sales Piece: How to Produce Brochures, Catalogs, Fliers, and Pamphlets* (John Wiley & Sons), and *The Copywriter's Handbook: A Step-by-Step Guide to Writing Copy That Sells* and *Secrets of a Freelance Writer: How to Make $85,000 a Year* (Henry Holt).

Questions and comments on *Selling Your Services* may be sent to:

Bob Bly
174 Holland Avenue, Dept. SS
New Milford, NJ 07646
(201) 599–2277

Be sure to request information on how you can sponsor a "Selling Your Services" talk or seminar for your company, group, or association this year.